The Long Campaign

The Long Campaign

A Biography of Anne Martin

Anne Bail Howard

University of Nevada Press
Reno, Nevada
1985

NEVADA STUDIES IN HISTORY AND POLITICAL SCIENCE NO. 20

STUDIES EDITOR
Wilbur S. Shepperson

EDITORIAL COMMITTEE

Don W. Driggs	Joseph A. Fry
Jerome E. Edwards	Andrew C. Tuttle

Library of Congress Cataloging in Publication Data

Howard, Anne Bail, 1927–
  The long campaign.

  (Nevada studies in history and political science; no. 20)
  Bibliography: p.
  Includes index.
  1. Martin, Anne, 1875–1951.   2. Nevada—Politics and government.   3. Politicians—Nevada—Biography.
  4. Feminism—Nevada—History—20th century.   5. Feminists—Nevada—Biography.
  I. Title.   II. Series.
  F841.Ml55H69   1985   305.4'2'0924 [B]   84–28062
  ISBN 0–87417–092–3

Materials from The Bancroft Library are quoted by permission of The Bancroft Library, Berkeley.

Materials from the Regional Oral History Office at The Bancroft Library are quoted by permission of that office.

Poetry from *Bread and Roses* by Diana Scott, published by Virago Press Limited (London) 1982. This collection copyright Diana Scott 1982. "Song of the WSPU" copyright L. E. M. Browne. "The March of the Women" copyright Cicely Hamilton.

University of Nevada Press, Reno, Nevada 89557 USA
© Anne Bail Howard 1985. All rights reserved
Cover design by Dave Comstock
Printed in the United States of America

CONTENTS

ACKNOWLEDGMENTS

I OWE THANKS to many people for their help with this project. The University of Nevada, Reno, granted me a sabbatical leave during fall semester 1983 as well as two summer stipends for research in 1980 and 1981. Staff members at the Bancroft Library in Berkeley were particularly helpful over a period of almost six years, and I am indebted as well to those who helped at the Fawcett Library in London, the Schlesinger Library at Radcliffe, the Sophia Smith Collection, the California Historical Society at San Francisco, and particularly the Nevada Historical Society and the Getchell Library at Reno. Several colleagues—Kathryn Anderson, Jerome Edwards, Mary Ellen Glass, Elizabeth Raymond, and Ann Ronald—read part or all of the manuscript at various stages and helped in many ways, as did Jacqueline Lowden, who typed the early drafts. My friends and family deserve particular attention for having remained friends and family through so long a project.

INTRODUCTION

In 1918, in the dusty heat of late summer, two women jolted across the rutted roads of rural Nevada in a canvas-topped touring car headed for mining camps and ranches, small communities and real towns at speeds sometimes as great as fifteen miles an hour. Anne Martin, independent candidate for the United States Senate, was campaigning, not just for the Senate but for an active political role for women. With the aid of her driver, Margaret Long, she was canvassing the big empty state for votes and for equality, and not for the first time, either.

Her pursuit was only one of many in an active life as a public person and a single woman. Martin and Long, comfortable enough in the remote corners of the sparsely settled desert, demonstrated how far American women had come in the fifty years since 1868 when a few of their forebears had tried to persuade Congress to include them as full citizens. Martin was forty-two, a small, plump, tidy woman in a loose suit, a sailor hat, and spats, her black hair beginning to gray, her sharply etched brows still black and unplucked. She was a world traveler with three college degrees who could boast of jail sentences on both sides of the Atlantic. Sharp-featured Dr. Long had come a great distance from her practice in Colorado and her days at Smith College and Johns Hopkins Medical School to coax the car up grades and across deserts, giving her time and her money to help her friend to public office.

Certainly it was a bold venture, one that would have fulfilled Charlotte Perkins Gilman's exhortation to "believe and dare and do." Believing and daring were easy enough; the doing called for help from voters, particularly women voters, who had only newly won the vote. In fact, in 1918 the large majority of American women were still without the suffrage: only in the western states—and only recently there—had women like Martin and Long persuaded legislators and male voters to listen to their demands for the vote. Martin could take credit in Nevada for organizing the state, stumping it, commanding an army of women to victory only four years before. And she could add to her experience of the world of politics long hours of labor in Washington as a lobbyist for the federal amendment.

Her Senate campaigns—she tried twice—attracted national attention, for Anne Martin was the first woman to try for the Senate, just as she had been the first head of the history department at young Nevada State University, the state's first woman tennis champion, and the first leader of the sassy National Woman's Party. But those two battles were only the best known of many in a long and active life. Persistent feminist, campaigner for political office, supporter of causes from child protection to world peace, Martin saw her life as worthy of note, as a long campaign for various sorts of justice.

She was one of the first Nevada women to attract national attention and attempt to make a mark in the world beyond her home state. Born in 1875, she was the classic New Woman, that developing creation of the nineteenth-century press—educated, independent, traveled, ambitious; but she spent much of her mature life searching for a replacement for the political struggle that had called her energies to full power—and to defeat. She knew, of course, that she had lost more battles than she had won. Whether her motives were altruistic or personal, for the community or for herself, she also knew that she had dared and done and it seemed for a very long time that no one else had noticed.

When she attempted in her fifties to record her life, she saw it as one affected by forces "rooted in the past, and brought to consciousness of this troubled age like a tangle of weeds and pond lillies scattered upon the pool's surface, without pattern, by a devastating wind." She wanted to tell "with disinterestedness and dispassion" of a life that was in many ways a kind of model of the striving of her sex for recognition, but one never marked with either disinterestedness or dispassion. She felt her story was worthy to add to the pattern of history as a tale of both an ordinary woman and a leader.

Anne Martin's peculiar mixture of pride for the things she accomplished and attempted and petulance for real or imagined injuries pervaded her efforts at autobiography, just as the same qualities affected her through a long and useful life. She began her biography presenting herself as an ordinary woman, thinking of herself as a leader; it is both as leader and ordinary woman that Anne Martin deserves our attention.

How did this woman, like many others of her changing times, become unlike her contemporaries? How did the ordinary woman become the leader?

Born to privilege, educated more thoroughly than the average woman of her time, Anne Martin came to believe that her very advantages made life difficult for her. Her status demanded a certain dignity, her education a use, her energies a cause. Although she found that cause for a period of ten years from 1910 to 1920, her goals grew steadily less realistic and her chances of success ever smaller. Yet at no time did she feel free to return to mere ladyhood—which she could well have afforded—and to living out a merely pleasureful life of golf and concerts, European trips and informative lectures at the posh and not-so-fine clubs she managed to find in various parts of the world or in the company of important people she both cultivated and antagonized.

Like many another woman of her era, she perceived that the very education she accepted as her natural right—thanks to the fairness and interest of her exceptional father—demanded that she perform. After schooling in Nevada and at Stanford, she tried college teaching of history and art history, she tried writing, she traveled. After her father's death the family's unwillingness to consider her opinions sent her away from Nevada for a series of trips to Europe and the Orient. She thought "the feminist iron" had entered her soul at the settlement of her father's estate, but she did not join the battle for suffrage until 1909 when her allegiance to Emmeline Pankhurst's Women's Social and Political Union in England gave her a ticket to jail and the future.

To come from Nevada, the state she often called the most male in the nation, to rise to national prominence was an achievement of a special sort. If her organizing of the successful three-year campaign for suffrage in her own state was only what another woman might have done, her continued interest and devotion to the cause were distinctive. Informed by a larger vision, joined in what seemed a useful life purpose, she continued to work for the federal amendment in Washington and elsewhere after Nevada women were voting.

By 1918 she was a veteran lobbyist, well aware of the power of the Senate and especially impressed as other Nevadans had been before her with the appeal for westerners of that men's club, all the more attractive to aspirants from a state too weak in numbers to carry any strength in the House. As a leader who had participated fully in the everyday work of the 1914 campaign for suffrage, she had visited every corner of the state during that long effort; moreover, in 1916 she had mounted a statewide campaign under the auspices of the National Woman's Party in an effort to defeat Woodrow Wilson, and she had labored in the ranks and higher offices of the suffrage drives throughout the country. She had picketed, she had been sent to jail for the cause. In those years of suffrage activity she had learned to speak in public, to organize groups, to plan campaigns. At a time when Nevada was trying to throw off out-of-state control, she was a native daughter who had learned every corner of her state first hand. By 1918, the suffragists could smell victory for the amendment as each vote and committee report brought the moment of enfranchisement closer. However Anne Martin's allegiances may have been pulled between the battle for the amendment and her own candidacy, her declaration for office seemed to her a fit next step for women. Anne Martin hoped to emulate Jeannette Rankin of Montana, who had followed suffrage leadership with a successful campaign for national office in 1916.

To suggest that Martin ever really entertained hopes of winning the more contested Senate seat seems to suggest that she was either politically naive or plain foolish. In the traditional rhetoric of politicians and press agents, of coaches and cheerleaders, her correspondence and her public utterances reflect an optimism she would have been silly to entertain. Her claims upon defeat that her one-fifth of the votes had been a victory for women may have been a cause for ridicule from men, but she believed sincerely that those five thousand votes had real significance, that they represented the first evidence of women voting as women for a woman. She resolved to try again. She failed once more.

Both attempts attracted national attention—perhaps more outside of Nevada than in it. Indeed, Nevada newspapers, far from demonstrating any chivalric restraint toward her sex, delighted in ribbing her great success in getting attention elsewhere and ridiculed her in personal attacks. One compared her with "the daughters of the Hun."

After her political defeats, she continued to work for women as a writer in a variety of publications in the United States and in England, but she devoted many of her efforts as well to support of Jane Addams and the Women's International League for Peace and Freedom. She left Nevada for the more welcoming climate of Carmel, leaving with not a little bitterness. As a delegate to the major conferences of WILPF and as a dedicated admirer of its leader, she worked for the cause of world peace, never forgetting her lasting concern with women's status during a period when only the most devoted of feminists still struggled for equal rights, equal pay, and power for women. Weakened by a heart attack that immediately preceded her mother's death, she turned to writing poetry, supporting WILPF until a personal difference in 1936 persuaded her to transfer her efforts to the People's Mandate to End War.

However much she may have turned to other homes, she remained a Nevada voter, returning from time to time, from cause to cause, to her native state. When in 1945 the University of Nevada granted her an honorary Doctor of Laws in recognition of her work for women, that simple act seemed to provide the justification she had needed. She returned loyally to her home state for most of the six remaining years of her life (in spite of the wind and the cold she hated), content with the simple public thank you that had made most things right. Even the private diaries that had long bemoaned the monotony of her life, the loss of so much—even these ceased to echo any unhappiness.

Since Anne Martin's death in 1951 little attention has been paid to her or her achievement. With the revitalized women's movement of the past two decades and the renewed interest in women's pasts and women's deeds, her name has emerged in local articles and regional publications. Two dissertations, a master's thesis, and a few articles on her life and career have appeared in the last decade. Both the *Dictionary of American Biography* (fifth supplement) and *Notable American Women* have printed short accounts of her life, and Ann Warren Smith's 1972 account of the Nevada suffrage campaign makes a small attempt at a memoir. Kathryn Anderson's more ambitious study of the two Senate campaigns is primarily devoted to an analysis of the rhetoric of those campaigns and an examination of the thinking displayed in Martin's later articles. Yet the sources for biography are rich. Anne Martin presented her suffrage materials to the University of California at Berkeley's Bancroft Library in 1940 and her remaining papers expanded the collection upon her death in 1951. Within the voluminous collection there and within smaller ones at the California and Nevada historical societies are materials that range from her childhood essays to the diary she started in her twelfth year, the sketchbook that recorded her adolescent pranks, the unpublished manuscripts of her many efforts at writing, the diaries of her declining years, and almost every piece of paper she ever touched in her public life.

The public and private worlds of this distinguished and yet ordinary woman reveal much about the seventy-five years she lived, years that saw the world change for millions of women. She was an actor in some of the changes, an interested and informed spectator to others. Scrutiny of this particular life may explain a complex woman and provide a broader understanding of her times, her ideals, her sex. It is the intention of this study both to present and to interpret that public and private Anne Martin as a woman of her times for our richer knowledge of our own.

CHAPTER 1

NATIVE DAUGHTER

A Nevada Girlhood in Empire and Reno

My lonely birth must have been the cause of a marked trait of independence.

—Anne Martin, Autobiography

The Whitaker school aims to turn the heedless girl into the thoughtful woman.

—Bishop Whitaker School catalog

IN THE SUMMER OF 1893 when Anne[1] Martin was almost eighteen, she complained bitterly to her diary: "Will I never have any ambition, will I never accomplish anything . . .? O, I must do something. I suppose I should live more for others, but I don't understand how. I must do something."[2]

Unlike her sisters or her mother, unlike many of her schoolmates, she was feeling the confusion that must have been common to many a young lady developing a new kind of consciousness, a consciousness only shadowed in the books she read, apparent to her only as troublesome doubts about her goals. She did not see her future as most young women did. She had goals both for the individual self that she wanted to be and for the selfless paragon of feminine virtue that tradition and her female relatives told her she should be. Her education, background, and privileges could have offered her the easy answers of a conventional marriage, but she wanted to do something, and the times were changing to help her develop into a woman of fervent ambition and real achievement.

Anne Martin's early years in fading Empire City, in San Francisco, and in the developing town of Reno were important ones for her later life. She developed a lifelong attachment to Nevada and she acquired the education and skills that would assist her later ambitions. Her parents, her education, her personal contacts with women, her reading, her particular shortcomings all contributed to her mature character as a strong woman, an independent leader with goals of her own.

Martin's brief and unpublished autobiographical memoir and the diaries from her adolescence chronicle the development of an independent spirit, trace the growth of a distinctive young woman. Surrounded by the strange contradictions that characterized the Far West at the closing of the nineteenth century, Anne Martin knew and enjoyed physical comfort and intellectual stimulation, adored an exceptionally open-minded father, and clashed with a mother who cherished the most conservative of Victorian ideals.

Martin's fragmentary memoir supplies a kind of cinematic montage of the world of her childhood—of the first family home as oasis in the parched country of the Comstock, of her father in black suit and snowy linen driving paired black horses across the dusty roads, of her "dainty . . . ladylike" mother conducting a home kindergarten.[3] The stereopticon view of her childhood projected by the double view of memory and of family mythology and seconded by her mature understandings of the same events was engraved against a background of a sun-blasted, sage-covered valley on the Carson River.

Before 1859 the little valley where Anne Martin was born was only part of what Mark Twain had called "a desert, walled in by barren, snow clad mountains . . . no vegetation but the endless sagebrush and greasewood. All nature was gray with it . . . [a] solitude of silence and desolation." The alkali dust was everywhere, and the valleys were torn with a steady wind and dust from the notorious Washoe zephyrs. A Washoe wind, Twain declared, " . . . is by no means a trifling matter. It blows flimsy houses down, lifts shingle roofs occasionally, rolls up tin ones like sheet music . . ."[4]

The discovery of silver in the nearby mountains had begun a rush of would-be millionaires to the area known afterward as the Comstock. Western lore has it that the excitement about the rich silver strike had emptied the settlement of San Francisco of most of its inhabitants as all who could hurried east to seek the Big Bonanza. In the center of the activity, Virginia City had grown from a canvas town of tents to a community boasting fine homes, elegant hotels, and even churches in only a few years. But however the little settlements rose and fell with the fortunes of the mines, the communities made little lasting impression on the wide expanses of land and sagebrush through which the residents moved from Empire City to Virginia City, from Carson City to the shores of Lake Tahoe. Virginia City's luxuries covered the vast emptiness of the land with only a minute patch of civilization, however much the riches from the depths of the mines seeded the wealth of San Francisco across the Sierra Nevada.

By the time Anne Martin was born in Empire on September 30, 1875, the town was already dwindling from its one-time high of 1,000 residents to the 150 who lived there in 1880. Like most mining communities, Empire developed rapidly to meet a particular need and declined just as rapidly when the demands on the nearby mines weakened as the precious metals were gradually mined out. But when William O'Hara Martin arrived in 1868, the town was still vigorous and vital, providing both wood for the timbering of the mines and mills to process the ore for shipment as bullion. Locals jokingly referred to Empire City as a seaport because of the water-borne traffic on the Carson River, jammed with rafts and thousands of logs destined for the mines. To prevent the cavernous excavations from collapsing on the workers, a square set timbering system had been contrived. This system consumed vast quantities of timber, timber that had to be brought from miles away. Even the coming of the railroad in 1869 did not immediately diminish the town's importance, for many of the mills ran on wood power and the river was still the best and fastest means of moving wood from the slopes of the Sierra Nevada to the Comstock mines.[5]

Traveling journalist J. Ross Browne recorded that the "quartz mills and saw mills had completely usurped the valley along the head of the Carson River; and now the hammering of stamps, the whirling clouds of smoke from all the chimneys, and the confused clamor of voices from a busy multitude reminded one of a manufacturing city."[6]

Eugenia May Bruns, a contemporary and friend of Anne Martin who lived in Empire until 1897, recalled it as "a bustling town of watermills, ore trains, wood drives, saloons, boarding houses, grocery stores [catering to] earnest, hardworking inhabitants and a few odd characters."[7] The little settlement edged the Carson, its hundred simple wood structures struggling up about the brick home of the superintendent of the largest mill, only a few cottonwoods shading some spots here and there from the fierce sun—a community in mining town terms, a town for its times. There the Stadtmuller store provided for William O'Hara Martin a job outside the mines, a partnership, and later a wife—and the first opportunity to secure his future.

Martin was the major influence on his daughter's life. Like many another daughter, she identified with him, adored him, longed to please him; like many another feminist, she credited his understanding with helping her to be what she was. But, like others before her, she discovered that the world at large did not value her in the same way he did, and her reaction was to try to change the world rather than discredit his evaluation.[8] She claimed later that his death shaped her future life, for it was then she discovered that her mother, her brothers, the family advisers treated her as if she were a mere woman like any other—incapable, dependent, voiceless.[9] Whatever hero worship informed her account of him, there is little doubt that he was admirable, honest, hard-working—a self-made man who had won his way at a time when substantial success demanded a certain amount of daring. Martin had maintained and improved his position in an area and an era when millionaires came and went almost as regularly as the ore trains.

Martin had arrived in the West as a child, brought by his parents to Grass Valley, California, in the 1850s. His father, Morris Washington Martin, had immigrated with his Irish wife by sea, crossing the Isthmus of Panama by land and finally settling in Cherokee camp in the California gold country. As Anne Martin explained, her grandfather's "studious tastes were ill adapted to conditions in the mining camps" and, his capital exhausted, Morris Martin died in Grass Valley, ten years after he had arrived, leaving a family of five to depend entirely on young William, then sixteen, whose education at Berkeley's Academy—later the University of California—ended with his father's death. In the course of some seven years of work in the California mines, William Martin established some security for the family and in 1868 entered the mines in Virginia City. Martin's service there was short; he moved to Empire before the year was out to work as a clerk in Stadtmuller's store. After he had negotiated a few successful contracts for wood, he became a partner and then more than a partner in 1871 when he married Louise Stadtmuller, an eastern-born visitor.

Anne Martin remembered in middle age that she had, as a child, "walked through ankle-deep sand to [her] father's office around great piles of wood, hundreds of cords of it, on the banks of the Carson River, [smelling] the odors of mingled dust and pine . . ." and she recalled her childish pride in learning it was her father "who was responsible for the mountain of wood." Well she might remember that lumber, for those contracts formed the basis of a fortune that proved ample to supply his widow and seven children with modest incomes for the rest of their lives. She remembered the men in "high rubber boots working with poles at the logs that jammed the great booms" at the end of the descent by flood and flume to Empire.[10]

William Martin was elected to the Nevada Senate in 1875 and was its youngest member, but he soon earned the respect of his fellows for what the *Carson Daily Appeal* extolled as "soundness of judgment and human sympathy in standing for the underdog and the masses." Martin, the writer claimed, had "a knowledge of public measures that has baffled some of the shrewdest lawyers in that body." Most of all, his daughter lovingly emphasized, the paper acknowledged his reputation for identifying himself with every measure affecting the interests of the people of the whole state. "'He has stood by the people all through the sessions.'"[11] At a time when "social conditions and standards of public and private honor were notably unstable, when legislatures were flagrantly venal and checques for one thousand dollars, and more, were freely passed about by lobbyists, no one ventured to approach him with a bribe," she continued.[12] Even allowing for the extravagance of turn-of-the-century newspaper writing, responses to his death in 1901 would seem to support his daughter's view.[13] He remained the standard to which she aspired. Whether she succeeded or not, she kept his image as ideal both in supporting the underdog and attempting to maintain her personal integrity. In her memory he was the champion behind the paired horses, the rescuer of the family, the understanding parent who cared for others beyond his family as he had cherished his oldest daughter.

Anne's mother, Louise Stadtmuller, was nineteen when she arrived in Nevada to visit her uncle and his family. The only child of Bavarian immigrants, she had enjoyed the privileges of a good education as well as some contact with the world of art and music in New York City before she journeyed west on the newly finished Central Pacific. Her marriage to Martin followed in less than a year.

Anne Martin's recorded feelings about her mother were far more complex than those relating to her father, for she both resented the need and accepted the obligation to care for her mother for many years, an experience quite common to the single, unmarried daughter. When Martin began her memoir in 1932, little more than a year had passed since her mother's death; she still doubted that she had paid all obligations.

From the beginning, according to Martin, the ties were close:

My mother often told me how I had brought myself determinedly, inexorably as fate, into the world, several days before my time, at six o'clock of a windy, dust laden Thursday morning (wind and dust have ever since been very hard for me to bear). The woman who helped my mother with her household tasks was for some reason not available. I lay alone nearly an hour with my mother, her life current flowing through me, while my father lashed his pair of black horses over the four miles of sandy road between Empire and Carson, in a desperate effort to bring the doctor and nurse to her in time. Brave mother, and fated child!

Although our temperaments were very different, and she liked better, as we grew older, the more conventional and domestic tastes of my three younger sisters, the more dependent characters of my one older and two younger brothers, a strong bond was woven between mother and daughter that windy September morning that lasted through her life, a bond that seems to endure through the inexplicable separation of death itself . . . My lonely birth injured neither of us. But it must have been the cause . . . of a marked trait . . . of independence.

Anne Martin noted the conflict of impatience on her own part and a "protective devotion" for her mother that caused her to give "hostages of loyalty and affection" against her own freedom.[14]

Martin's sense of herself as a kind of radical outsider, protected only by her understanding father, is repeated regularly in her autobiography, colored by the disillusionments of a feeble middle age; not surprisingly, the diaries that recorded these days in their own time seem to present a lively girl, a father's favorite who did not seem to resent the others or question the mother's devotion, a happy and independent child who enjoyed life.

Anne Martin recorded almost wistfully her earliest recollection of that childhood in Empire: "the garden of grass, bordered by cumulus topped cottonwood trees, an oasis in the desert jungle of sagebrush and sandy roads outside the picket fence, sloped downward toward the Carson River; the odors of pungent sagebrush, damp grass and bittersweet woods mingle . . . But the sensation that is most vivid at this hour is one of awe at the evening silence broken by the rhythmic roar of the stamp mills,—the distant 'Mexican' and the 'Morgan.'" She marked the "silence and mystery and awesomeness of the spring evening, mingled with the distant roar of the equally mysterious work of man."[15] (Many years later, she attempted a novel about water problems in Nevada with the steady pounding of the stamp mills as background for her opening chapters.)[16] She remembered the afternoon sunshine on the sugarloaf foothills to the west and, of course, her father, "behind his pair of black horses," a Swedish nursemaid, a Chinese cook, the fire on the Christmas tree that her father extinguished—a multitude of pictures.[17]

More specifically, she recalled the efforts her mother made to offer the children the opportunities that might have been denied them by the isolation of their home. Inspired by the work of Hannah Clapp and Elizabeth Babcock, who had started a private school and kindergarten in Carson City,[18] young Mrs. Martin spent each morning with Harry, Anna, and Gertrude offering "pre-school advantages" with a regular program of activities: "mat weaving, songs played to the accompaniment of the parlor organ, . . . and Sheldon's 'Object Lessons,'[19] that encouraged the then original idea of placing in the child's hands the objects themselves to feel and describe, including live biological specimens, so far as possible." Anne Martin credited her lifelong love of animals to these first lessons from her mother, when the family dog served as object for the classes. Perhaps other credit goes to the studies, for Martin recorded that she learned her "ABC's very quickly, before the age of four," and that her mother had called her the "most precocious of all the children," an opinion in which her father concurred.[20]

Sundays the family drove to Carson to the Episcopal church, past the prison, and she recorded a "childish stirring of sympathy for the prisoners who, her father told her, were not all bad men, and for the little children [in the orphan's home] who had no fathers or mothers." At the church, the child was taken with the ceremony and the hymns, especially "Jerusalem the Golden, with Milk and Honey Blest," but also with the chance to see and speak to others after the service.[21]

Such social occasions were rare, and the mother's efforts to educate her children were augmented, at least in Annie's case, by her father's steady concern. It was he who singled her out as "the brightest of all the children," while her mother, "whose sons were close to her heart, would be silent"; it was her father's simple punishments for lapses of responsibility and honesty that stayed with her for decades. Her father's pride in her scholarship later urged her on to study, his acceptance of her tomboy behavior allowed her special privileges over her sisters—a pony and later a horse, a dog, a bicycle, a camera and darkroom equipment. Her mother let her know regularly that she was not behaving properly for a girl.[22] Certainly the "daintily dressed" mother might have complained of a girl who rejected her sisters' games with dolls" . . . which were only make-believe. I would play by myself, with my pony or the carriage horse in the stable, or with hammer and nails build play-houses, greatly to the distress of my mother, who wanted me to sew with my sisters."[23]

In this attachment to her father, Anne Martin resembled other female achievers and many woman suffragists, as Barbara Welter notes: "The father assumes direction of his daughter's education and character while the mother is relegated to the role of . . . nurse-housekeeper for the younger children. The girl and her father develop an extraordinarily close relationship as part of which she feels that she compensates for the son she is sure he wished her to be." Welter goes on to observe that in later life these women "achieve more than most of their contemporaries . . . [and] are occupied with finding a suitable definition of woman's nature and role."[24] William O'Hara Martin did have a son only a little older than Anne, but Harry, although he had some small success after his father's death, seemed to have far more problems with his father than Anne did.

Although Mrs. Martin later supported her daughter and became herself a believing suffragist, at the time Anne was small Mrs. Martin seemed to accept the standard Victorian view of women expressed in that "Cult of True Womanhood" so treasured throughout the country, proclaiming "four cardinal virtues for women: piety, purity, submissiveness and domesticity."[25] Mrs. Martin came to Empire City as a kind of protected pioneer when the West offered to women who settled there opportunities seldom available in the East, but she brought with her the prevailing attitudes of her age, an age influenced by what Dorothy Gray has called "the dismal grey of Victorianism that was falling across the East like a long twilight."[26]

Unlike the earliest arrivals, who kept house in tents and helped in the heavy work of home building and homemaking, Mrs. Martin started her married life in a small apartment and moved quite early to a brick home; she escaped the heaviest labor and she soon acquired the luxuries that softened her life for many years—the two servants at Empire were but the first of many hired to lighten the burden of her large family. Louise Martin ruled her house efficiently, the evidence shows, but her oldest daughter continued to believe that the "determined discipline was applied far more to her daughters than to her sons. This trait was undoubtedly due in part to her German ancestry, in part to woman's traditional beliefs as to man's superior position and ability."[27] Clearly Mrs. Martin was a woman of some reserve to wait so long as a year before marrying in Empire, for the notorious shortage of women in the West seemed to produce—at all levels of society—immediate engagements and instant marriages.[28]

Whatever the reasons for her traditional beliefs, her collisions with the headstrong daughter were frequent enough to convince Anne Martin that she was "the black lamb in the fold," as she put it in her later poetry, but one who regretted her behavior and would long to have the chance again "to sew to please my mother."[29] Hard-headed Annie may have collided with her equally strong-willed mother and in an ill and embittered middle age seen herself as a "black lamb," but her father's special attentions compensated. She recounted trips to see General Grant at the International Hotel in Virginia City and to hear the memorial service for President James Garfield, and she remembered the drive home down "the juniper studded canyon and over the plain known as 'American Flat.'"[30]

To assume that because she was raised in Nevada Anne Martin escaped the onus of Victorian thought about women would then seem to be quite false; to assume that her childhood and adolescent experiences were duplicates of those of eastern girls would be just as false. In some ways she enjoyed freedoms not possible for others of her age simply because she lived in the West and because, in a community short of contemporaries, her parents made special efforts. But the standards set for her, the ideals toward which her mother and female relatives strove, seem in no way different from those of other comfortably fixed families of the time. Whatever indulgence she enjoyed as a favored child, she was expected to be the proper young girl, at least in the eyes of her mother, the most constant influence upon her early life.

There is little evidence that Louise Martin was especially harsh with her. Annie recorded her particular tasks with no particular resentment, seemingly accepting such duties as helping with the younger children, caring for her dog with not more nor much less complaint than that of any other child. She was spared the need for heavy chores, for even as the family grew William O'Hara Martin was well prepared to offer luxuries as well as necessities. Anne Martin remembered the last Christmas Eve in Empire when her father came home early with a gift of diamonds for her mother.[31]

In 1880, when Empire City shrank to nearly nothing as the mines that fed it faltered, Martin sold his property, disposing of everything he owned, and left the mill town for San Francisco, taking his young family—now grown to include four children—on the "Reno" train of the Virginia and Truckee to connect with the Central Pacific. Anne Martin recalled

> the night odors from the sagebrush flats mingled with fresh breezes from the river—the gathering of friends and neighbors to wish us Godspeed— the all night journey from Reno to San Francisco, my first experience in a sleeping car. Child as I was, it was with a feeling of depression and foreboding that I left Nevada and the next morning from the deck of the ferry boat got my first view of foggy San Francisco Bay and of the city itself—a feeling that returns to this day when I arrive there, even after having gone through the experience hundreds of times.[32]

While Martin offered no details about the family's stay in San Francisco, a Reno newspaper noted in William Martin's obituary that after two years "his early business training at Empire made his love for Western Nevada so strong that he returned to [Nevada] in 1883 . . . and went into the mercantile business which he conducted profitably for years."[33]

Reno, a young town by any measure, was growing steadily and boasted a variety of civilized refinements when Martin returned with his young family to build a business down by the railroad tracks and an elegant home on the banks of the Truckee River on Mill Street. The home was ample in every way, twelve rooms in three stories with basement and room enough for carriages and ponies, for crystal chandeliers and imported mirrors, for, finally, seven children and visiting cousins as well as prominent visitors from all parts of the country.

By 1883, Reno had developed into a railroad center town that, while still dependent on the products of the mines, was struggling toward its own existence and a commercial status that would allow it to grow more steadily than the more colorful communities in the state that rose and fell with the luck of the mines. Bertha Bender Brown, whose family moved to Reno in the same decade, recalled that in her youth it was known as "the dirty little town on the Truckee."[34] "Every business block in Reno contained half a dozen or more saloons," Samuel Bradford Doten observed.

> The streets were unpaved, full of chuckholes in summer and mud-holes in winter. In the business district ancient wooden awnings overhung the wooden sidewalks, shutting off light from the stores; and one of the routine operations performed every summer on the sidewalk was the chopping away of knots with adzes, because the irregular projections tangled up too much of the unsteady feet of the sojourners in the town.[35]

But Doten praised the "Athens of Nevada" as both " . . . a wild town of the old west, where pistols and knives were rather freely used . . . [and] a town of high ideals, earnest work, and Christian fellowship."[36]

Families entertained at the Nevada Club, where young people gathered for dancing and supper.[37] Fine homes rose along the Truckee and up to the north the university buildings crowned the hill. Not far to the west of that site on another hill stood the Bishop Whitaker School, since 1876 the boarding and day school for the families who could and would afford private schooling but were not ready, as some had been, to send their daughters off to California or "back East" to learn.

In this town of some fifty square blocks and at this school Anne Martin grew to womanhood. Her years—1882 to 1894—in Reno until her departure for Stanford University were crucial ones for her development. During that time she received the superior education that encouraged her to study more and she established the habit of independence and the custom of confidence. She learned the joys of reading and the pleasure of scholarship; she learned the pleasures of the out-of-doors and the joys of a healthy body. Bishop Whitaker's School for Girls offered her a sturdy start for future learning.

One of few such institutions in the Mountain West, certainly the only such school in Nevada, the Bishop Whitaker School, later known as Whitaker Hall, was founded in 1876 under the leadership of Bishop Ozi William Whitaker to provide the necessaries of high school education for Nevada girls. Largely built by donated eastern money, the school was the last structure on the northwest city limits.[38]

By the time the Martin family returned to Reno, Whitaker was well enough established to offer high school classes for day students and boarders and had added a preparatory department for younger girls. At one time all three of the older Martin girls—Anna, Gertrude, and Clara—attended, traveling the two miles in the family carriage.

And a fine building it was, "filled with luxuries uncommon to schools at the time." Whitaker boasted five pianos and an organ, a steam-heated dormitory and classrooms in two roomy buildings.[39] The bishop hoped that the girls came to his school not only to obtain a small amount of French or music, the ladylike advantages, but "to fit themselves for womanhood, to purify the heart through culture of the mind."[40] Bishop Whitaker described his curriculum as a means of "turning the heedless girl into the thoughtful woman,"[41] aiming "to develop the pupils into refined, cultured, Christian women well fitted for the duties of practical and social life." Moreover, the school sought to form "true womanly character" through careful attention to the manners, morals, and health of the students in an atmosphere where "discipline never relaxes into the indulgence too often found in home life."[42]

The school offered a thorough academic program taught by young women brought from eastern schools. In the preparatory grades "reading, elocution, writing, spelling, and especial attention to English composition . . . and the formation of a correct taste in reading" occupied the girls.[43] In the upper school pupils could study Latin, French, German, plane geometry, mental philosophy, history of art, and rhetoric as well as drawing and music, both vocal and keyboard. Simple restrictions were made upon dress, and the school insisted that parents "see that their daughters are clothed so as not to interfere with the free use of lungs and muscles."[44] The student body came from all over the state—from Cherry Creek, Pioche, Mason Valley, Fish Springs, and Tuscarora as well as from the larger towns—and many of the students had been personally sought out by the bishop. While the rules were strict, the pleasures were many, ranging from picnics and parties to excursions on a special car of the Virginia and Truckee to Steamboat Springs.[45]

Diaries from 1888 through 1894 and a pair of sketchbooks from 1890–91 record the days Annie Martin spent at Whitaker School and catch a private and personal view of a girl growing and questioning, not quite certain about many things, happy to record her days. Here is the record of tomboy Annie who loved to climb trees and play softball, who loved her bicycle and rode astride her horse, who developed pictures on glass plates and made etchings—and played pranks at school. Here, too, is the uncomfortable young lady who dreaded dances and being a wallflower, who formed strong emotional ties with girls a bit younger than she was, and who even at the university wished the chemistry class had "no boys." The sketchbooks (one was confiscated for some months) that the fourteen-year-old Annie kept record the defiance by the girls of an unpopular principal in a series of drawings that preserve the high spirits of a lively crew led by a boisterous and bright Annie.

The 1888 diary, a gift from her cousin Fred Stadtmuller, lasted only a short time. From its accounts of the minor events of a twelve-year-old's world emerges a short picture of its author, an orderly child who kept careful track of letters sent and received and of the disposition of her fifty-cent allowance, an honest child who accounted for occasional expenditures "due to carelessness." There is the first appearance of "Dick," Victoria Godfroy, best friend and sometimes difficult ally, a boarder from Virginia City. Although the reading she recorded seems precocious—H. Rider Haggard's thriller *She* and a large dose of Thackeray—the events recorded are familiar ones:

—I let off a firecracker today in the schoolroom and Miss Pease rushed in and thought it was a door that slammed . . .
—I played marbles with the boys and won . . .
—I had a dandy time on a bike. It just fitted me . . .
—For once I knew my music lesson. Miss Quaiffe didn't say anything about it but I imagine it took her breath away . . .

One day she graded the Latin papers, but two days later failed in Caesar; she watched cheating on the moral science examinations but confided "if this wasn't secret I wouldn't say so."[46]

Anne seemed to have ignored the diary in 1889 to begin drawings for her schoolgirl epic of events in what she called the Johnny Rankin Album, a carefully drawn collection of drawings supported by narrative to chronicle particular pleasures and the minor rebellion during the very short term of Father John R. Rankin as principal. Carefully recopied into a standard, sewn composition book quartered to four inches by six to leave on the cover a flying fowl of some sort, the album starts its spirited journey on the cover where the bird—most likely a goose or duck—is converted to an eagle, as the opening ditty attests, carrying Father Rankin in its beak:

There was an eagle flying south,
With Johnny Rankin in his mouth,
When he found out he was a fool
He dropped him on the Bishop's school.

Annie dated the album 1890, although the sketches are often of earlier events and there is a separate book of draft sketches for the final version, one written and drawn with great care, the penmanship superior to her usual work, the drawings considered, planned, and executed precisely.[47]

Father Rankin seemed to have problems from the very beginning as records in the archives of the Episcopal church suggest; indeed, Amy Pease, who was left in charge after the bishop left in 1888, "expressed concern over how to tell the parents of the students that [he] was to take charge. And Rankin came with the idea that the school was not going to go well."[48] By the time Annie Martin began her records of pranks, Rankin was firmly established as butt for the girls' humor, even after he quit as principal (in 1889) and became vice-rector and bookkeeper as well as teacher.[49] Surely one of the earlier drawings—"Come into my room a moment. I'd like you to know I'm principal"—strikes the general spirit: an exaggeratedly skinny old man with a pointed beard berates a stubborn girl in pigtails. On occasion the book is called the Pap Rankin Book and the recurrent image is of a group of girls laughing behind an old man's back.

Drawn with a good deal of skill (Annie was proud of her drawing ability and worked hard at the private lessons her parents provided), the book is a record of minor rebellion and misbehavior of the lively young women who saw an easy mark and struck at it. Rankin is the primary victim, but others of the teachers come in for a share of caricature, the artist admitting that "the personages . . . are not so hideously ugly as pictured."[50]

The scenes of life on Seminary Hill are charming ones of students and teachers as well as of the persecution of poor Father Rankin: straw rides and picnics, baseball games and class experiments, special literary evenings of the Bronze Lamp literary society, and confrontations with authorities that include both Annie and various friends. Annie was clearly full of spirit and respected by her friends, who regularly elected her to any open office.

Two writers on Anne Martin have made much of the juvenile rascality of the prankster revealed in the album: Kathryn Anderson concluded that Martin "saw herself in non-traditional ways during her early school years, always portraying herself as defiant, mischievous and non-conformist,"[51] and Carrie Townley noted that "the girl established a pattern of defiance at the establishment and those in authority—certainly Johnny Rankin helped her learn that masculine authority was not frightening and could be challenged."[52] From these suggestions both writers reasoned that the drawings demonstrate her difference and illustrate her exceptional qualities. Certainly they show artistic skill and picture some lively events. But the cheerful good spirits are shared by the entire group, Annie being perhaps a leader, but not consciously revolutionary—a clown and a rascal, but hardly much different from the rest. Nineteenth-century girls of fourteen and fifteen were often treated as just that—girls, and Anne Martin and her friends seem to have thought of themselves as children. Even though regular attendance at dancing school was standard, the girls hardly ever seemed to act like young ladies—except under coercion.

Annie Martin was proud of her part in the pranks, but she certainly did not perform alone. To suggest as Townley does that "Anne Martin's defiance of the establishment seems to have begun with the year she spent under the control or lack of control, of the ineffective Father Rankin"[53] singles her out of what appears to have been a rowdy bunch, few of whom later defied the establishment in any sense at all.

But school officials held the entire class back, partially as a result of the rebellion. Anne Martin's diary reveals little concern about the delay but it offers some sense of the end of the year ceremonials of that day: she recorded the flutter of practice and fittings that preceded the performance in June by the Del Sarte class, for example.

Draped in appropriate classic tunics of cheesecloth, the young women of the school demonstrated their skills in attitudes adapted to recitations. Del Sarte, a system of gestures and movements to accompany elocutionary performances, included, as novelist Maureen Howard remembered, "all the gestures of life boiled down, jelled to a routine and practiced first to the right . . . then to the left":

Calling (hand cupped to the mouth), Looking (hand over the eyes), Hearing, Greeting, Farewell, then into the deeper emotional material: Rejection, Fear, Love (both open and guarded variety), Laughter (head tossed, eyes dancing), and . . . Sorrow. Sorrow was posed with the head sagged, eyes covered with one drooping arm while the other was thrust back in Limp Despair.[54]

Annie's record of her last year at Whitaker reveals a girl not quite ready to be a woman, an obedient child willing to go through "the usual program of duets" with her brother and sister for guests, a hard-working student beginning early in the term on her reading for the prize essay on Hawthorne—"we have to do a great deal of reading and I will enjoy that part of it"—and an appreciative friend. When she learned that Ray Baker had driven cattle to earn money to take her to the fancy dress ball, she soberly predicted ". . . if he keeps on, he will make a nice man" (diary, 1891). Not quite sixteen, she was still more child than woman:

Dick [Victoria Godfroy] and I have got into the habit of sending each other bugs in notes. I caught an interesting specimen. He was quite lively. I did him up in a neat little package and Dick opened it up in Latin class. Then the bug and she were both quite lively. (March 22)

Although family affairs intruded from time to time (her brother Harry left for a "new chance" in San Francisco after "acting shamefully at Carson"), she continued to enjoy her new horse and enjoy "great fun" once "way out" to "ride as the boys do," and to take great pride in writing the prize essay at school and to get the most from a summer vacation with relatives in San Francisco. When the family decided in late summer of 1891 that she would leave Whitaker and attend the university, she was momentarily saddened to "leave all the girls . . . especially Dick," but in accepting the decision—she had thought for some time the school went "too slow"—she again proved a responsible and obedient child.

Anne Martin's earliest years were happy and full ones. She was protected from want and loneliness and she was encouraged to learn, to be independent, to work with others, to make friends, to be responsible. If she showed no signs so early of an interest in women's rights and women's status that is not surprising. Still a child in her own mind and in the minds of her parents, she was ready to enter the adult world of education with all the advantages that a loving and comfortable home could offer her. Her position as oldest daughter required some behavior she could not seem to manage, but her place as favored child—brother Harry seemed to have a good many problems with the family—gave her privileges as well. An understanding father who indulged her individuality surely helped to give her confidence in herself as did her success at learning and leading. A fond if conventional mother may have made young Annie conscious of some difference in herself, but Mrs. Martin appeared to have respected the special quality of her energetic and hardworking daughter, as demonstrated in later years when she publicly supported her grown daughter's varied rebellions. Anne entered the Nevada State University prepared to learn and to achieve. As the nineteenth century moved to its close, a new world for women was beginning. She had a part to play in that new world and her beginnings had prepared her well.

CHAPTER 2

A MODERN EDUCATION

Nevada State University and the World of Women

> She must be enduringly, incorruptibly good; instinctively, infallibly wise—wise not for self development, but for self renunciation . . .
>
> John Ruskin, *Sesame and Lillies*

> Will I never have any ambition? Will I never accomplish anything? . . . O, I must do something . . .
>
> Anne Martin, Diary, 1893

ANNE MARTIN spent five years in college—two of those years at Nevada State University so close to home and three at the brand new Leland Stanford Junior University in California. Those years set her apart from other women in a number of ways: they gave her an education that taught her to expect much from life, acquaintance with other women of ambition, confidence in her abilities as a leader and as a scholar. She was fortunate to have both the leisure and the money to take full advantage of new opportunities for women both at home and at Stanford. She matured, she learned, and when she finished graduate school in 1897 she seemed at first to have found a clear direction for her life as a teacher.

When Anne Martin enrolled there in 1892, Nevada State University was barely five years old, "just a bit of land, partly reclaimed from the desert," according to Samuel Bradford Doten, a place "inconceivably bare and bleak" in comparison with the "green success" of Whitaker

School, its few buildings set above fields and pastures to the south and edging the unbroken sagebrush to the north. In a nearby hollow cows "mooed lustily in the midst of recitations" and the "odors and flies and wind-born debris helped to give the university the atmosphere of a genuine 'cow college.'" Intruding into the beginnings of a campus came at intervals cattle, horses, sheep, and even hogs to assist in the clipping of the new-made lawns.[1]

Although Anne Martin was just past sixteen when she entered, she and Louisa Lucas, also from Whitaker School, managed to qualify as sophomores after entrance examinations.[2] Anne looked forward to more challenging classes, but she was still able to maintain close ties with her friends at the old school, for the walk was a short one between the two campuses. At the university many of the faces were familiar: her favorite cousin, Fred Stadtmuller, was completing his studies there; Hannah Clapp, a longtime friend of the family from their days in Empire, was at work in the library; girls from school were students as well; most of the staff were friends of the Martins.

"It doesn't take very long to get right down to hard work at this University"—one of the earliest entries in the 1892 diary reflects the demands of her first-term program: geography, English, algebra, chemistry, German, and Latin. The new university student paid less attention to her diary, perhaps because of the heavier load, perhaps because she was newly enthusiastic about tennis. The new sophomore emerges as a serious student and forms new kinds of friendships, but it is still clear that she thinks of herself as something less than a grown woman. While she commented on sober events at university functions, she still skipped rocks on the ponds with her little brothers, cherished a note from Dick: "Annie and I are *mad* though she seems to dislike me yet I love her just the same" (diary, 1892).

Almost imperceptibly changes came as the world widened in her second year at the university, for the diary for 1893 reflects a growing maturity, a serious concern for her own character, her own goals. She gave little thought at this time to the standard sort of future—marriage—even though Carrie Belknap, whom Anne particularly admired ("she can run faster than I can") had announced wedding plans and Anne's sister Gertrude was attracting boys at all the parties where Anne suffered through the dances. The transition from an all-girl school to the mixed classes at the university was apparently only partially eased by years of attendance at dancing school and parties.

She chided herself for her ambition, but she longed most of all

> . . . to have an independent fortune on the income of which I can live comfortably and do as I please without too much managing. Then the first thing I would do would be to go in quest of a country town where they have beautiful springs and no wind all summer long. There I should build a cottage—one after my own heart, planned of course by myself—by the river (the town must have a river). And there I should live independently, governed by no law but my own conscience, which must, by that time have attained a tolerable degree of enlightenment. (May 1893)

Certainly she had begun to meet women who were models of independence, and she had clearly decided that she would be no beauty with multiple suitors; in fact, she had congratulated herself on encountering on a streetcar in San Francisco a "flashy girl" who had once attended Whitaker Hall—"It's a pity such a pretty girl can't remain virtuous and modest. To me there's comfort in the thought I'm not pretty" (August 1893).

Pretty or not, Annie Martin was beginning to have a steadier concept of herself that recognized certain virtues and saw particular faults. Sometimes she confused the two, but references from her friends help to reveal the future feminist: Edythe Newlands, daughter of a Nevada senator and a lifelong friend, saw the determination—"She could imagine me in later life talking women's suffrage or something of that sort. 'And you would just pound it into them'" (30 July 1893). In charge of buying tickets home for the younger children on the Central Pacific after the usual summer stay in San Francisco, she cautioned herself, "No cheating on the fare. Central Pacific is the meanest and most grasping company." And she recorded as a "compliment" from a friend: "She said I could take people down better than anyone she ever saw. I suppose she means I'm sarcastic, as Dick always said" (April 1893).

In the midst of it all, a serious concern for women and their problems began to emerge, a mulling over of questions that were argued about her sex, and she recorded the effects of the influence of women around her. Steady as before in keeping lists of the books read, she began in the 1893 diary to raise questions about them, to record opinions and to respond, sometimes rather curiously. She supposed that she knew what John Ruskin was talking about in *Sesame and Lillies,* that paean to woman as queen of her sphere, as head of the home:

> . . . woman's true place and power . . . she must . . . be incapable of error . . . She must be enduringly, incorruptibly good; instinctively, infallibly wise—not for self development, but for self renunciation: wise—with

the passionate gentleness of infinitely variable, because infinitely applic-
able, modesty of service—the true changefullness of woman.[3]

Annie's response is to wonder, "Will I never have any ambition? Will I
never accomplish anything? . . . O, I must do something." The call to
feminine submissiveness merely sharpened her sense of her need to do,
and the virtues she sought for herself were rather less humbling ones: "I
must be honest first, honest, sincere, fair and charitable" (August 1893).

Not surprisingly, the novelist George Eliot became a center of her
attention after she read *Middlemarch* and discussed the work in some
detail with Hannah Clapp. Annie was apparently considering a study
(perhaps for her English class) to settle a question of whether "the life
and works of George Eliot exert a good or bad influence." The topic
sounds as if it might have been one posed by Professor Thomas Cowgill,
who appeared in the diary as a righteous sort likely to object to the
irregularities of the writer's life. Clearly, Annie admired George Eliot:
"[she] must have been a noble woman as she created such noble
characters—look at Dorothea Brooke—however, the converse does not
follow." She went on to record Miss Clapp's comment that although
accused of being manly, "at bottom [Eliot] was a womanly woman, that
nature made her so and the works of nature are unchangeable." References to Eliot abounded: the novels were topics of party conversation,
and when she exerted her will upon her horse, Chub, Annie compared
herself to Grandcourt in *Daniel Deronda*—"I drove him, holding him so
hard my arms are still lame." At no point did the young lady from the
proper home offer the slightest criticism of the author who spent much of
her life living with a man who was not her husband; she responded to the
morality of the works, ignoring the irregularity of the life. How much of
this openness of thought she owed to her father's influence and how
much to the contacts she made with women less conventional than her
mother is unclear. Her reading, the comparatively open attitudes of the
social world in which she moved, and the contacts she had with forward-
seeing women had important effects on her: the nineties were a time of
great change and ferment in the thinking of women throughout the
country and she had the ideal opportunities for getting the most from that
commotion in her privileged position.

Hints of the restraints common to her time flickered in the diaries—
her father objected to the character of some of the young men at a concert
she attended and brother Harry's exact misbehaviors were hidden from
her. But she enjoyed considerable physical freedom in her daily life.
The rides on Chub gave her the freedom of the countryside, her bicycle

carried her to school without the escorts she had required as a youngster, and she frequently drove the family carriage to return guests throughout the town. Times were changing for western women: during the decade her acquaintance Eugenia Bruns remembered a horseback expedition she and friends made to Bodie, California, where the women's bloomer outfits attracted the entire town,[4] and Bertha Brown recalled a pioneer bicycle trip from San Francisco to Los Angeles.[5]

Anne Martin particularly enjoyed her bicycle, the machine Duncan Crow has called one of the major liberating forces for women both in the United States and England,[6] and her references reveal the strange child-woman she was at eighteen. "After your bump of self esteem has been rudely handled and your opinion of yourself badly lacerated, nothing so soothes your spirit and heals your wounds and causes your estimate of yourself to rise again as a run on your smoothly running bicycle over an even road" (1893). Yet, young as she was she was noting, observing, watching the condition of women in a way that would suggest that from some of the growing attention to the nation's press, from some of the "New Woman" hullabaloo of the decade, she was drawing some conclusions, longing for more than to "live independently," developing a sincere desire to "do something."

However remote Reno may have seemed from the world of restless women reaching for something outside the home, Anne Martin's personal excursion into difference was not unique. At this period of her life her concerns strongly resembled those of other young women who grew to be leaders in the suffrage cause. New ideas directed their thinking, new goals animated their ambitions. Inez Haynes (later Gilmore, still later Irwin) was two years older than Anne Martin and lived in Massachusetts, but she, too, kept a diary and her reading was strikingly similar to Martin's, her recorded ambitions equally reflective of the changing times. Both women became early members of the radical branch of the suffrage campaigners, the National Woman's Party, in later years.

Like Anne Martin, Inez Haynes had grown to young womanhood in a large household full of relatives and ideas. She had one aunt who was a minister, another who was a spiritualist. "I heard discussed every possible system of ethics, every possible theory of humanitarianism . . . I was conscious then of no impressions, I realize now they had a profound effect."[7] Like Martin, who had high goals, Haynes longed to "cultivate self sacrifice and heroism, honesty and chastity, patriotism and fortitude, meekness and purity."[8] Like her later associate in the NWP, Haynes recorded a certain discomfort around men.

Both young women read the same sorts of books: Marie Bashkirt-seff's journal, *The Heavenly Twins* by Madame Sarah Grand, Plato and the Latin classics, the novels of George Eliot, the essays of John Ruskin—a mix of accepted moral teaching and new ideas. Bashkirt-seff's journal, an immensely popular work for years after its first appearance in Europe in 1887, revealed the real life of a young woman of talent and ambition who died before she could achieve the greatness she sought. In its open and intense celebration of female individuality and ambition, in its romantic excesses, the journal raised quite a commotion in a world devoted to female submissiveness, to the sacred shrine of sacrificing womanhood.[9] Little of the Victorian ideal of modesty greyed Marie's flamboyant pronouncements. To read Marie's adventures, to share her ambitions, was to escape the dilemma of the young woman who knew she could learn, believed that she could yearn for achievement, but plainly saw that all those around her expected her to stay true to no greater glory than motherhood, no other ambition than wifehood.

Ambition in Marie or in Anne or in Inez denied the prevailing beliefs about the proper nature of woman, beliefs concisely put by Eliza Linton's *The Girl of the Period,* widely accepted on both sides of the Atlantic as a summation of Victorian goals: "passionate ambition, virile energy, the love of strong excitement, self-assertion, fierceness and an undisciplined temper, are all qualities which detract from [the ideal of] womanliness."[10] All the condemned qualities helped describe Marie, whose journal refreshed many a young woman restless under such elegant restraints.

Anne Martin likened herself to Marie. The young Russian wrote of constant competition with another young painter she called "Breslau" (she could not or would not record the rival's real name), who was the winner to subdue, admired and envied, a symbolic adversary to spur Marie's ambitions. Martin found Breslaus all her life, noting even at eighteen that "there's consolation in finding I am not the only one so afflicted. With my customary egotism, I have always thought so" (diary, February 1894).

Both young women could have found in *The Heavenly Twins* a disturbing picture of woman as a "mere cork of a creature on the waters of life." In a series of exempla detailing the dangers of womanhood, Grand particularly touched home with her account of twins, male and female, who were like enough to change positions and clothes from time to time to reveal the unjustness of varying attitudes toward the sexes, attitudes that often repressed the freedom and intellectual curiosity of the girl on the basis of mere gender.[11]

Both young women feared that marriage would impede ambition: Haynes called marriage a privilege, not a duty, adding it was an "unphilosophic thing to marry."[12] Martin included no man in the rosy future she envisioned, living "independently, governed by no law but my own conscience." Both admired George Eliot's high-minded heroines who sacrificed themselves for principle. Eliot's heroic women, a modern critic has observed, "had intelligence, imagination, passion, and a keen desire to live life to the fullest. Yet each fails or languishes through a mistaken sense of duty, or through death, before the book is done."[13]

Most of all, the diaries of the two young women reveal a hunger for independence, a refusal to accept the pallid role assigned to women, two goads to achievements beyond the ordinary. Similar objections to the accepted female role mark the records of M. Carey Thomas, later president of Bryn Mawr,[14] and Crystal Eastman, lawyer and writer, both later members of the NWP, which Anne Martin headed in 1916. Just as Anne Martin's father encouraged her to camp out, ride, and learn to shoot a rifle,[15] Eastman's father supported the young girl's demand for physical freedom from long skirts and her insistence on equality in the family.[16] It is no wonder that within the next twenty years women like these would jolt the suffrage campaign to new life.

A new kind of woman was emerging throughout the country, a woman nourished by open-minded parents, sharpened by higher education, alerted through her reading to a consciousness of the realities of feminine existence. Resistance to the accepted modes of behavior started young in these women, less in overt actions than in their private thoughts and burgeoning ambitions.

As she matured, Martin's relationships with women in Nevada were many and varied: she was able to observe quite a cross section of advancing womanhood even in so small a community as Reno. Some of the teachers at the school became personal friends when Anne Martin ceased to be a responsibility and could be accepted as an equal. The once dreaded Miss Ewin, caricatured in the childhood sketches, became a valued friend, as often the object of Annie's trips to Whitaker as Dick, a matron there by 1893. Two women in particular—Hannah Clapp and Mila Tupper Maynard, suffragist, teacher, minister, and writer—were models of female independence that could have inspired her to ambition.

From the time they married, the Martins had known Hannah Clapp, best remembered in Nevada as the woman who put up the iron fence around the state capitol in 1875. Clapp had made herself a personage many years before she started to work at the university. A lifelong feminist, she had journeyed west with a revolver and a bloomer dress and had even managed to meet Brigham Young. But she was more impressed with Mormon women, whom she saw as "miserable slaves" of "the licentious knaves" of that polygamous faith.[17] When the Martins met her in Carson City, she was well established in a home of her own and was the head of Sierra Academy, a private school that in its first financial success proved her business skill. The school was famous in the area and its board of trustees included major officeholders, one of whom was Senator William Stewart. In her twenty years at Carson, Clapp constructed far more than a fence around a building, for she had established friendships with powerful men and had earned a reputation as far more than a schoolmarm. She had, like so many others in Nevada, both enjoyed the fruits of financial success—a fine home, extended travel—and suffered the loss of practically all in the depressions that attended the depletion of the mines.[18] Sixty-three years old when the state university was moved to Reno from Elko in 1887, she managed to persuade Senator Stewart to have her appointed as one of two faculty at the new school, beginning many years of service in various capacities.[19]

Hannah Clapp was a regular visitor in the Martin home for all of the years that Anne Martin was growing up. Voteless, she was nevertheless an ardent worker for "the benefits of political patronage" as close adviser to Senator Stewart.[20] She was working to get the vote as a participant in nearly every organized women's movement in her life-time, beginning with the 1883 introduction in the legislature of a resolution favoring woman suffrage.[21] In 1891, with her lifelong com-panion Elizabeth Babcock, she held the first meeting of the Queen Isabella Association, a kind of women's auxiliary to the Columbian Exposition at Chicago, a group that aimed to erect a pavilion designed by a woman architect to offer a nursery and kindergarten for children. Among the women she recruited was Anne Martin's mother, who served as treasurer. At the university, Clapp was adviser and Anne Martin president of the Adelphi Literary Society, which was devoted to the "promotion and cultivation of literary talents . . . and to [improving] the moral, intellectual and social condition of our members."[22]

Anne Martin enjoyed the many visits Clapp and Babcock made to her home, but she recorded some problems as well: "Miss C. and Miss Babcock are dear old ladies, but they are very funny. You sit between them, and both get to talking at the same time on different subjects; it is very hard, under the circumstances, to be polite and listen to both" (17 January 1893). Perhaps because she found Professor Cowgill unsym-pathetic to women she sought out Clapp for discussions of George Eliot;

at any rate, the pair presented Anne with a complete set of Eliot's works "bound in half calf" for Christmas the last year she was in school at the university (list of gifts received, diary, 1894).

Although it was Clapp who talked most to Annie, Babcock was almost always along and offered in her own life an example of service and hard work. Founder of the first kindergarten in the state and a full partner with Clapp in the early days of Sierra Academy, the less hardy Babcock had become ill and dependent the last few years of their thirty-five-year friendship. Kathryn Totton suggests that they were an accepted couple for many years, their friendship "part of the Nevada scene."[23]

The Clapp and Babcock household offered Martin an alternative example to routine marriage, but if the devoted elderly couple were not enough to impress Annie with the complexity of a woman's world that might conceivably include a life much different from her mother's, there were other influences as well and Annie was well aware of them. Clapp was a suffragist and an independent actor in a world she confronted directly as her male contemporaries did, but however she may have been admired in the family circle, she was a woman of limited abilities and restricted education, indebted to her political connections for her very position. Perhaps the best of the examples of what an educated woman might do was demonstrated by Mila Tupper Maynard, not only educated but accomplished and confident as well.

Mrs. Maynard and her husband, R. A. Maynard, arrived in Reno in 1892. Both were Unitarian ministers. Mrs. Maynard was a graduate of both the state normal school in Whitewater, Wisconsin, and of the university course at Cornell in 1889 with a Bachelor of Letters and a special diploma in philosophy.[24] By 1893 both Maynards were well enough acquainted with the town to offer a series of lectures, while Mrs. Maynard did some teaching at the university in German and literature.[25] Mila Maynard remained a friend of Anne Martin for many years. A woman well ahead of her time, Maynard was then at the beginning of a long career as lecturer and writer who pursued the offbeat as well as the popular. Her interests were varied: she could speak on *Trilby* to the Twentieth Century Club and publish a few years later one of the earliest serious studies of Walt Whitman, a poet little loved by the academics of his time.[26]

Anne Martin attended several different series of the many lectures the Maynards gave in Reno. Her occasional responses in the diaries suggest she particularly enjoyed the literary series, one that featured Tennyson and included other contemporary British and American writers. Her

ticket to the lectures was a treat from her parents, but it was a pleasure
disapproved of by her English and history teacher, Professor Cowgill,
who saw the Maynards as a "heathenizing influence . . . as the all
importance of Christianity in connection with Dante wasn't brought out.
But the money part seemed to offend him particularly," young Annie
complained. "He talked so earnestly that I almost forgot whether it was
his or my business he was discussing" (diary, 1893). Cowgill's arguments, she continued, "didn't shake my faith a particle," and the
passage continues to record her approval of Mrs. Maynard's "absolute
freedom of thought in thinking about God," particularly praising the
older woman's comment that "whenever we admire and seek for Truth
we are worshipping and seeking God." This controversy between Anne
and Cowgill—both professor and Episcopal minister—points up the
intellectual freedoms allowed the girl by her father in spite of her
mother's more conventional attachment to the church. Anne was free to
choose her own service and she took that opportunity when the
Maynards were in town.

It was easy to prefer Mrs. Maynard to Cowgill, for he had irritated the
girl in class by offering topics like "Our fancies are as giddy and infirm
as women's are," subjects she termed "like Professor Cowgill—always
making a sly hit at women." He was ". . . coarse-fibered, vulgar, a man
who thinks his position as a clergyman gives him license to express
himself freely in a mixed class of students" (22 January 1894). Perhaps
more distantly, Doten comments that Cowgill, "living a life of austere
simplicity among his books . . . was misunderstood by many of the
students of that period."[27]

Mrs. Maynard, on the other hand, was easy to understand: "Although
you know she is very learned and intelligent, she doesn't let you feel it
overwhelmingly," Annie wrote in 1893. "She always meets you on your
own ground—she can adapt her mind to yours so readily, and always
finds some truth or some good in whatever you say." For the girl's
sincere admiration, Mila Maynard returned her own attention. She
encouraged Anne to apply to her own school, Cornell, and she introduced her to young women who were making their own way (31 January
1894). In the summers she organized the female students in the town
into a vacation club for outings and discussions (July 1894).

Rather surprisingly, Anne Martin mentioned not a word about suffrage in her many references to Mrs. Maynard, even though the latter
had clearly stated ideas about the question and was by 1895 a leader in
the revived movement in Reno. Indeed, it was this Mila Maynard who
"gave a splendid address" for almost an hour at the legislative session

that eventually passed a first resolution for removing the word "male" from the voting regulations.[28]

Whether she planted suffrage ideas in the girl's mind or not, Mrs. Maynard surely offered her mature companionship, intellectual stimulation, and liberating open-mindedness on many a subject. Her continuing success as a public person must have impressed a young woman longing for a goal for her energies.

If she learned of female independence and loyalty from the Misses Clapp and Babcock and of intellectual achievement from Mila Maynard, Anne Martin learned dramatically of the dangers facing the unprotected woman in the fate of her drawing teacher, Alice M. Hartley, a newcomer to Reno in 1894 who had established a studio in the bank building and had sought unsuccessfully to join Reno social circles. An entry in the diary for 1894 opens: "I feel sorry for Mrs. Hartley. She is an artist of merit—the best teacher that has ever been here, and yet she can't get enough pupils to pay her expenses, I wish that I might help her in some way. I feel that I am doing good work with her" (9 February 1894).

Mrs. Hartley was apparently befriended by the Martins, for Anne records introducing her to her favorite aunt "with whom she was charmed." As later events revealed, Mrs. Hartley had found another admirer in the person of state senator M. D. Foley, a noted womanizer, about whom Anne had wondered when she questioned "whether to refuse Dr. Darling and men like him to dance or not. Yet we all dance with Mr. Foley as he has money and social position" (1894). Still, whatever Foley's reputation, the Martin family was "electrified," in Annie's words, on 24 July "to hear that Mrs. Hartley had shot Senator Foley and that the shot proved fatal in a few minutes." She found it

> easy to imagine the cause of the shooting in a case where Senator Foley is concerned. He had wronged her, she was penniless, about to leave, in need of his assistance, which was refused. He must have been unbearable, so the interview terminated in the shooting . . . I think every woman in town is partially responsible for this horrible affair. They shunned and snubbed her on account of the stories afloat, when she was trying to be respectable. Her course of action is a resultant [sic] of several forces, the determining one the unmercifulness of her sisters.

This remarkable outpouring written only a few hours after the event reflects not only on the shock to be expected when a close friend is involved in violence but reveals her close knowledge of the case even before news accounts had appeared. Mrs. Hartley's studio was in the upper floor of the bank building, one level above Foley's own office, and it was there the shooting happened.

There was melodrama enough: Mrs. Hartley was pregnant as a result, she claimed at her trial, of the senator's having plied her with liquor in February; ready to leave town and dependent on him for help, she had admitted him to her studio one last time, her pistol already loaded. Anne must have heard how Mrs. Hartley emptied the gun into the retreating senator, how he stumbled down the steps to a doctor's office, crying out, "Doctor, I am shot and I am killed," how Mrs. Hartley was found, revolver still in hand, admitting, "I have shot Mr. Foley and I am glad," or, in yet another version, "I hope that he will die."[29]

Surely before Anne made a last shopping trip to San Francisco to buy her college wardrobe, she listened to the controversy and read the *Nevada State Journal* editorial that admitted, "M. D. Foley had his faults, but who has not?" and continued to comment on the wealthy senator's habit of being "close in his dealings with people."[30] William O'Hara Martin was both a pallbearer (the Foleys were family friends) and a member of the coroner's jury, but forty years later Anne Martin credited him with helping to get Mrs. Hartley's sentence lightened.[31] Anne's responses might well have been affected from the beginning by her father's views, his defense of a woman he clearly thought respectable enough to employ for his daughter's instruction; whatever the reason, Anne's sentiments were strongly in favor of the unfortunate murderess. In August, before the trial that enthralled the community in September (after she had left for Stanford), Anne again recorded her feeling that "every woman in this town by her coldness and arrogance toward Mrs. Hartley during her first few months residence is partially responsible for this terrible, terrible trouble" (August 1894). Years later Anne Martin called for "sex solidarity" among women voting for reforms; in 1894 she seemed to realize how important acceptance could be for a woman and to blame those who had forced Mrs. Hartley into dependence on the apparently all too willing senator. Martin's sense of the root of the problem oversimplifies Mrs. Hartley's predicament, but it indicates how strongly she sensed the importance of community among women.

This "terrible, terrible trouble" engendered by the shooting was resolved later in the year when a jury convicted Mrs. Hartley of second-degree murder; after the birth of her son in November, she was sentenced to eleven years in the penitentiary. She served two years before she was pardoned in January 1897, again amid great controversy.[32] Although Anne Martin was not in Reno during the entire time, she was certainly kept informed by her regular letters from home and from her many Reno friends. She was in Reno in 1898 when Mrs. Hartley, with no little nerve, sued for a share of the Foley estate for her son. She lost the suit but won a new husband and, as Mrs. W. S. Bonnifield of Winnemucca, returned to as much respectability as she might hope for.[33]

For all the womanly concern about sisterly coldness toward Mrs. Hartley, the young woman who packed her shirtwaists and her black corset, her tennis rackets and her books for her first semester at Leland Stanford Junior University in August 1894 was still very much a girl in many ways, however dignified she may have sounded as Anna Henrietta Martin, A.B., when she finished school. She was not quite nineteen, and she was still a bit of a tomboy, proud of her athletic prowess and not particularly fond of ladylike pursuits or a young woman's restraints. Bookish and shy with men, she preferred literary conversations to dances, but not necessarily out of choice. She wondered in her diary after she had attended graduation at Whitaker Hall:

> During the dancing a grave problem confronted me. Whether a girl not pretty, attractive, or popular should submit to tyrannical social restrictions which compel her to face the whims and neglect of men in marked contrast to her younger sister, who is certainly not a wall flower. O, what I suffered! . . . My answer to the problems was that an unattractive girl should not place herself in a position where social customs are such as to cause her humiliation . . . I am not going to dance any more. (June 1894)

The "tyrannical social restrictions" didn't keep her from her secret pleasures of wearing riding trousers and her brother Bill's hat to go "on a beautiful spin on Harry's wheel," nor did she restrain herself at graduation from trying to "rouse the regents" with a discussion on the system of college electives. The tyranny seems to be more related to fulfilling social obligations expected by her family from time to time.

If she was hurt by the "whims and neglect of men," that mattered only when she was forced to seek such attentions. Most of her friends and associates were young women like herself, and the closest was the younger Victoria Godfroy, Annie's favorite of all the girls at the hall, the recipient of mischievous and of romantic notes, the center of Annie's affections for many years. The only letter from early years in the extensive "out" correspondence at the Bancroft Library is an invitation in Martin's hand asking sarcastically for an explanation of Dick's refusal to "go violet hunting" (dated 1893). Dick was an uncertain sort of friend, one who might refuse invitations and turn her eyes elsewhere to the sadness of Annie, who observed at a party "Dick and Evelyn, oblivious of everything but each other," and how "Maud Rives . . . is the

only friend I have" (1893). Little changed before Anne left for Palo
Alto; the visits to the hall continued and Anne tutored Dick in geometry
(Dick did not go beyond Whitaker Hall but remained as a matron and
part-time teacher), even though on occasion there is a note in the diary
about Anne's returning "all the love letters." And the letters continued to
move between Nevada and California during the first year Anne spent at
Stanford.

Theirs was a friendship in the traditional spirit of the ardent companionship recorded among so many nineteenth-century girls and women
who had been known to long for "an Eden of eternal adolescence,"
feelings often misinterpreted in our own age, when such terms as "fall in
love," "make love to," and the like imply more explicitly sexual
relationships.[34] As Carroll Smith-Rosenberg has pointed out, a "romantic rhetoric . . . surrounded the concept of friendship," and terms of
sentimental affection abound in expressions between women just as they
do between men and women: "the twentieth century tendency to view
human love and sexuality within a dichotomized universe of deviance
and normality . . . is alien to the ideas of the nineteenth . . . [and]
fundamentally distorts the nature of [women's] emotional
interaction."[35] Smith-Rosenberg goes on to speculate that by the twentieth century "a number of cultural taboos evolved to cut short the
homosocial ties of girlhood [but] nineteenth century American society
did not taboo close female relationships but recognized them as a
socially viable form of human contact—and, as such, acceptable
throughout a woman's life."[36]

Although she apparently had a brief romantic interlude shortly after
her graduation from Stanford and maintained a long romantic and
political correspondence later in life with a married man, Anne Martin
found most of her lasting friendships with women. Perhaps this tendency had its beginning in the young college student who did not choose to
compete for male attention—although she would compete for almost
anything else. It would be wrong, however, to assume too much from
these early preferences.

To say that at graduation she was a country girl as she had been a
country child in Empire City would be incorrect. The company that
filled the Martin home was drawn from various parts of the country.
Before she attended Stanford, Anne Martin met David Starr Jordan, the
young president of the university, in her own house as a guest of her
father. Every summer the older children stayed in San Francisco where
the lunches at the Palace were social pleasures among a determined
number of "advantages" happily accepted: trips to galleries, museums,

concerts, and similar excitements that the city could offer along with holiday celebrations and fires.

Anne Martin had been a good student her two years at the university; she had studied its basic course successfully (there were no electives except a choice between French and German) and if she had not been greatly challenged by it she had expanded her intellectual horizons with her own extensive reading, with her inquiries into and trials with religion, and with her contacts with mature and educated people. She had seen by example that women could accomplish much in the world. Her venture to Stanford was a second step into the kind of education that would separate her from other women who stopped learning sooner and sought less from the world than she did. In Palo Alto she could expect to meet new challenges both to her burgeoning intellect and to her personal independence.

CHAPTER 3

THE BEST OF EDUCATIONS
A Finish at Stanford

No training is adequate which falls short of the best.
—David Starr Jordan

I have estimated intellect all too highly . . . Feeling is important, after all.
—Anne Martin, Diary, 1894

LIKE MANY ANOTHER young woman of nearly nineteen, Anne Martin was a mixture of uncertainty and determination, of fear and eagerness, of silliness and sense when she arrived at Stanford. To a twentieth-century woman she would seem naive, still tied to girls' games and girlish affections in spite of her wide reading and advanced education. Pictures made of her that year show her small, piquant face peering uncertainly forward between the exaggerated sleeves and the tightly pulled back hair, stylishly "up" from her childhood pigtails. Although she had considered colleges in the East briefly, her decision to attend Stanford marked her later career and helped direct her life, already one somewhat distinguished from that of others her age.

By 1890 young women were finishing secondary school at a steadily growing rate; they had always been more likely to finish than young men—9,000 women to 7,000 men in 1870, 57,000 women to 38,000 men by 1900, as Carl Degler points out. Going beyond high school was another matter; more than four times as many men as women managed the second step by 1900.[1] Although not all educated women became feminists, almost all the women who fought for suffrage and continued to champion women's rights were educated beyond the average.[2]

Leland Stanford Junior University, founded by one of California's richest men, was, like the new University of Chicago, a coeducational institution from the very first, for Leland Stanford himself had made clear to the board of trustees in 1885, when "the farm" was still unchanged countryside, that it was "of first importance that the education of both of the sexes shall be equally full and complete and varied only as nature dictates. The rights of one sex, political or otherwise, are the same as those of the other sex, and this equality of rights ought to be fully recognized." Trustee James M. Shafter repeated the determination of the founders to support a right "that has received partial recognition in other institutions; here it is declared in its full extent and is to be literally enforced."[3] At the start, it was.

While coeducation was no new thing in the last decade of the century, Stanford made a public and publicized point of its devotion to the goal, even though the purposes of education for the female students reflected traditional views of women. It was not for the wide world that the women were to be educated, but, as the founder insisted in his opening day address, it was "of special importance that those who are to be the mothers of a future generation shall be fitted to mold and direct the infantile mind at its most critical period."[4] If these views were little different from the prevailing ones of the century before—and some decades to come—of woman's taming function in a world that was "only a large home,"[5] the opportunities were exceptional at Stanford, and access was open to both sexes to profit from Jordan's dictum, "No training is adequate which falls short of the best."[6]

Anne Martin's entry as a major in history reflected the choices of most Stanford women to emphasize the humanities and to concentrate on languages, history, and English, the most popular choice. A solid 20 percent of the women in the first decade of the school found majors in science, mathematics, chemistry, and the biological sciences even though Martin's friend Lou Henry recalled she was the "only girl geology major" when she entered.[7] While some clubs and societies initially excluded women, female students were admitted to those groups most strongly developing from the curriculum—zoology, history, Spanish clubs—and the women founded their own musical organizations and debating societies early. Intercollegiate competition in debate, for example, often included women.[8]

Perhaps it was reassuring that Dr. and Mrs. Jordan were somewhat familiar and that relatives were nearby, for there were in September "two very homesick girls" in the Roble Hall room that Gertrude and Anne shared. ("Anna" seems to have returned in school records, although she was clearly Annie to friends and family for a long time yet.) Typically sociable around women and happy in groups, Anne Martin joined not only a sorority but also the Women's Athletic Association and the Saturday Night debating society, and she took part in the class farce. Lou Henry was a fellow officer in the athletic association and remained a friend of Martin's for almost fifty years, in spite of many separations and the rocky record of Anne Martin's battles with Lou's husband, Herbert Hoover.

Not all of the new social life was easy, and Martin recorded conflicts with new-made friends in a December diary entry: "I have made such violent adjustments in my ideas of late and my moral feelings are still shattered—and I am still prone to make the same mistakes—set my ideals too high, expect too much." By the close of the year and the diary—the last she kept for several years—she wrote about the changes in her thinking: "I have estimated intellect altogether too highly . . . My trouble with Florence has been the striving after the brain understanding before we had the heart, the soul understanding—with Bertha it was different—but I love them both. Feeling is important, after all" (diary, 1894). Martin apparently had made another romantic attachment, like those of her long girlhood, and the comments reveal once again the conflict she continually saw between the calls of feeling and those of reason, calls she saw as inimical. As an undergraduate at Nevada, she had argued for prose over poetry because the former was the medium of reason and, while "reason is not power, it is an instrument of power." Ever subject to emotions she wished to control, she ever cherished reason as superior.[9]

Anne Martin's participation in the life of Stanford is well documented in the student paper, the *Daily Palo Alto,* and in the yearbooks that record campus life; also, her cousin Henrietta, who graduated in 1895, kept a scrapbook of activities that surely included her cousin from Reno.[10] "Netty" had always been close to the Reno Martins—her mother was Anne's favorite aunt—and there were new acquaintances to be added to the family group. Gertrude, for example, a year younger and always more socially at ease than Anne, joined fewer organizations, but she met her future husband, T. T. C. (Tom) Gregory, at Stanford in her early years. Tom's older brother John became a particular friend of Anne at this time. Nettie worked on the paper with Otis B. Wight, who later married the third Martin sister, Clara, a later student at Stanford. The family group remained close at Stanford and Anne remembered her days there fondly.

It seems likely then that Anne Martin shared her cousin's friends and games. "Progressive Observation," an amusement familiar to the Martin girls from schooldays, was a feature of social events; it involved the blindfolded recognition of liquids, smells, and so on, with samples ranging from prune and tomato juice to smells like paregoric and nitre.[11] And certainly life at Stanford, as attested to by letters from students and by the student paper, was not all work, nor had it been from the beginning, even though one female student was careful to note occasional receptions, "occasional because it is not intended at Stanford that play shall gain ascendancy over work." After the first effort, when the men of Encina Hall invited the women of Roble to a dance and were primly refused, "it being more proper that the girls give the first dance," subsequent affairs were held at the women's hall. The young faculty— almost all of them under forty—held regular "at homes" for students, as did the president himself.[12] Even though an early edition of the daily newspaper spoke editorially of the "usefulness of old students to first year men" and President Jordan addressed the all-male societies, when the class of '96 was organized, Anne Martin was chosen to be its secretary.[13]

As always an active athlete, Martin held first place during her first year in tennis, and in 1895 maintained her position by defeating a Miss McCray in a four-set battle in which "every point was a hot one" for the championship in ladies' singles.[14] After Christmas in Reno Anne Martin could have heard her mentor, Mary Sheldon Barnes, speak on "Historical Ideas of Womanhood" and must have known of Dr. Jordan's lectures on "The New Woman" to the class in evolution in March. Years later, Martin could remember hearing Dr. Anna Howard Shaw speak in the Stanford chapel, appearing there with the aging Susan B. Anthony: "It was the only time I ever saw 'Aunt Susan.'"[15]

If Anthony spoke, the *Daily Palo Alto* paid no notice, but it did report Dr. Shaw's arrival and four days later quoted her recalling how Elizabeth Cady Stanton and Lucretia Mott had "a vision of a time when women would be barred from nothing and they determined to have that vision realized."[16] She might also have heard Carrie Chapman Catt in October remind an audience that included Mrs. Jane Stanford that "women are in every way capable of suffrage" and remark that in the beginning days of the country "women . . . could not sing or speak in church . . . Now the church would be crippled without women."[17]

Not only were there many speakers on woman's changing role, but Stanford publications were concerned with woman's state. Surely she agreed with the editorial that deplored the action of Johns Hopkins University in closing its rolls to women "who have become scholars in the strictest sense, [barring them] from a chance to reach the highest scholarship in certain lines."[18] It would seem certain that she was aware of the Women's Congress in San Francisco held in April 1897 while she was finishing her thesis. It was there that President Jordan praised women (however redundantly) for working "under sealed orders": "The need of woman's influence is the strongest plea for her full freedom. The influence of women is fully as important as that of men and most of it is for the future."[19]

During her three years at Stanford, Anne Martin enjoyed as much liberty as the freest of young women in her class, but it would be misleading to think that her personal freedom was not considerably less now that she was a young woman. Although few rules were stated, the university assumed a certain propriety on the part of the woman admitted there, valuing her for her civilizing influence (and the new school had need of some civilizing as the pranks recorded in the school newspaper suggest). Neither male nor female students were subjected to the kinds of rules of conduct that became common on university campuses in the years that followed. As Jordan insisted in an article in the *North American Review* in 1897, the belief was that the university should not assume a parental role but must respect the student's ability to behave properly: "Students are expected to show both within and without the university such respect for order, morality, personal honor, and the rights of others as is demanded of good citizens. Failure to do this will be cause for removal." And a young woman assured her mother: ". . . we have no rules of action whatever and we may do just what we please, restricted only by criticism and the sure fact that if we overstepped the bounds of propriety too far we should have to go." But as Roxanne Nilan has observed, "Jane Stanford kept a close eye on the social conduct of the students, particularly the women."[20] Some students did have to go: Will Irwin, author of the senior farce in which Anne Martin appeared and later the second husband of Inez Haynes, was actually expelled for a prank and later reinstated. (Mrs. Stanford's concern changed direction later. It was she who insisted effectively in 1899, when female enrollment grew to 44 percent of the student body, that only five hundred women be admitted to avoid the stigma of being a "woman's school.")[21]

In Martin's time, women participated fully and made the most of the opportunities. Of Anne Martin's baccalaureate class, several were career women, and some combined marriage and career, serially or simultaneously. Perhaps because they sensed some special quality in the group (21 of 137 were in *Who's Who* in 1926), members of the class of

1896 gathered and composed material for a book about themselves thirty years after graduation called *Stanford '96: An Accounting in 1926*. Privately printed for the members and friends, the book was edited by Sarah Comstock, a free-lance editor and writer and a long-time acquaintance of Anne Martin. Two-thirds of the forty-five women in the class became teachers after graduation, three librarians, four writers, two doctors. Of the group only five married immediately after leaving Stanford to devote their lives to the home. Anne's Whitaker School friend Fredricka Lord, for example, taught school in Gold Hill and Elko before she married but remained active in Red Cross work and headed the Pacific Division of the Survey of Nurses before she died in 1919.[22]

A good many of the graduates remained unmarried, for the generation that came of age in the nineties included a high proportion of women who never married. (That proportion was never higher than it was for women born during the last four decades of the nineteenth century.)[23] Married or single, Stanford women seemed to have been happy with their university experiences. As Susan B. Stokes put it thirty years after graduation, Stanford "opened my eyes, made the world outside a reality, converted life into an immense laboratory."[24]

Stanford offered Anne Martin the chance to compete with women and men of high accomplishments in a school dedicated to quality, one open at the time of her attendance to the development of women, one alive with the ideas that were changing the attitudes and goals of women all over the country. And she responded to what was offered her enthusiastically, taking part in all she encountered, from the senior farce, in which she played the lead, to the tennis court where she excelled, to social organizing she enjoyed as a member of the prom committee and as an officer of the student guild.

Academically, she was particularly impressed by a woman who, as director of her thesis and as a successful and innovative college professor, became Anne's academic mentor and role model—Mary Sheldon Barnes. Fifty years afterward Martin recalled her work and her acquaintance with Barnes; she styled her teaching after Barnes' as far as she could, using the Stanford teacher's study guides and techniques to bolster her own insecurity in the craft. Her autobiography mentions very little more of her other activities at Stanford but draws particular attention to Barnes. Mary Sheldon Barnes had joined Stanford the second year of its operation, arriving on campus with her new husband, Earl, a former student many years her junior. Her demanding history classes were developed around sets of primary sources and featured give-and-take discussions that could prove "disconcerting to precise, note-taking students" accustomed to the traditional lecture method. A frail, dark woman who died in 1899, two years after Anne Martin finished her M.A., Mary Barnes insisted students study in an "independent and solitary way," using her questions as guides to problem solving, and she demanded of them that they learn to observe, weigh evidence, generalize, and exercise creative historical imagination.[25] Several years later, Earl Barnes helped Anne Martin in England, assigning her small research tasks at the British Museum while she was trying to find her way as a writer in England (diary, 1903).

Like many others of her class, she elected to stay for graduate work, achieving her M.A. in history one year after she received the A.B. She wrote a carefully researched thesis on the causes of the Baden revolution, working in both English and German under the direction of Mary Sheldon Barnes. If her thesis is not startlingly original, it is nevertheless workmanlike, carefully documented, clearly written, the kind of detailed if not original work that was expected.[26]

At Stanford she had ventured into a larger world, and she had made friends, some of whom were to last her through a long life. Of particular importance to her were the Herbert Hoovers. Although the future president proved a disappointment as an important friend, Lou Henry Hoover never wavered in her personal loyalty to Anne Martin, even though she later argued with Martin over suffrage tactics and over Martin's bitter attacks on Hoover on many issues. Theirs was a friendship buttressed by family association through T. T. C. Gregory, Gertrude's husband, who worked for Hoover during relief efforts after World War I. Anne Martin found in her relations with Lou none of the disappointments or slights that she perceived or imagined from other friends over many years. Martin also enjoyed the attention and, perhaps, the affection of a man she could respect in John Gregory, whom she had met during the Palo Alto years and whom she was later to identify as "almost a fiance." His accidental death in 1899 seemed to have sent her away from her first professional position and left a scar that remained unhealed for years.[27]

Anne Martin's six years of education had separated her from the mass of women, had prepared her for a life of accomplishment, had included the best that money and effort could bestow. She had grown both intellecutally and socially. As she had been a leader at Whitaker School as a child, she was a leader at Stanford. Young as she was, she was ready to face the challenge of a career. Her reading, her education, and her experience at Stanford combined to give her a proper education for the future. But her ties to Nevada and her family were deep and strong. Half a century afterward she recalled how the sight of wild violets she had always associated with Nevada had affected her. During the last months in Stanford's lush acres of oak and wildflowers, memory called her back from the softer climate she wished to prefer:

> I was walking our Faculty Row to consult Mary Sheldon Barnes about my master's thesis . . . My mind on my thesis . . . I was suddenly transported to another world by a glimpse of wonderful blue in a patch of wild grass growing on the edge of the sidewalk. I fell upon my knees and spread the grass apart. In what *specie eternitatis* had I seen those heavenly-blue, star shaped little flowers, on long stems, with grass-like leaves? In a rush of tears I remembered—not in another world, not eternity, but in our grass grown garden in Empire . . .[28]

A longing for home and a true affection for the lively family she had left behind combined to send her back to the large home on the river, the rides in the desert, and her first paid occupation at the state university. Whether she might have been more ambitious for a job at a more prestigious school is uncertain; surely she had little difficulty finding a position at a campus where she was well known as an outstanding student and as the daughter of a firm and generous supporter of that school. She was not quite twenty-two, more adult no doubt than she had been when she left as a homesick girl, but perhaps happy enough to return to her home state. All of her life she returned regularly to Nevada, from travels throughout the world, from suffrage activities, even after her mother's death. She loved Carmel with its crowds of artistic men and women and its closeness to San Francisco where she had family with whom she kept close ties. Even in her later years, in spite of the wind and the cold she hated, Nevada called her. The beginning of her short teaching career was only the first among many returns of the native daughter.

CHAPTER 4

"FEMINIST IRON"

The Long Search for a Vital Connection

It is no wonder that the feminist iron entered my soul from the day of my father's death.
—Anne Martin, *Autobiography*

It is easy to become the dupe of a deferred purpose.
—Jane Addams, *Twenty Years at Hull House*

ANNE MARTIN was not quite twenty-two when she returned to teach at the Nevada State University—to teach and to return to the family and home she loved, to an occupation that was in every way suitable for a young woman of her education and ambitions. She was well prepared for a career for life, and still young enough to consider marriage. But instead of culmination, the next years saw her withdraw from the new career to spend year after aimless year—almost a decade—in apparently pointless travels, occasional study, and unproductive efforts to find a purpose in life, to make "a vital connection." Perhaps the loss of her "almost fiance" in 1899 drove her from teaching, perhaps the death of her father in 1901 made accomplishment seem less important. She tried more study to little effect, she tried writing with little success, she saw much of the world. Whatever the reason, the ambitious young teacher of 1897 was adrift, caught in the snare of preparation for a goal she could not choose for the better part of a decade.

Certainly her first paid occupation was suitable. As Carl Degler has observed, "teaching attracted women because it was a socially accepted job . . . it was, after all, an extension of woman's traditional work as the rearer of children."[1] By her own declaration Martin's feminism was still latent (indeed the word was just entering the language in the last decade of the nineteenth century). She had been impressed by Mary Sheldon Barnes, her Stanford mentor, a woman who had achieved an important position at a prestigious university; Hannah Clapp was still part of the Martin circle of friends even though her teaching days had passed and she was serving as librarian in a post perhaps more suited to her training. Martin was well prepared. Among the twenty-eight faculty members at the school were seven women. These seven held four M.A. degrees, a higher proportion of advanced degrees than the male component. Only Professor Walter McNabb Miller, an M.D., President Stubbs, whose doctorate was honorary, and one other professor held the highest academic degrees.[2] The annual register claimed five thousand books in the library in the basement of Morrill Hall (only one-tenth of Stanford's holdings) at the time and offered the opportunity of working for a master's degree in some departments.[3]

President Stubbs marveled that "for a commonwealth with a population of fewer than 50,000 people to maintain a University of three hundred and more students annually reflects the highest honor on the state."[4] Still essentially a prescribed curriculum with few electives in the liberal arts division, Nevada's program demanded strong doses of composition (six semesters of rhetoric), basic science, foreign language, and history. "Miss Anne Martin and President Stubbs" shared a department of history and political science the first year, and hers became a separate department in 1898. Unlike most teachers at Nevada who taught fifteen to eighteen hours a week (the energetic Professor Miller was in the classroom or laboratory for twenty-eight), Martin was responsible for only eight hours of class each week in the university and three more in the normal school for a yearly stipend of $900,[5] a comparatively high salary for the times.

Martin's classes were small ones the first year, the largest, Political History of the United States, enrolling twenty-five, while History of England drew only three. Among her students in her two years of active teaching were men she would later encounter in her political years, including future judge and U.S. senator Patrick A. McCarran.[6] In holograph notes for her autobiography that were not included in the typed version, she recalled how frightened she had been of questions from the class when she first began teaching[7] and she righteously included as "one lapse from mental integrity" that she could recall an occasion when she was teaching Mary Sheldon Barnes' *Outlines of General History* in her "first callow year . . . and used [Barnes']

Teacher's Manual for expanding the outlines of the hour's work, without telling the class the source." She wrote that "when I realized my fault I acknowledged it, to the increased confidence of all concerned."[8] Although she excuses herself from self-righteousness in the passage, she seems particularly sensitive to the practice, one common enough among inexperienced or lazy teachers in any institution and one for which teachers' manuals are intended (or so Mrs. Barnes' manual was); but Martin wished to use the incident: "if my father and my life have taught me anything, it is that honesty and sincerity are the solid rock on which to build one's personal relations: that any other course is not only intolerable to one's self, but ineffective,"[9] thus managing to be both moral and pragmatic.

Whether her mental integrity lapsed again or not, she records nothing else of her teaching career. One of her students, Charles Paul Keyser, who graduated in 1899, provided another view of the young teacher in an interview conducted in 1971. Keyser remembered that "she was not a brilliant person, but she knew how to make a speech, and she was a great dig. She went into things and worked." President Stubbs backed her desire to offer a major in history, and, Keyser remembers, "Dr. Stubbs . . . persuaded three of us to take this course of Anne Martin's as a sort of demonstration . . . Well, I'd go, and she'd give us notes to read, and we'd come back three times a week to her lectures, and so on, and discussions, and . . . would argue with her, and talk about what we thought of what we read . . . And finally she called an examination and she flunked us all three of us." All of the students complained. In the ensuing battle, President Stubbs backed up his teacher, for he had promised not to graduate anybody who did not pass her requirements. One student left without taking the degree, but Keyser was granted a second chance at an examination with the same results before he finally persuaded Stubbs to give him his diploma since his mother had come all the way from Elko to see him graduate. "Well," Keyser concluded, "Anne quit. She threw up her tail and went away." Although Keyser passed a token test in the fall from Martin's successor, Jeanne Wier, he remembered that after that school year Anne Martin "went into a decline, she told me afterwards . . . I looked her up . . . we were friendly enough, as long as she lived. But we just couldn't see eye to eye on her ideas of standards, and I couldn't do for her what she wanted me to do."[10]

Keyser's account is of a single class and recalled after more than seventy years, but it would seem to reflect common enough problems among young and earnest instructors not too sure of themselves and afraid and uncertain about allowing any deviation in assignment and task. The rigidity displayed was typical of Martin's early behavior in the suffrage campaign and in the dogged persistence she showed throughout life in pushing things she believed in. It is typical, too, that she could remain friends, to one degree or another, with those whom she disagreed with.

Whether she was a success as a teacher or not, she became a part of the university and its world for those two years, teaching and participating in campus life both as a member of the faculty committee on the university system[11] and as captain of the faculty ladies' basketball team. One match with the seniors was reported in the *Gazette* as one in which "the learned ladies of the faculty and the learned seniors took off their dignity along with their street clothes and the game was red hot all the time."[12] In 1899 she was elected to head the Alumni Association, a group she had helped form in 1894, and she was promoted from instructor to assistant professor.[13]

At home, her father's lingering illness clouded the happy life at the big house on Mill Street, but one improvement lasted long enough for the family to entertain "quite a company of friends" on the silver wedding anniversary of the elder Martins and to spend a month in the summer at Deer Park Inn at Lake Tahoe.[14] Family photographs from the period show well-dressed and smiling Martins of many sizes at the lake.[15]

Whatever Anne Martin may have planned for a university career, however she may have entertained other ideas, a single event seems to have changed those plans and stopped some hopes. Charles Keyser recalls that when he saw her afterward (that is, after his problems with her course), she confided "she had been having quite some trouble" at the time of the controversy. "She said she had worked hard and wasn't up to standard anyway, in getting all this thing together. And then she said the man she wasn't engaged to, but was almost a fiance, was drowned in a boat in San Francisco Bay while this was goin' on. I didn't know anything about it."[16] John Gregory had been a classmate of hers at Stanford, and had stayed on, as she had, for graduate work in 1896–97. They had shared various activities and had continued their friendship in the large family group that included the popular Gertrude and her fiancé. How deep the attachment was is hard to tell. A much later photograph[17] of Martin at the Nevada Historical Society bears an explanation on the back in the handwriting of her niece, Edna Martin Parratt: "the ring is not a wedding ring, but an engagement ring turned around." The ring is probably a token from Henry Turner, a later fiancé whom she refused to marry, according to her niece, "because she could not see herself darning his socks."[18]

Stanford '96 pictures Gregory and comments that he had at the time of his death in 1899 "an excellent start in the profession [law] for which he was gifted, showing a clear and judicial mind, combined with earnestness and a capacity for hard work," and tells of his death in an outing with six other Stanford men 3 June 1899.[19] Certainly he was the kind of young man who would have appealed to Anne Martin, one whom she could have met intellectually and respected. Surely he is the John referred to in a diary entry in 1901 when she records a visit from Gertrude's Tom: "I rummaged through Gertrude's desk and came upon a picture of John I had never seen and the best—good, true, honest, manly fellow. The tragedy and the uselessness of it all came home to me again, when I thought I had forgotten. And I was no use the rest of the afternoon."[20] In the same diary she recalls a conversation in which a friend categorizes her as one who has "lost the man [she] loved."[21] Almost forty years later, Martin wrote a poem recalling a person who had not seen her heart "an open door," which would seem to recall such a loss, and family tradition upholds the view that she had been disappointed in love.[22]

Whether because she mourned Gregory—friend or fiancé—or because she still felt inadequate in the classroom, she did not teach in the fall of 1899 but sent for a Stanford friend, Jeanne Wier, to take her courses and asked for a leave of absence, granted by the board of regents 21 September.[23] A little more than a week later she had gone east with Edythe Newlands, according to the local paper.[24]

Although she later claimed to have studied at Columbia, she did not pursue a degree there and she is not recorded as attending any degree program. All of her life she was to use "studied" loosely: she "pursued a course of lectures" at Oxford and Cambridge, she reported later,[25] but, again, she was not listed as a regular student. It is likely that she was in attendance at the extension courses that were being developed at the English universities at that time, particularly in the summers, and for which no academic records were kept in official university files. At any rate, a sketchbook preserved at the Bancroft Library bears her name and that of New York's Chase School of Art.[26]

Whether she seriously considered attempting professional art work or not, she did attend sketching classes, drawing from her fellow students in what seems to have been an all female class, and from a male seminude model in what must have been considered rather revealing drawers. Here she had the advantage over women only a few years before her. Until the nineties, young women who would study anatomy had to learn from plaster casts, or, in some instances, had to content themselves with cows for models.[27]

She tried the special programs in the summer at the British universities, which still granted no degrees or fellowships but received guests—in Cambridge, for example, at Newnham.[28] But then neither Newnham nor Girton nor any college at Oxford for women conferred degrees upon any of their students until after the First World War, even though women could be admitted to examinations.[29] Clearly, Martin's studies in England were at a very general level, probably not directly related to a change of career, and they were left rather vague in her own accounts of her life.

Ever duty conscious, Anne Martin would probably have been disturbed with any tagging of this first trip as a part of the Grand Tour that so many Americans of the age saw as the culmination of a proper education. Yet it is clear that the study meant attending lectures rather than examinations, spending days and weeks rather than months, enjoying the tourist sights more than intellectual delights, most of the time properly in the company of a familiar couple from Nevada. On her travels Martin took up her diary again, writing as she had apparently not written since her first days in Stanford five years earlier.

The tour was only the first for Anne Martin, whose restless wanderings took her to many parts of the world throughout a long life. In later biographical sketches she was to refer to travel in the Orient, but the early years of the century her travels marked familiar tracings of the culture route—Germany (where she was comfortable with the language), France, England (where the Hoovers offered a homelike stop that she enjoyed frequently over the years), Italy, Ireland (for a nostalgic trip to the O'Hara family home country), and, in 1906, Egypt. Usually she traveled with another woman, although she occasionally made part of a trip alone, even on the first one, when she clearly relished her solitude.

That first trip was, for much of the time, in company almost too familiar. With family friends she traveled to Leipzig and then to Berlin, enjoying the company for the first part of a very close and very valued younger friend, Alonsita Birney (Walker). Although she later identified Alonsita as merely "a great friend of mine," she does not appear to have come from Reno or from Stanford.[30] But she replaced Victoria Godfroy as special and adored "smash," to use the then current college term for sentimental attachments.[31] By the time Anne Martin began the journal, however, Alonsita was on her way back to the United States while her anxious friend checked on the arrival of her ship (diary, 1900, p. 10). The departure of the younger companion forced Martin to rely on the Walter McNabb Millers, perhaps only endured and especially resented when Martin and the parents became a threesome of incompatible adults along with two small Miller boys.

Walter and Helen Miller had long connections with Anne Martin: Anne's diary had posted the engagement of the Whitaker School teacher ("Guthrie" in Annie's diaries) to Professor Miller, whose confirmation the girl had found amusing in 1888 when she was wryly anti-Episcopalian. She had noted the baptism of the first Miller child as well: "[the baby] was not old enough to realize the ridiculousness of it all, I suppose" (diary, 1894). The girl who had heard the "astonishing news" of the engagement was still amusing herself skinning the cat on the school gym bars, but the woman who accompanied her former teacher on the trip had spent many years around the Millers.

Clearly the party traveled in style, with a fräulein to care for the two boys; still, it was not a happy trio that found lodgings in Leipzig in October, and the tensions had been building over the months of travel. In fact, Martin enjoyed playing devil's advocate in the Millers' quarrels, and she had to admit once that "there are times when I feel the very devil in me and must hold him down with a firm hand."[32]

Understandably pleased that she was taken for sixteen by a German she engaged in conversation (at twenty-five she was rapidly approaching traditional spinsterhood), Martin fancied herself "distinctively American in my gray slouch hat, closely cut coat, short skirt and well fitting patent leather ties, unlike the German shoes . . . [but] he probably prefers a good haus frau like the rest of them!"(diary, p. 10). She was a demanding guest and a severe critic of servants in the German pensions the Millers and she frequented, taking them to task on the one hand for "stupidity": "I order fire, bath, fruit and coffee, and they come inevitably in the following order: coffee, though I detest breakfasting until I am dressed, bath next, fruit last. And their idea of order is to make disorder invisible" (diary, p. 9). On the other hand, she wrote consolingly of the young women, as she had of the family's Irish maids at home: "their poor arms, sleeves rolled up to the elbow, exposing them to the weather and making them raw with cold" (diary, p. 5).

She criticized the Millers for everything—the handling of their children, their behavior at concerts, their taste in music. Although she would later object to her sisters for "kow-towing to their husbands,"[33] she prayed that "heaven deliver me from a man who has been so brow beaten and subjected by his wife that he loses all initiative and power of planning and making decisions" (diary, p. 14). She described a sharp interchange in which she observed "Mrs. Miller's eyes pop and chill, her lips press together, and whole manner stiffen" (diary, p. 16). After she had gone her own way, she explained Mrs. Miller as one whose "whole character hinged on self. Self was the guiding, the shaping principle. She must lead, she must be looked up to" (diary, p. 16). Obviously the two personalities of young Martin and the more mature Mrs. Miller had collided many times, but Martin could still prefer traveling to returning home, as she wrote at the beginning of the diary with the prospect of her return in view: "No more of Europe, pictures, music and German University for many years to come, probably. But home, family and some months of study and writing will help me formulate the ideas and impressions that have been stirring in me of late" (diary, p. 2).

Life on the German trip was not all clashes with the Millers and unsatisfactory service: Martin recorded the attentions of various young German men, but she seemed concerned about their becoming too attentive. Her affections were more warmly given to the recently departed Alonsita, on her way home on the *Nordlund,* while Martin remained at the lectures in art history, at which the professor appeared "like an athlete entering the arena" (diary, pp. 10–11) before she moved to Berlin and the pension where both had stayed before. Martin remembered that she had given herself up to the pleasures of Alonsita's companionship, and "lost my head like a very schoolgirl of eighteen" (diary, pp. 24–25). Although she looked back at this diary three years later and condemned herself as a "selfish little egotist" (diary, p. 54), she offered a thorough view of the ensuing weeks of the signal journey that took her on her own to Paris and yet another friend. "Miss Hall," who became "Ada," was a soothing companion for the last days of Martin's visit.

Hall was in Paris in the company of a friend ("Miss Nicholson is good, but commonplace") and shared the delights of Paris, recorded by Martin after she had returned home, as the "most memorable of my whole six months in Europe." Martin recalled the joys of being sympathized with and understood: "I would be uncomfortable a moment, but it was good to be with Ada if we did nothing but stare at the fire, she in the arm chair, I on the floor with my head against her knee" (diary, pp. 42–43). While Martin had been the more mature member of the couple with Alonsita, whom she always treated as a rather pretty and amusing toy, Martin obviously enjoyed changing roles, allowing Ada to find in her "a fascinating little thing . . . just beginning to feel [her] power over

men, and to use it." Martin must have relished being told, "You're very
charming and appealing with your clever brain and your dear little
person—your curly fluffy hair and Irish eyes" (diary, pp. 42–43). There
is no questioning in the diary pages Ada's acknowledgment of the
"plucky, self-sufficient little American with the attractive devil-care
toss of the head." Ada's description was flattering to a young woman not
too experienced with compliments of the sort and the words must have
been cherished. More exciting was Ada's claim that their relationship
was "like a good marriage," which showed she could understand that
"life is very lonely 'tout seul,'" and raise the troubling question "but
when we grow older and are no longer attractive and everyone else has
husbands and children to love—do you think we can face it?" (diary, p.
44).

Perhaps modern readers may read too much into the loving entries in
the light of generally held modern attitudes about women with women,
but Anne and Ada seemed to find their close communion compatible
with regular concepts of heterosexuality: a poor marriage is condemned,
but it is not ruled out. As Smith-Rosenberg's research shows, strong
emotional ties, deep concern, true affection, and romantic language
characterized relationships that were deeply felt, and most likely without what moderns would call a sexual character.[34]

"What is life?" Martin wondered. "It is feeling. I used to believe it
was thinking" (diary, p. 45). Once more she revived the battle between
head and heart that her reading helped to dramatize and make significant
at emotional periods of her life.

The journey home only strengthened her sense of a changed view
within herself and her life before her. Still relishing Ada's praise and
affection, she boarded ship in December to meet her parents in New
York, visit Niagara, and spend yet another week with Alonsita. Almost
as soon as she returned to Reno (4 January) she turned again to the diary
to record those events over and over again that spring. The voyage had
offered still more of the personal conquest she had longed for:

> Couldn't write anymore on the steamer between seasickness and Sir Henry
> . . . how I liked being liked for my red cape and giddy self:—It was all so
> interesting and exciting, from the Countess and Sir Henry's devotion, to
> Mr. Corbett's American chivalry and Mr. Day's American humor—right
> up to the last moment . . . with Sir Henry at my side and I distinguished the
> little figure of my mother, the fluttering handkerchief, and the tall gray
> figure of my father, with the new white in his beard across the space of
> waters between—and to actually have been made love to by a countess,
> proposed to by a baronet—me! the staid, severe student, and distant

professor of two years ago! I've got that in me yet, but I'm more Celtic, more volatile, more Bohemian, more expressive than I ever imagined I should be. Nevada may crush it all out of me, however, but I'll fight against it. (Diary, p. 35)

Even returning to her family from New York created problems, "the agony of no longer being my own mistress, of having to account for my movements and submit to a time limit on them—and the agony of having to rise at 6 and breakfast at 8! Wheew! What a selfish old pig I am . . ."(diary, p. 38). And the contrasts were greater by the time she returned to Reno, where she hated "dusting and washing dishes (no servants to be had) after *ordering* things to be done; the contrast between taking my place as the useless, helpless, lackadaisical and indifferent member of a useful and busy family aggregation, and taking my small world of England and Paris by storm as the bright and plucky and fresh and talented little American, a person of Consequence. Ah me, how short was my glory, how soon was my star set" (diary, p. 39). Such irony in dealing with herself was rare as she grew older, more discouraged, more separate.

Reno must have been a tremendous letdown. Jeanne Wier had firmly established herself as a rising young faculty member, offering more courses than Martin had, devoting her considerable energies to the work that her friend had begun.[35] Perhaps Martin's changed position at the university offered the first instance she had as an adult of "not holding things," a term she used over and over in the fragments of autobiography. She had not as a child held the affection of her cousin Dan, and she continued to feel pushed out of organizations, personal lives, and just rewards until the last years of her life.[36] Certainly, throughout the long months before she began to offer occasional lectures in art history, she turned her thoughts back to those six months of excitement abroad.

By March she had listed "Hints for Stories" that reveal family strains. All of her life she was loyal to her parents, however much she may have criticized her mother's lack of faith in her, and she could complain about her father in only the most roundabout fashion, even while he was alive. But among the hints is one for a story of an "idealistic and artistic daughter on Pullman home to Nevada accompanied by practical parents," another on the conflict of a "college bred and travelled girl of genius appearing late at the breakfast table of practical and Philistine parents" (diary, pp. 47–48). Her estimate of herself and her criticism of her parents developed as the hints did.

When the *Reno Evening Gazette* celebrated its acquisition of Merganthaler typesetting equipment on 1 April with a special edition, Anne Martin contributed an article on "A Morning in Petticoat Lane," the earliest extended piece of her journalism available. Half tourist guide to East London's famous market, half political and economic analysis, it exhibits some of her lasting concerns and curiosities—a sincere if impersonal interest in the problems of the poor, albeit with a condescending air, a fascination with the crowd, and an awareness of social conditions as political issues. Her patriotic preferences for Americans and her hope for the better life in her own country emerge as well. Although her article suggests some awareness of social conditions in New York (she would have been a rare educated female visitor to that city if she had not at least visited one of the college and university settlement houses), it reveals a familiar tendency to believe in the superior opportunity in the United States. She describes the crowds, for example, finding the heterogeneity of the American mass far more encouraging than the "impassive features . . . dull eye, heavy mouth and jaw" of the Londoner, a "low type of man mentally and physically," a victim of complete hopelessness. There was "no firmness about the sullen mouth that stood for hope, aspiration, and the desire and will to rise out of the slough of poverty and sordidness. And the pity of it was that they did not know their own sad case." If she romanticized American crowds in a particularly Nevada way—"here an actor, there an unfortunate gambler who has met misfortune or ill health, here again a bonanza king"—she saw in them "a different light in the eye . . . a more vigorous poise of the head, an independent shrug of the shoulder" that suggested "men may be born into the slums in the United States . . . but it is not written that men must die there."[37]

Such a venture into East London would suggest Martin made a conscious effort to see the other side of life, or, perhaps, had developed an interest in social work, another of the more acceptable occupations for women. Carl Degler sees that movement as a direct outgrowth of the education of increasing numbers of women, observing that "the striking thing about the most famous settlements of the later nineteenth century . . . was that they were run and staffed mostly by . . . college trained women who wanted to put their education to use and, above all, wanted to expand their talents and find an identity beyond the family."[38]

Jessie Bernard claims the interest in social work reflected a new interpretation of the sacrificial duty that women had been trained to perform, an escape from what came to be called the "family bond": "in developing a new definition of the female *ethos,* advocacy of self interest was, of course, unthinkable. So the new point of view had to be couched in terms of duty. Duty, however, to one's self."[39]

The woman yearning for independence could listen to the voice of duty ("O, I must do something," Anne Martin had written at eighteen), but she might break the umbilical cord and serve herself by serving others.[40] Just as Catherine Beecher had extolled teaching as an acceptable extension of the duties of the mother and had been influential in making teaching acceptable for thousands of American women,[41] so the pioneers of settlement—the Jane Addamses and the Lillian Walds—extended the family to include the slum populations of the nation's cities. "The new concept of self," Bernard concluded, "took the traditional *agape* guise as social service of one kind or another, as settlement workers or social reformers, as pioneers in welfare plans."[42]

As a woman devoted to social reform, Martin may have considered social work, which Bernard views as "an expression of *philos*, . . . social reform as an expression of *agape*."[43] Martin's sincere urge to be of service may have led her into testing the possibilities of such a course. Perhaps the woman who could not feel comfortable with housework was not ready for so direct a confrontation with the needy, but she certainly knew women who had followed that path. During the decade that she spent searching she met such women over and over again, and the majority of her associates—Alice Paul, Lucy Burns, Maude Younger, to name only a few—in the National Woman's Party some years later were former social workers.[44] Toynbee Hall, the first settlement house in the world, was the object of a visit during her time in London.[45] Martin collected large numbers of pamphlets dating from the 1890s and the first years of the new century, all concerned with social issues, with efforts to come to terms with them, and with settlement projects.[46]

Whether her plans for writing were to include more of the sort of essay she published in April 1901 or not is hard to say: she retained a lifelong interest in the British social reformer Josephine Butler, ending her career with articles on Butler and what was then called the White Slave Traffic. Her view of woman's mission and role remained compatible with the view that gave energy to the new social movement: she always supported the doctrine of spheres that saw men and women as essentially different, each working in a separate sphere, her moral superiority, her greater sympathy offering the female special qualities to soften public life, and demanding of her special responsibilities for the poor and the weak.

For all of her momentary sympathy with servants and expressed concern for the betterment of the poor, she was not personally suited to making some of the choices her contemporaries were making, serving as the women she would know later did. She was not likely, like Maude Younger, to turn a five-day visit to a settlement house into a lifelong career,[47] or go to work in a factory as did Alice Paul,[48] or offer herself, as Beatrice Webb did, to work as a "plain trouser hand" in East London sweatshops.[49] She enjoyed her creature comforts, enjoyed them perhaps a little guiltily, but she clung to them. But in 1901 she was still uncertain of what to do, as she was to remain for several years before the British suffragettes captured her imagination, her dedication, her unused energy.

Sometime in the summer of 1901 she joined a group of other women and naturalist John Muir to climb in the Sierra Nevada. A letter from Muir the following December attested how proud he was of his "Sierra Club girls," and he reminded Martin that she had not been forgotten and he hoped that the next trip would "prove as pleasant as [the] first was."[50] Still more excursions occupied her, for when she took up the brown diary again in 1904, she noted and regretted "not having jotted notes in my drives across the Nevada deserts and Indian reservation, my Sierra Club trips to Yosemite and Tuolumne Meadows, the Kern River Canyon and Mount Whitney. How refreshing to breathe a few whiffs of desert or mountain or forest air" (diary, 1904, p. 70).

There was plenty of time for such trips because there was little to occupy her at the university, even after her return to the staff in the fall of 1901. Although the register of the board of regents announced some twelve hours of courses to be given by Assistant Professor Martin in the history of art,[51] a later report indicates that fewer were actually taught. It would seem likely that Jeanne Wier's usurpation of the history department (certainly Martin thought of it that way in later years) was the beginning of what became a lifelong battle between two former friends. Apparently Martin taught nothing in the fall, for the president's report of 1901–1902 observes that "the work in art history was organized in January 1902. The only subject it was possible to offer was the History of Painting with special reference to the work of the Italian masters."[52] A university bulletin in 1902 reported an evening lecture with slides on Titian, but, to judge by the salary that she received, Martin did no more than the single course and perhaps some lectures before local groups.[53]

Her failure to teach in the fall may well have been influenced by the death of her father in early September, by the loss of the man she had idolized from childhood. His death could have been no surprise: he had been back and forth to San Francisco for some years, sometimes staying as long as three months. A week before he died, he "called the members of his family to his bedside and bade them goodbye. He was ready and anxious to go rather than have his suffering prolonged."[54] Anne Martin remembered that this "most fair minded and impartial of fathers, to daughters and sons alike, adored his daughters":

> Toward the last he must have been brooding over some memories of family life, for he murmured once "My sweet little girls!" And then he lifted up his head and spoke the words, "Abraham Lincoln," and then again with a look of surprise, as if in recognition, "Abraham Lincoln!" and then, nothing more.[55]

The funeral from the home was a simple one in accord with his request. And while the *Gazette* observed that he had "left everything in the best possible condition for his family," Anne Martin disagreed violently with her brothers and the family advisers when the estate was settled.

She recalled that after his death "more than one working man and widow, or old servant, came to my mother and told of his firm and kindly intervention against the rapacity of bank or insurance officials, to secure these people sums justly due to them," but, she continued, "It was probably inevitable that his widow and his children should not be so protected . . . my mother was induced to sell one hundred shares owned by his estate for one hundred per cent less than their real value . . . His estate was thus deprived of thousands of dollars, the just fruits of his work." She closed her diatribe with a complaint that "it was one of the ironies of life that he would have been the first to appreciate that from the day of his death I was never again to know the family peace of old nor financial security," even though she admitted that she had always been "economically independent."[56] Martin offered no substantiation of her charges against the banks. Some of the bitterness about the settlement of the estate surfaced in her references to her mother when she accused Mrs. Martin of "loving her sons best, giving them free scope well nigh to ruin both her and my own financial security, as these memoirs will reveal."[57] While the promised revelation never appeared in the memoirs, her memory of the time is marked firmly in her claim that it was "no wonder that the feminist iron entered my soul from the day of my father's death."[58]

Her father gone, as eldest daughter she no doubt assumed responsibility within the household as support to her mother. Her brother Harry had married two years before, there were still young children in the home, and there was a job at the university. Although she apparently taught in the fall of 1902 and the spring that followed, again her work was limited, her pay listed in the annual report as only $20 in September of 1902. In the spring she offered "illustrated lectures on the work of Raphael,

Michael Angelo, Andrea del Sarto, Correggio, Titian and others."[59] In January of 1904 she asked for and received another leave until September 1905, but she apparently decided not to return to teach, for her name does not appear in the register for any year after 1903. Teaching, it would seem, was not the occupation she had been searching for so avidly.

What was she to do? She had money enough to travel; her responsibilities at home were less than they would be in the future. She claimed her freedom from home and home ties during these years, spending much of her time in Europe traveling with a variety of companions or alone. She clashed regularly with her traveling companions, and just as regularly blamed herself for the problems.

Hard as she tried to respect one, she would complain that "she rubs me the wrong way and hurts my self-esteem and when I object disposes of the question in the most summary manner by accusing me of egotism." But, she conceded, ever ambiguous in her feelings, that the companion's "opinion is worth listening to even when it hits the hardest . . . New England conscience backed up by years of rectitude and unselfish conscientious devotion to duty" (diary, p. 53).

Still, Anne Martin enjoyed the second trip, when she and her companion landed in Ireland in July, some four months after she had left her family on the dock in San Francisco. She satisfied her longing to search out her Irish roots with an expedition alone to the country of her father's ancestors, even to the graveyard where there were O'Haras buried. Ireland was "like the fabric of a dream, emerging from mysterious and befogging mists. Its softness, its wildness and then its simple calm beauty and restfulness set my Irish blood circulating" (p. 53). If her Irish blood did not call her to spend more time there, her friendship for Lou Henry Hoover kept her returning to London where the Hoovers, back from some years in China, were at the center of social activities among the Americans in the English capital. Martin both appreciated the Hoovers' hospitality and envied their activity, both hoped for their continued friendship and wished not to need it. She found herself alternately "very lonely and desolate and then very cheery and happy," concerned to observe that "resourceful as I used to think myself, here in London I've no resources within myself, but dash from museum to concert, concert to theatre, theatre to art gallery, and never settle down to assimilate and repose."

Apparently unwilling, as she had been before, to accept the life of a mindless traveler, she sought meaning. "I am in vital contact with no one, nothing. I am necessary to no useful work in the world, to no useful person—and until I can bring my life into vital connection with some-body, or some work that is worthwhile, my existence is worthless to my family and friends and a burden to myself" (p. 76).

But these pangs of conscience lasted only briefly; she enjoyed the pleasures of London. After the outburst about her uselessness she devoted a long paragraph to the description of the processions honoring the visiting royalty from Portugal, showing herself willing to endure "a long wait and cold feet" until the "six-horse carriages all went dashing by, preceded by the horse guards, and in the case of the Prince of Wales, accompanied by a musical burst of 'God Save the King.'" And the concert at Queen's Hall made her "tingle yet" as she recalled it (diary, pp. 78–79).

She could relate with enthusiasm the whirl of activity in London as Lou Hoover's guest, but then congratulate herself for leaving it: "I am filled with virtue still when I think of how I left Lou . . . to go off and pay a duty call . . . and then to come home to spend the last Saturday evening with Anna in my cozy rooms." Whatever that virtue was, the desire to be on her own overwhelmed it. "It all shows how selfish I am, how used to following my own pleasures, to willing my own life—that I should plume myself on virtue and unselfishness for performing a very obvious duty, and spend this evening as friendship, and not duty, should suggest . . . without question I am a very bad case."

If she credited herself for not accepting her chance to depend on Lou, become part of Lou's life, she worried about the possibility of marriage most of all (the entry was written at the time of her sister Clara's wedding). Oddly, she seemed to expect marriage, even though she mentioned no name, even though she was by then twenty-nine. The use of the conditional in so careful a writer is perhaps significant.

> How could I throw my own life into some one's else, and give up and forbear, as a wife? The things that are hardest I must learn to do, and bear; this, so far, has been my lesson in life. And this last, too, must come, but not this year I hope.

The "I hope" is surprising in context, as if she did not control her own choices, as if the calls of duty to be the ordinary woman, the traditional spouse, the classic wife were demands forced upon her, even if she expresses them conditionally. Apparently all of her liberal religious training, all of her open-mindedness about the possibilities of women, all of her hopes for accomplishment had not rid her of that lingering onus of the cult of true womanhood, that demand to be sacrificing, to be

good, to serve, a prospect she dramatically presented as particularly
unappealing:

> The suffering must come first, anyway—the baring of self to the bone, the
> facing of my life and relations with people and problems as they are—the
> humiliation, the abasement, the submission—oh, it is all coming. Give me
> the strength to meet it, help me grow in character and worth this year, this
> month, this week, or life must be a failure. (Diary, p. 81)

If there is feminist iron in such a soul, it is not very well forged. Like
others, she was a victim of the occupational disease among women of
her generation and class that demanded she accept the womanly responsibility as moral model, as mother or sister of charity to the world and
still respond to the needling need to meet the demands of self that had
been nurtured by opportunity and education. Jane Addams had suc-
cumbed to it, recovering her health and designing the direction of her
life in the discovery of a cause in the settlement movement. As Anne
Martin's pleasures were diminished by her sense of her failure to be
useful, Addams some years earlier had found her delight in travel, her
admiration of art only deepened her sense of uselessness and eventually
forced her to act to satisfy the conscience that was fiercely alive. For
Addams, the spectacle of a bullfight in Spain was the catalyst for her
step into action:

> It is easy to become the dupe of a deferred purpose, of the promise the
> future never can keep, and I had fallen into the meanest type of self
> deception in making myself believe that all this was in preparation for great
> things to come . . . Far from following chariot of philanthropic fire, I had
> been tied to the tail of the veriest ox cart of self seeking.[60]

Anne Martin's life was almost entirely devoted to the pursuit of "culture," already something of a demand she could not entirely counte-
nance, however much she enjoyed the events that fed that demand.
Attracted always to art—she had particularly enjoyed her rooms in
Queen Square, for one was "the former dressing room of William
Morris himself, perhaps, with its open garden spaces at the back" (7
October 1904)—she both insisted on her trips to galleries and felt wrong
about the real joy she found in them and in music. Although she was
doing small jobs (little research assignments in the British Museum) for
Earl Barnes, she needed something greater than these, some grand cause
to offer her definition. Victorian woman enough to fear her growing
sense of self, however shadowy, she was New Woman enough to

remain independent and to understand her need for solitude, independent action, and a fulfillment that did not fit into the standard pattern. Perhaps she did not perceive how each of these independent actions was one more step from the traditional role, its "humiliation," its "abasement," its "submission," but her actions for some years continued to swing between some sort of work and the pursuit of still more study and training. With no clear goal, she continued to be trapped by what Jane Addams, quoting Tolstoy, called "the snare of preparation," spread before the feet of young people, "entangling them in a curious inactivity at the very period of life when they are longing to construct the world anew and conform it to their own ideals."[61]

Martin was not ready, as far as her records can show, to get more closely in touch with the world of things as they are. The bits of information on the years that follow speak of little direction: after London she went to Germany, then to Venice to enjoy "John Bellini," her favorite Italian painter. If she had joined the Fabian Socialists by this time, and that seems likely from her associates, she did not feel compelled to write about it. Hers is a record written and photographic of horseback riding and golf, of visits to country houses and museums, and of occasional musing about creative work: "I kept puzzling how I could find myself in my work and find expression and be helpful. Could I write a story about a lonely girl trying to find herself . . . Perhaps I could accomplish this by trying to write the story myself, if I could bring myself to begin it" (diary, p. 72). In a larger sense, she was waiting to begin her useful life.

A datebook kept in London, pictures preserved, and scribbled notes about appointments show no new direction for the wanderer in 1906. By that fall she was a member of the American Circle of the Lyceum Club, although she was not yet a resident, still staying on at Brunswick Square in familiar Bloomsbury: "Tuesdays, McLeod' Charleton, Sundays, Gray' Thanksgiving Dinner—Lou." For 1907, on yet another trip, only scattered lines record wages paid her chauffeur and appointments at the British Museum.[62] On 23 November she wrote of attending a lecture by Shaw at Essex Hall on Socialism, and other entries note "Suffrage debate Lyceum; Thursday Socialism debate" among the lunches and drives of time-passing, day-killing activities.

It would seem that by 1907 she might have become more seriously interested in Socialism, for one of the regular companions noted is Mary Fels. Mary and Joseph Fels, who had made a fortune in soap, were members of the Fabians, as was George Bernard Shaw. Fabian headquarters were in Clement's Inn, close by the future home of the

Women's Social and Political Union. Some time after the Lyceum Club
opened in 1904, Anne Martin became a resident of the fine building
across from Green Park at 128 Picadilly, in the club that declared itself
to differ from the ordinary social ladies' club "by the fact that membership is confined to women who had published any original work of
literature, journalism, science or music, who had university qualification, or are wives or daughters of distinguished men." Qualified on
several points, Martin may have sought the club's proferred help to
members of "advice and where possible, by disposal of their work."
Special circles were established for smaller groups and the Lyceum
Alpine Club was the headquarters for women mountaineers. One of the
club's goals was to establish "centers of intellectual and artistic life in
various countries of the world, and by the affiliation of these centers to
promote interchange and thought between the cultured women of all
nations."[63] A women's section of the Fabians met at the Lyceum,
according to the WSPU *Votes for Women.* Suffragettes were active
there, some years later forcing the cancellation of a banquet for Earl
Crewe, responsible for arrests the night before.[64] Such was the ambi-
ence of Anne Martin's London.

In later years, Martin referred to her time in London as "writing for
the English papers," yet she preserved nothing except a copy of a
typescript of a letter to the *Manchester Guardian,* the diary, and the
notebook, an odd oversight for one who still had her childhood essays
when she died at seventy-six. Undated manuscripts in the Bancroft
collection appear to have been offered for sale under the name of "Anne
O'Hara" from about 1907, but there are no printed copies that would
indicate success of publication. Apparently the wanderer was home in
1908, as she was from time to time throughout the restless decade, for
some thirty-five years later in a diary entry she recalled "a ride on a
stringy Arabian in 1908 to the foot of the Sierras in Reno and family
dinner in [the] old home . . . Dick, Mother, Margaret, myself in riding
suit" (diary, 21 June 1943). Several undated photographs show Martin
on horseback, both in her Reno drive and dressed for lessons in Brighton
during this period. There are snapshots of her as a tiny golfer in an
overwhelming landscape, mementos from Fabian summer schools, a
black-bordered card from the American embassy advising her that
"because of the death of His Royal Highness Edward the VII" she would
not be presented at court.[65] She was home in 1909, for example, when
she had Isaac Ball of Reno arrested for shooting Jaspo, her sister
Margaret's cocker spaniel, after it had killed one of his chickens. When
the case came to a hearing, Anne Martin offered to pay for the chicken,

giving up the cause of punishment for Ball after arguments that the fowl had been "a pet chicken that would jump on the shoulder of the old man and pick corn from his tongue."[66]

Yet by 1909 Martin had found a direction in the battle for votes for women. That is the date she usually offered for her first participation, although she kept records of suffrage demonstrations from 1907. She could hardly have missed them from the Lyceum Club. Her collection of pamphlets on suffrage dates as far back as 1904, but she was ever a collector of materials, old and new, a magpie who lived in later years completely surrounded by books and papers.[67] Mary Austin, already something of a celebrity, placed Martin's earliest efforts in 1910 when Austin remembered meeting Martin at the Hoovers'. Her account of their early friendship shows the nature of that drifting decade. As Austin recalled the time, "Anne Martin was trying to write and not doing very well at it. She had very little capacity for hard work, but was getting involved with the women's franchise interests."[68] Martin's own account, carefully refuting Austin's slight, emerges in Helen McKnight Doyle's 1939 biography of Austin with a somewhat different tone. Doyle recounts how Martin and Austin "went about a good deal together," and Martin remembers Mary at the Hoover dinner parties where "she was quite the center of attention." As the account goes, "Mary realized that Anne had ability, both as a lecturer and writer," and she suggested that they go to some quiet spot in the country and work together:

> Anne was to act as an amanuensis, Mary telling the stories and talking over her work with her. Then each would spend the morning writing, meet for lunch, read what they had written, spend the afternoon tramping and planning for the next day's work.[69]

It was Mary who went to Bramley in Surrey and found quarters for the pair in the "homes of artisans," rooms Martin found "shabby and comfortless" and made even less attractive by the odor from the tannery and inedible food. When Martin objected, Austin insisted that "Anne should develop character by learning to disregard living conditions." Martin escaped by inviting herself to a visit with an English friend.[70] Whatever the reason for parting, the two remained friends until Austin's death in 1933, arguing frequently, but always resolving those disagreements.

The incident shows essential differences between the two and emphasizes Martin's unwillingness to be uncomfortable, much less suffer inconvenience for art. Roughing it in the out-of-doors was a matter of choice, and Martin was capable of handling crude conditions; living in discomfort was another matter. She took care to have shelters nearby, alternate exits available. Writing with Mary Austin demanded a kind of discipline she was not ready to accept. Although in later years no one questioned her tenacity, her wholehearted commitment to her activities, in 1910 she could not force herself into the labor of writing as a trade—certainly not in smelly rooms on inferior food.

Always attracted to the aristocratic and wealthy, always a bit of a snob in spite of her populist views, always working from a sense of *noblesse oblige* (whether that *noblesse* was of blood, money, or intellect), she must have found membership in the WSPU appealing. Even years after she had left militant activity in England, it was the aristocrats that she liked to recall knowing. In this she was perhaps not exceptional, for many women offered sincere support for causes without questioning the system, believing in abstract solutions while disdaining their maids.

From 1899, when John Gregory died (if he was indeed a person of significance to her), until 1909, the date she gave herself for her first involvement in suffrage, Anne Martin wondered and wandered to little purpose. To her credit, she was uncomfortable about accomplishing little, but she found it hard to direct her efforts. That decade of search would seem to have ended by 1909. She had found a cause, and she approached thirty-five free from either the economic need to work or continued entrapment in the "snare of preparation." Had she less comfort to keep her amused, more needs an inheritance could not meet, a husband and a family that she seemed to have dreaded (and had successfully eluded, however unconsciously), she might have acted sooner—or not at all. However little contribution she had yet made to the world, she accepted the need to perform—slowly, perhaps, but inevitably.

She had developed into a well-read, well-traveled woman who was comfortable in a variety of social circles, critical of friends and associates and of herself, a woman embarrassed by her own inaction, deeply in need of a compelling cause. That cause, or perhaps Cause (to grant it the capitals its supporters raised), caught her and thousands like her in a ten-year battle.

She was ever a creature of her times, not until her Senate campaign a member of the vanguard. The times were changing for suffrage both in England and America, and the times provided the "vital connection" that directed her life for a decade of campaigns until 1920.

Young Annie Martin depicted herself at work on "The Johnny Rankin Album" in this 1890 sketch of the Whitaker School in Reno. Nevada Historical Society, Reno.

Anne Martin was a graduate student in history at Stanford when she posed for this portrait in 1897. Courtesy, The Bancroft Library, Berkeley.

As president of the Nevada Equal Franchise Society Anne Martin led the state suffrage campaign in 1914. Nevada Historical Society, Reno.

Anne Martin (fourth from left) posed in a hayfield when she and Mabel Vernon took the suffrage campaign to rural Nevada. Courtesy, The Bancroft Library, Berkeley.

The candidate poses with a dog outside National Woman's Party headquarters in Washington at the beginning of her first Senate campaign in 1918. Nevada Historical Society, Reno.

Martin rides in front with her driver, Dr. Margaret Long, touring the state with her niece, Edna Martin Parratt, and a fourth woman, seeking votes in the 1920 contest. Nevada Historical Society, Reno.

Speeches from the car, like this one in Fallon in 1920, were regular features of Anne Martin's campaigns. Courtesy, The Bancroft Library, Berkeley.

Martin's last years in Carmel, California, were shared with her cocker spaniel, Punkin. California Historical Society, San Francisco.

CHAPTER 5

JOINING THE CAUSE

A Nevada Recruit in the Pankhurst Army

Shout, shout, up with your song!
Cry with the wind for the dawn is breaking.
March, march, swing you along,
Wide blows our banner and hope is waking.
—Cicely Hamilton, "The March of the Women"

For it is the grandest movement the world has ever seen.
And we'll win the *Vote for Women* wearing purple, white and green.
—L. E. Morgan-Browne, Song of the WSPU

ANNE MARTIN usually offered 1909 as the year of her first association with the suffrage movement and called up, late in life, scenes that seemed in retrospect to be crucial to her. Thousands of women in England and America joined the final suffrage battles in the decade before 1920. For many the experience was finished with achievement of the suffrage. For Martin, the experience launched her in the way that she would go for the rest of her life. She demonstrated, organized meetings, learned to speak in public. Her English labors forecast the suffrage work to come in Nevada and the nation. That year in England she was like many others in responding to the flash and color of the dramatic furor excited by a new group of militant women who enlivened the wearying struggle for the vote. Her recruitment to the cause changed her life; her choice of a particular battalion of that suffrage army affected her career in years to come in ways she could not have predicted when she joined, happy finally to have found a purpose for her life.

The Women's Social and Political Union by that year had become the most visible suffrage brigade in the English-speaking world. Headed by Mrs. Emmeline Pankhurst and her daughters, Christabel and Sylvia, the WSPU had come from Manchester to London with a reputation for lively demonstration and publicity seeking that promised a future of action less ladylike than that of the staid National Union of Woman Suffrage Societies headed by Mrs. Millicent Fawcett. Like their American cousins, the English women had been seeking the right to vote for some fifty years or more by the turn of the century. Although women could vote in some municipalities and hold certain restricted kinds of public office, the parliamentary franchise seemed no nearer than it had been for years. In both England and America, the drive for the right to vote seemed stalled, the women weary, and the goal still out of sight. Scores of loosely united suffrage organizations struggled to maintain group spirit until the WSPU emerged to spark new life into the movement.

Mrs. Pankhurst, widow of a lifelong reformer whose generosity to various liberal and radical causes had diminished his material estate, was a charismatic leader, supported brilliantly by her two daughters, Christabel, trained in the law, and Sylvia, champion of working-class women in East London. The WSPU forced the Cause onto the public stage as no other group had done before; the public attention WSPU won offered encouragement only a few years later to an American group inspired by the Pankhursts' success that gave Anne Martin her first national attention.

When one reluctant British battler recalled the imprisonment of Christabel and Annie Kenney in 1905, she admitted that the single incident "forced her over the brink" to support of the cause: "I could not keep out of this struggle . . . It did not attract me; it bludgeoned my conscience. I could do no other than become one of those who were heaving the wheel of reform out of its rut."[1]

Millicent Fawcett, longtime leader of the nonmilitant suffragists in England, admitted that the Pankhursts had sent the suffrage question "sweeping like a flame throughout the country," and Beatrice Webb, long unconcerned with the vote, announced her conversion to the cause. Later, Lady Constance Lytton would claim that Christabel Pankhurst, who shared the center of that agitation with her mother, was "the sunrise of the woman's movement . . . The glow of her great vitality and the joy of her being took hold of the movement and made it gladness."[2]

Whether "heaving the wheel of reform out of its rut" or sending flames throughout Britain, the WSPU emerged in 1905 (while Anne Martin was still aimlessly wandering) from its modest political beginnings as only one of scores of suffrage societies in Britain. It became a suffrage army with Mrs. Pankhurst as commander in chief of a militant corps of suffragettes whose performances for a fascinated public drew thousands of English citizens to consider the question—they could no longer ignore it.[3] William O'Neill has observed that there was a need then for a new organization, "for firm direction and unity of action," a need met by the WSPU, which was never democratic but united by the charismatic power of its leader: anyone who disagreed with Mrs. Pankhurst was "encouraged, indeed forced, to leave it."[4]

Whether Anne Martin was a member or not, she could not have missed the publicity attendant on those first arrests. Christabel Pankhurst, an inspired orator, and Annie Kenney, a former mill worker who had been effectively adopted by the Pankhursts, went to jail for disrupting a political meeting and overnight became national celebrities, the first of many martyrs to the Cause.

Martin was certainly in London in 1907 when a WSPU march on Parliament was broken up by police who used excessive force.[5] She may well have belonged to the Lyceum Club group of suffragists who had been meeting there that year[6] and it is possible that she was the "Miss Martin" listed as a subscriber to the WSPU in its first annual report for the year ending in February 1907[7] and in subsequent years. By 1910, when she was first arrested, she was definitely one of the Union's faithful.[8] When she joined is less important than why she did; why this particular group appealed to her is important, for her decision to join affected her life for many years in ways she cannot have foreseen. There were alternatives if she was interested in suffrage: like the United States, Britain had numbers of groups working separately and together to gain the vote for women.

Martin could hardly have condoned in any other circumstances the acts for which Christabel Pankhurst had been arrested. After a peaceful effort to have a Liberal politician answer a question on votes for women, she had attempted to hit the policeman restraining her, and, failing that, "managed to spit at one."[9] The particular action mattered less than that women of her own sort were moving from mere ladylike discussion to something more, something close to vigorous action denied them by the times. She would have agreed with Mrs. Fawcett that the WSPU had done more in a few months to "bring the movement within the region of practical politics than I and my followers [had] been able to do . . . in years."[10]

Martin required something spectacular to move her to action. Like her friend Beatrice Webb, she had grown up without suffering many of the restrictions normally placed on women, a fact that Duncan Crow has suggested in writing of Webb "proved that personal experience had most to do with attitudes adopted," demonstrating how "the behavior and attitude of the individual Victorian father towards his daughters" determined their "adult approach to the true position of women in life."[11] Martin's unusual ambition and confidence nurtured by her father had been dealt a blow by the settlement of the estate, but that injury did not stir her to action. The English militants did. Her early contacts with independent women and their problems and her glancing attention to feminism as a college student had not forced her into activity, even though her efforts to write, her search for a "vital connection," were producing little at the time the WSPU elbowed its way to center stage.

In later years, when she was trying hard as leader of Nevada's campaign for the vote to forget her militant forays, she was willing to have only her membership in the Women Writers Suffrage League listed among her previous affiliations,[12] and it may have been this group, formed about 1908, that first drew the would-be writer. Ever a seeker for celebrities, she would have relished its February 1909 meeting at which John Masefield and Henry James read from their works to raise money.[13] She was already acquainted through the Fabians with Keir Hardie, the parliamentary champion of the cause who had led the International Labour party contingent in the 1908 suffrage parade[14] and with Mary and Joseph Fels, active supporters of the WSPU.

Certainly the company was the sort she sought. Margaret Haig (Lady Rhondda), later publisher of *Time and Tide* and the central figure in a battle to be seated in the House of Lords, wrote in her autobiography that participating in the WSPU was "almost the done thing in our family," and serving time in prison an activity worked into a busy life: "Florence Haig, though loathing every minute of it, went at such intervals as she could afford to spare from her own trade of portrait painting."[15] She recounts how she went to watch "Aunt Lotty get to prison,"[16] notes that her mother went, and that she herself finally became involved after much arguing with her father: "I persuaded him to let me go, anyway, for a bit."[17] Lady Constance Lytton was a regular prisoner. At first released from the routine sentence both because of her rank and her fragile health, Lady Lytton took another name and was force fed, only to be freed when her identity was learned. Her case drew attention as demonstrating one set of rules for the rich, another for the poor, but it remained clear that the majority of protesters were women of rank and position, as a popular limerick testified:

There's a lady whose name's in Debrett,
She became a great suffragette
She walked and she talked
She wrote and she spoke
But Adam is adamant yet.[18]

To Anne Martin, then, it was no contradiction that she should seek to be presented at the Court of St. James the same year that she almost went to prison.[19]

The WSPU specialized in pageantry. Ever impressed with pomp and ceremony (as the diaries attest), Anne Martin was sure to respond in some way to the massive processions that the combined suffrage societies, urged on by the WSPU, organized from 1907 on. From a gathering of three thousand women in 1907, the ranks grew to hundreds of thousands by 1911[20] in one demonstration that *Votes for Women* estimated spread over "seven miles of marching womanhood."[21] The displays could be spectacular. Ray Strachey commented that ". . . for a time some of the pageantry of the Middle Ages came back to the streets as women made lovely symbolical standards worked in silk and velvet . . . militants, always more extreme about everything, paraded in costume, some on horseback, others representing the professions and occupations of women, or the famous women of the past."[22] Colors were particularly striking: in the summer the women's white dresses contrasted with the multicolored banners; whenever possible, those women who had university degrees wore academic regalia, caps and gowns and hoods of the rich ceremonial garb of the University of London and of Trinity in Dublin. Ladies who seldom traveled three blocks on foot marched miles for the Cause.

The demonstrations drew huge crowds, some spectators who came to cheer and others to jeer. The shows continued in spite of the weather: women were counseled to be sure to "wear something that doesn't need to be held up,"[23] and one parade continued in such a downpour that it became known in suffrage annals as "the mud march."[24]

Along with aristocratic members she wanted very much to know, with pageantry she admired, the WSPU offered immediate action, certainly attractive to a young woman exhausted with ten years of seeking for a focus for her energy. Militant strategy was to keep the issue in the public eye constantly, to keep pressure on Parliament with continuous contingents of petitioners—and to keep the police arresting women, jailing women, martyring women if necessary to gain the vote. Women chained themselves to grates in Parliament, women demanded to be heard, and all of these actions brought the police—and public sympathy.

By summer 1910 Anne Martin had qualified as a speaker, proud to record her rehearsals in a photograph of her against the summer bushes and wicker furniture of a garden; the caption reads "Making a Speech for Taunton, Somersetshire, 1910."[25] While women could not vote, they could express their needs at election time, supporting those who promised action on the long-delayed suffrage. If she had qualified as a speaker, she had taken the required WSPU ten-week course especially designed to help women learn public speaking. (Mary Austin later claimed to have been her teacher; she was certainly offering more than moral support.) How many speeches she made, how many demonstrations she joined remains uncertain. Her desire to play down the WSPU connection in the years of the Nevada suffrage campaign and the Senate campaigns led to a number of evasions. In her autobiography, however, she remembers two, the first one mentioned either in 1909 or 1911 (spring of 1910 saw a truce between the militants and the government):

> London, and the hawthorn trees in bloom in May in Hyde Park—and I standing behind a barricade of policemen fronting the House of Commons in a swirling mob, wondering how I could break through to join Mrs. Pankhurst's group seeking admission to the Prime Minister at the door of the House.[26]

By that time, demonstrations had begun to display an almost ritual structure: although the leaders would seek through other sorts of pressures from sympathetic men to push for legislation in Parliament, regular deputations would form to petition Prime Minister Asquith, who would just as regularly refuse to admit them to his presence to respond to their demands. The women, chosen from volunteers or by invitation, would meet for a Women's Parliament, usually in Caxton Hall, sometimes in the open air of Parliament Square; they would resolve to petition the government once again for votes, and they would then move to "rush" the House of Commons. Policemen, acting under the orders of Home Secretary Winston Churchill, would just as regularly block their way. Sometimes a small band would manage to reach St. Stephen's Porch entrance to the House, but most frequently none would, and their repeated efforts would bring clashes more or less violent with the police, who would arrest the petitioners for refusing to leave. Crowds of hecklers jammed the sidewalks, offering advice to police and suffragettes alike, relishing the little conflicts. Once arrested, the women would almost ceremoniously accept bail from Frederick Pethick-Lawrence, WSPU treasurer, who was, in the words of Dame Ethyl Smyth, "ever ready to take root in any police station, his money bag between his feet, any hour of the day or night."[27]

In the first few years—1905 to 1910—the prisoner experience was a terrifying ritual, for the women would demand status as political prisoners and, once refused, begin the hunger strikes that would be answered with the violence of forced feeding, accomplished by forcing a tube down the throat or up the nostril to nourish the unwilling woman on liquids. Exhausted, ill, often actually injured by the brutal process, the women would serve their short terms and emerge as qualified martyrs, entitled to wear prison garments in subsequent demonstrations and a specially designed pin featuring prison bars—only to return after the next deputation. The organization made the most of releases as well as arrests: special parades and breakfasts welcomed the returning members. Fearful of a death among the women but adamant in its treatment of them, the government enacted what came to be known as the "Cat and Mouse Act" so that ill women could be released to recover and be re-arrested if they caused trouble again. But the women—including the Pankhursts themselves and other top leaders of the WSPU—continued to go to prison and endure the treatment until they were finally granted first-class status.[28]

Their conscious martyrdom brought criticism from many, but even the conservative suffragists—"constitutionalists" in British parlance— objected to the treatment of the women. Mrs. Fawcett was quick to observe that the "brutal severity with which some of the militant suffragists were treated . . . gave all parties another subject on which they were in agreement," noting that "minor breeches of the law . . . were treated more severely than serious crime had often been." Mrs. Fawcett was appalled that "a sentence of three months' imprisonment was passed in one case against a young girl who had done nothing except to decline to be bound over to keep the peace she was prepared to swear she had not broken."[29]

Militancy in 1910 had not yet developed into the organized violence that erupted throughout Britain in bombings, arson, and window smashing. Heckling speakers was a tradition in British politics, and, as Pethick-Lawrence explained in his book, *Women Fight for the Vote,* tactics similar to those of the militants had been employed during previous campaigns for extensions of the suffrage in 1832 and 1867.[30] If the marches on Parliament were provocation—and all seemed to agree they were—government's reaction was still out of proportion. The vicious cycle of petition and punishment followed by provocation and more severe punishment, O'Neill suggests, "appeared to prick the heart of mankind in some secret, vulnerable place. Seemingly men felt diminished when women struck the attitudes and employed the robust vocabulary that were traditionally male prerogatives." As response grew more savage, "government entirely abandoned those standards of civility and that tradition of amiable controversy which were England's pride and the world's envy."[31]

When Anne Martin volunteered for the 18 November rush on the House of Commons, she could certainly have expected some roughness and perhaps anticipated arrest; she could hardly have envisioned what actually happened that day, remembered ever after as "Black Friday." The first deputation after a truce of eight months, during which only peaceful marches and gatherings had kept suffrage spirit high, the 18 November deputation was in direct response to Parliament's failure to include the reading of a suffrage bill on the agenda of its short term before Christmas. Martin, who had already made an appointment for surgery on an old injury to her arm, almost missed the event, the only one she ever described in real detail. In an account in the Reno paper two months later she claimed that she saw the action as "my last chance to take part in a movement for the enfranchising of half of the English race"; she thought ". . . the experience might help me in the movement to gain suffrage someday for the women of my own state of Nevada."[32]

In the delegation were women from some of the conservative groups and such well-known women as Mrs. Garrett Anderson, sister of Mrs. Fawcett, Mrs. Hertha Ayrton, widow of a South African premier, and a Miss Nelligan, all of them over seventy, who marched in the first group with Mrs. Pankhurst. Martin joined the third group of twelve (a number within the law), moving with sympathizers toward Parliament Square where, near Westminster Abbey, "thousands upon thousands of people" (or so it seemed to Anne Martin) were "massed together . . . beginning to overflow . . . blocking our way . . . We were able to crush through almost to the very door of the House. There we were blocked by a solid row of big policemen's backs."[33] What seemed to be near safety was shattered by commands to "move." "Police used bodies, elbows, and fists with great effect; great rough powerful men, they tossed us all, young and old, from one to the other, hurled, kicked, and knocked many down . . . The crowd into which I was thrown was pressed on toward

Westminster Abbey." For Martin, the mauling was fairly brief: going to stand by a fellow demonstrator attempting to address the crowd, she was hauled off by two policemen to nearby Cannon Row Police Station, but not before she had seen "a little nurse in uniform being knocked from one policeman to another."[34]

Others in the square were not so lucky: for six hours the women and the police surged back and forth, for the police were under orders from Churchill to make as few arrests as possible, to wear the women out. As David Morgan has written, "nothing quite like it had been seen before in the precincts of Parliament:"

> For six long, violent, sometimes brutal hours there raged in Parliament Square what can only be described as a battle between the police and not the unemployed, the homeless or the destitute of whom there were plenty, but middle- and upper-middle class women of all ages: the very women, in fact, who could have been mothers, wives, or daughters to the M.P.s the police were protecting with such vigor, once they overcame their deference toward "ladies."[35]

That deference failed rapidly, as the police were not the usual Westminster force, rough enough themselves, but less experienced men from East London.[36] When the House rose and the struggle ceased, 115 women and 4 men had been arrested, Anne Martin the only American, then not completely aware of the extent of the violence that day.

In the melee were passersby, suffragettes, policemen, and the ever present hooligans who enjoyed the opportunity of grappling with the women. So severe was the treatment that a special commission was appointed by Commons to investigate violence that ranged from twisted arms to sexual assault. The most frequent complaint was the "twisting around, pinching, ripping or wringing the breast . . . done in the most public way to inflict the most humiliation."[37]

Although some of the women had reached the House, Prime Minister David Asquith had refused to see them, in spite of demands from friends of suffrage inside and a rousing defense of "militant tactics" by Keir Hardie, who pointed out that "women had been waiting quietly for some time hoping for justice: they are being treated with a good deal of contempt to which no other section of the community would submit if applied to them."[38]

At the police station, Anne Martin was charged with "obstructing the police in discharge of their duty" and conducted to a large hall where thirty women cheered each new arrival, one of whom called the place "a haven of rest" after Parliament Square. Bailed out by Pethick-Lawrence—even though Herbert Hoover had been waiting hours to rescue his wife's close friend—she felt "curiously pleased with life" when she appeared the next day at Bow Street for her hearing, carrying only a handbag and an umbrella instead of the hand luggage more experienced women had brought. While she protested to herself that "honour forbade accepting the option of a fine . . . as it was conceding that an offence had been committed," she and the rest were dismissed,[39] "brought before the Magistrate in batches, scolded like fractious children, and discharged."[40] While Churchill officially announced that "no public advantage would be gained by proceeding with the prosecution," Martin—and the London press as well—firmly believed that the action was politically motivated to ensure Churchill's re-election in the coming months.[41]

So ended her first clash with the law, her first threat of prison. The newspapers in the United States gleefully printed her name, and the Nevada state press responded, in some confusion, to the brief notoriety. The *Tonopah News* proudly reminded readers that she was "the sister of Harry M. Martin and W. O'H. Martin of Nye County Mercantile Company of this city."[42] J. C. Hopper, an old family friend, wrote the next day, making passing reference to "scandalized relatives" and expressing his amusement and concern:

> Upon my word, Nan, it was a struggle between tears and laughter, with lapses during the day towards weepiness, but after all my risibilities have the best of it. I don't believe that the "Bishop's girl" would scratch even a Bobby—and with 800 American Jackies looking on and cheering.

But whatever the exaggerated story that had reached him, he saw the incident as one to be expected of one who as a child "rode the wild pony and went bumping her nose over the pavement."[43]

After she had sent her own account to the local newspaper, the hometown editor, noting "diverse opinions presented to the paper in the interim," commented:

> Miss Martin's story may be accepted as the plain, unvarnished truth. No one who knew her during her long residence in this city could do otherwise. It is well that the truth be told . . . not all the women who have espoused the cause are proceeding like ruffians descending on a banquet. There is much to be said on both sides.[44]

Although she held a ticket for the deputation for the next week to the prime minister's home at 10 Downing Street, Martin spent that time having the postponed operation, cheered in her nursing home by being singled out in *Votes for Women* as "a native of the States . . . brought into the Suffrage movement because it appealed to her as the greatest, most unselfish, and most vital movement for the cause of justice since the American war on Slavery."[45] She returned to chair meetings at which such important leaders as Annie Kenney spoke, and she wrote of a later deputation when, she reported, "I had on fencing armor, as I knew from former experience that I would need it."[46] She wrote letters to English newspapers affirming the positive effects of suffrage in Wyoming and Colorado, letters heavy on quotation and rather short on argument.[47] Thus she was still participating when the women began to switch tactics after Black Friday, having sworn, as Christabel Pankhurst phrased it, that "property rather than their persons, might henceforth pay the price of votes for women."[48]

As Martin reported of her second deputation, "Many of the women had bags of stones and they were at Caxton Hall ready for any woman who desired ammunition. As Mrs. Massey, at one of the deputations of the previous year said, 'we prefer to break a window and be promptly arrested to having our bodies broken by the police.'"[49] At first a defensive tactic, the vandalism grew finally to organized window-smashing raids on London shops, to bombing of post boxes, destruction of art works, burning businesses, and the eventual spectacular suicide of Emily Davison, who threw herself in front of the king's horse at Ascot in 1913.

In Martin's experience, the suffragette battle was, in the words of a popular marching song, "the grandest movement the world has ever seen,"[50] in which women would "March, march, many as one, / Shoulder to shoulder and friend to friend"[51] in the words of another.

If militant violence shocked the British public and incited the British government to a bafflingly brutal response, that very outrage sparked new life in the movement. Even to so condescending an observer as George Dangerfield, the militant interlude, which faded into superpatriotism with the outbreak of the war, was "a strange, unlovely, but valuable phenomenon" that sought the solidarity of women: militant methods were "bad and mistaken, but their ultimate motives shine, as a lamp shines through a fog."[52]

Somewhat dazzled by the shine, Anne Martin returned to the United States to tell other women how "women of the working classes as well as those of the aristocracy were rubbing elbows metaphorically in a common quest for suffrage," preferring, as she often did,. to see the movement as a broad one.[53] While it is true that there were working women involved, the majority were women like herself and so the metaphor was loosely constructed. Even within the Pankhurst clan one daughter, Sylvia, had gradually moved to bread-and-butter goals in her work in East London. But Martin truly believed in the breadth of her cause, and she had made it her own by the time she left England, impressed by both the effectiveness of militant actions and fully apprised of the cost of them.

Anne Martin's ten years of doubt and confusion, her travels and her efforts at journalism, her uncertainty about a goal ended with that final touch of a conversion—the word is not too strong—to ardent feminism. Those ten years had contributed to her late maturity and her lifetime thinking: it is important then to evaluate that experience, to consider how it shaped her life for another decade of vigorous political activity.

Her inheritance had proved both a blessing and a hindrance, for the ease it brought allowed her to choose. Choosing was not easy for her, in spite of her awareness of many models of female accomplishment: she knew of the settlement movement, but she did not join; she was prepared for college teaching, but she deserted it after little experience; she deplored her own lack of ambition, but she could not seem to concentrate on steady effort to produce results. While she termed herself a writer, and made other vague reference to publishing in an English newspaper, she preserved nothing from that time but the simplest sort of ineffective fiction and run-of-the-mill summaries written too late from other news accounts. Her adventure with Mary Austin revealed how her love of comfort precluded the steady work of writing. Further study was possible had she been firmly directed at any discipline. Her association with the Fabian Socialists may have grown from her continued adoration of her late father's progressive ideas, but her writing at the time reveals no intellectual response. With the Fabians she could make a superficial effort at genteel reformist thinking in the pleasant company of women much like her, attend the summer schools, and acquire a few more names to drop: the Webbs, Keir Hardie, the Felses.

Once affiliated with the WSPU she could not fail to know of Sylvia Pankhurst's work with the working-class women in East London, but she found the political activism in fine company with Christabel and Emmeline Pankhurst and the comforts of the Lyceum Club fronting Green Park more suited to her tastes.

Perhaps the very slowness of her awakening to the suffrage cause honed her next decade's effort, when no one could fairly fault the steadiness of her dedication or question her willingness to work for personal and social goals. Perhaps the joy of finding that long-sought cause, that call to her talents and imagination, gave her a new sense of purpose that could unite her longing for home with her need to act. Less than a year after Black Friday she was once again in Nevada, this time with a clear purpose for the coming years.

CHAPTER 6

LEADING AT LAST

Commanding the Fight for Nevada Suffrage

I know only woman and her disfranchised.

—Susan B. Anthony

. . . there are enough broadminded and courageous women, enough just men who want fair play to carry an amendment through in Nevada.

—Anne Martin, 1914

ANNE MARTIN returned to the United States in time to carry the Nevada banner in a suffrage parade in New York City in 1911.[1] Such public participation marked a suitable return to the nation and the state, for her next years would see her carry the state to suffrage through an intensive three-year campaign that marked her most successful leadership. She ran the campaign in near military fashion, but she perfected her organizational skills, learned the daily demands of canvassing, made mistakes and mended most of them. She became a near celebrity, a leader perhaps overconfident of her abilities.

The New York parade Martin marched in reflected the experience other American women had gained in England: Harriot Stanton Blatch, leader of the New York effort, and others had been struck by the success of involving the public in their cause by such displays. Like their English counterparts, American women had been petitioning for the suffrage for more than fifty years. Although some western states offered the franchise to their women, efforts to extend it further were discouraging. In spite of years of organization and effort, equality seemed farther and farther off as state campaigns ground through slow processes of amendment. Dr. Anna Howard Shaw, earnest but aging head of the National American Woman Suffrage Association (NAWSA), offered no new strategy for the new century.

Encouraged that woman suffrage was more acceptable in the West than in the East, a revitalized Nevada Equal Franchise Society had emerged in 1909 at the suggestion of Mrs. Katherine Mackay, then heading the New York Equal Franchise League. Mrs. Mackay's Reno credentials were impeccable: her husband, Clarence, was the son of John Mackay, a true bonanza king and one of the few that enriched the state that had done the same for him. Although the second-generation Mackay spent little time in Nevada, the name carried a certain magic, a spell to which Professor Jeanne Wier, Martin's former friend and her successor in history at the university, responded. After some false starts, and with the aid of an impressive committee of important Reno people, the group had formed in January of 1911 and elected Mrs. Margaret Stanislawsky as its first president in February.[2] Almost everyone approached was willing to serve, although at least one sympathizer apologetically refused for the good of the cause. A. A. Hubbard of Reno explained to Wier: ". . . as I am a prominent worker in the Socialist party (also for municipal water works) it would lose the cause of suffrage many votes if it was seen that a Socialist was on that committee. The Socialist party is already pledged to equal suffrage, however, and anything that I can do for the cause I will gladly do."[3] Possible Socialist connections were to prove a problem from time to time during the campaign, and when it was all over the Socialists claimed credit, pointing out that the strongest votes in favor came from the heavily Socialist mining camps.[4] At the time no one seemed to mind Anne Martin's Fabian connections; perhaps no one knew the nature of the group.

Through the efforts of a few lobbyists, including Professor Wier, Mrs. Stanislawsky, and Carson City attorney Felice Cohn, a resolution favoring woman suffrage passed both houses of the Nevada legislature on 18 March, only three days before adjournment. According to Nevada law, passage again in 1913 and a statewide referendum would be required before the vote would be a reality for Nevada women.[5] The three-year process was not peculiar to Nevada, but it did demand continuous effort over a period of time and the sort of organization that few women had learned. Impressed with the first success, Dr. Anna Howard Shaw, writing from the national organization, urged Wier to conduct a low-key campaign, based entirely on mailing literature, to avoid creating an "antagonism which might be perfectly dormant if not aroused."[6]

University president J. E. Stubbs, even before the first passage, had fussed that nearly every senator and representative from Washoe County (Reno and environs) "expressed himself in private as opposed . . ." and Stubbs believed the reason was that "if the women vote, it will put a new and vital moral power into the elections of this state."[7] His comments reflected the firm beliefs of suffragists throughout the country and of opponents whose businesses may have wished to avoid close moral scrutiny. But the prospects were still promising when Anne Martin returned to Nevada late in 1911 determined to throw her considerable energies into the local cause.

Hopes for a successful Nevada campaign were brighter in 1911 than they might have been a few years earlier for a number of reasons. After fourteen years of struggle during which not one additional state had been won for suffrage, Washington women had captured the vote in 1910 with a quiet but carefully organized campaign modeled on the newer publicity-seeking approaches of Mrs. Carrie Chapman Catt, who had profited from a visit to England during the height of the WSPU agitation, and of Mrs. Harriot Stanton Blatch, who had revitalized the New York effort. Perhaps it was just as important that Oregon had lost after an even quieter campaign, muted to avoid attracting too much attention from liquor interests, forces all suffragists believed were opposed to the voting of women. Within months, California staged a drive, successful in November, that, as Eleanor Flexner put it, gave other states "something to shoot for in brilliance, flexibility, and scope," a paradigm for other states in its attention-getting techniques, its meetings, its spectacles. Most of all, it was marked by support from all over the nation, not only from the National American Woman Suffrage Association (NAWSA), but from other groups and from women all over the country.

Until the last week, California women campaigned in rural areas and in small towns to prevent the liquor interests from buying large segments of votes in San Francisco and Oakland. The most spectacular event—a concert and speaking marathon in San Francisco's Union Square—was held the day before the election. The organizers cinched their victory by mobilizing poll watchers in every precinct, securing both volunteers and hired detectives for the vaults where ballots were stored in big cities in order to prevent any miraculous increase in votes against the measure.[8] Both style and technique of the California fight became part of the Nevada campaign.

Anne Martin assumed duties as press secretary to the Nevada Equal Franchise Society in the fall of 1911. Her chance to lead—always for her preferable to anything less—would not come until 1912. Meanwhile she spent some time on her return writing an article she never managed to place for reasons obvious to any reader who has to weave through shifting point of view, only slightly veiled personal references, and a strained mixture of the colloquial and the pretentious. The very faults make it interesting here, however, for what it reveals of this woman of thirty-six, snared so long in preparation for a work she had reason to value for the rest of her life. Ostensibly a kind of defense of Reno, probably intended for an English audience, it exposes the author more than it presents the still raw town and demonstrates her interests and her attitudes.

This "normal Western town," she wrote, boasted a social life "probably the most democratic in the democratic West," but it is clear the author somewhat disapproves of that:

> the expressman who delivers one's trunks upon returning from a long journey . . . having known one from childhood riding about on an Indian pony or one's brother's bicycle, salutes one breezily . . . the idea of familiarity or disrespect never entering into the matter . . . the plumber rings at the front door . . . all the monthly collecting for bills . . . is by means of the front door, and the Japanese servant . . . So democratic is it, that in the early days, if one's parents did not allow one to attend public dances to which the butcher boy secured admission by paying twenty-five cents, if one were educated at a private instead of the public school, one was considered "high-toned," a term of disparagement.[9]

Not content with such blatant self-excuse, she continued to recount tales of Bishop Whitaker's saloon sermons and of only two of the famous four bonanza kings, whom she remembered as "labourers in the mines who never forgot old friends," and she commented on the fine "western spirit of enterprise and democracy where men found their place on merit" to form "a kind of local aristocracy" that refused to accept divorcees, "no matter how well fixed."[10] Thus the claim to respectability and social standing, all in the name of extolling "social democracy," edged out the putative subject.

While she could praise aspects of her hometown (fine homes "above the rushing Truckee River"), while she commended the city's placement ("suggesting Switzerland"), she rhetorically questioned how "decent respectable people" could live in a place that "glories in her notoriety . . . clinging to divorce laws that encourage collusion, fraud, immorality or bigamy, which insidiously attack the family and the home for the sake of gain."

Obviously, the free beliefs of suffragists she had met at home and abroad had not shaken her innate conservatism, and the daring young woman who sneaked out to buy cigarettes in Paris was momentarily squelched. Reno's main street appeared to her a "glaring Midway Plaisance, tempting young and old day and night, a crime ridden place." She deplored the notorious Johnson-Jeffries fight of 1910, a fight that had "precipitated race riots, the moving pictures of which were prohibited in Europe and the rest of America . . . and even in El Paso and Barcelona." She was righteously incensed over her hometown where "even the negro and the tramp could vote" and "men of property and pillars of the church" believed the money from vice "'good' for the town." Clearly, she suffered a strong culture shock on her return to schizophrenic Reno, a town whose respectable citizens could blink, for money's sake, at what the world called sin and vice.[11]

All her association with the intellectual Fabians, her freedom in her protracted student days, and her on-again-off-again rebellion against the bonds of womanhood had not set her off particularly from her sisters. She almost cherished an essential snobbery, a racism common to her sex and class, and a lack of practical sense about the world that would surely have disappointed her adored father.

Yet precisely because she was all these things her accomplishments in the several long campaigns that became her life are particularly surprising: she would find herself forced daily to overcome her natural feelings, to open her mind (however briefly), to accept unexpected challenges with at least surface decorum in pursuit of her ambitions for herself and for women. To believe that the new and ever changing population of Nevada was very largely made up of "saloon keepers, 'tinhorn' gamblers, stock brokers and stock gamblers, desperadoes and soldiers of fortune, the many types who spend their lives wandering from one mining camp to another for quick profit and adventure,"[12] and yet to go out in that electorate, often alone, at other times with only a single female companion—that kind of action in the face of that kind of belief requires courage, deserves respect, and demands recognition. If there was self-dramatization in the press release that chronicled the campaign, if there was press agent puffery that glorified Anne Martin, that created public figure surrounded a real woman of strength and character, and the stories grew from a basis in solid truth.

Very few members of the Equal Franchise Society were present at the meeting in February 1912 when an absent Anne Martin was elected president, but no one seems to have challenged the election.[13] First efforts of the tiny group concentrated on education, expanding the weekly "Equal Franchise News" Martin had begun to send to papers all over the state. From most, the response was positive. In Reno, the *Nevada State Journal,* essentially a Democratic paper, happily accepted the regular column, while the *Evening Gazette* offered a caveat: the editor "disclaimed all responsibility for the sentiments" expressed by the suffragists and invited opposing views.[14]

Nevada women faced a number of serious problems in the three-year battle for the vote: not only was there the difficulty of the three-stage amendment process, but the very success of women in neighboring states had alerted opponents to the diligence of suffragists. In Nevada, the mere matter of canvassing was extremely hard, as Anne Martin pointed out regularly to those who did not know much about a state that had almost sneaked into the Union in 1864, its acceptance based more on its nonslave status and its rich silver than upon any real qualification for statehood.

Then one of the largest states in the Union at 110,000 square miles, its 80,000 citizens in the second decade of the century were scattered in small communities and mining camps, the largest city claiming only 20,000 at the most. It was a territory "one quarter larger than Great Britain" with a transient population that included only 20,000 male voters, even though half the population was male and of voting age. The state had "the lowest urban and most scattered rural population" in the nation, "the highest proportionate male population, the lowest proportionate population of women, and the largest 'floating' or transient vote in the whole country . . . due to mining, railways and irrigation construction and other transitory occupations." Moreover, many settlements were not on railroads, located to serve the mines rather than particular areas or communities, so that campaigners would seek out voters by automobile or stage and even on horseback. To reach the one hundred votes at Austin in the center of the state required a journey of two days over the desert on a narrow-gauge railroad.[15]

Because the state was so large, the towns so small and male, few women had any organizational experience beyond the local level, although a federation of women's clubs and an active Women's Christian Temperance Union drew some workers.[16] Press work and education, then, were particularly important.

By spring of 1912 some forty-nine editors throughout Nevada were receiving suffrage news and Martin sent dispatches to suffrage newspapers throughout the nation as well as to newspapers in major cities.[17]

Anne Martin's comfortable financial state made it possible for her to travel to women's meetings throughout the United States, and she was quick to seize every chance for publicity for the cause and, perhaps not merely incidentally, for herself.

She was an attractive personality for newspapers: educated, traveled, poised, a short woman with a full figure (then no disadvantage), black curly hair and intense blue eyes; she was an articulate speaker and a colorful personality for the interviewer. Her English experiences captured the reporters' imaginations; her western origins and her equestrian skills appealed to them. During her first year in office, the "bright eyed, rosy cheeked" leader who charmed a *San Francisco Post* reporter was widely publicized as "a power in two continents" by the *San Jose Mercury,* copying a subheading on a Reno headline, and the *Philadelphia North American,* where, conveniently, an old Stanford classmate, Winnifred Harper Cooley, worked, included her among notables in the 1912 suffrage convention. The *Reno Evening Gazette,* generally not particularly friendly to the cause itself, eulogized her as "a woman on horseback" who rode "for freedom," but observed that during the time that she "sits in her library, reads, writes, thinks . . . [then] she is a power."[18] By January 1913, when the *New York Times* called her "a spectacular figure among the suffragists," she had achieved a sort of local fame as well.[19]

Her experience with the militants was more interesting than helpful. Newspaper reporters found it colorful. In almost every interview she was obliged to repeat her early assertion that "there is not the least probability of our resorting to militant methods . . . In America we use American methods allowed by our circumstances," and although she often quoted Mrs. Pankhurst's "until we get the power to make the law we shall break the law," she repeated her intention to conduct a ladylike campaign.[20] By June 1912, when Mrs. Pankhurst and the Pethick-Lawrences had been sentenced to nine-month prison terms for conspiracy, however, she wrote a long article for the *Evening Gazette* to present "An American View of English Militancy," eschewing their methods while deploring American correspondents who "made merry over Englishwomen serving months in prison with hard labour for fighting for liberty." "Americans," she wrote, "honor and revere Patrick Henry, Daniel O'Connell, Mazzini, and Garibaldi. So," she declared, "do we honor and revere these noble English women."[21]

While their president was attracting national recognition, the women of the Nevada Equal Franchise Society were organizing throughout the state. Each new society began at a single meeting prompted by a letter from Reno headquarters to a prominent woman of the town. At the meeting the women moved to plan small gatherings and fund-raising drives, public demonstrations and town parades. Suffragists concentrated on personal contact with voters, however hard that was when the usual gathering place for men was the saloon, a man's space, off limits to respectable women.

Anne Martin met in person with these leaders, some of whom became lifelong friends. Others were impressed by her presence and skills, as Maud Gassaway was, who wrote to Martin to thank her and added: "I notice that you always make a *point* and then proceed to *clinch* it. That is much more effective than flowery oratory."[22] It is not surprising that the proper Miss Martin, a lady in well-tailored outfits, soft of speech but educated, was successful with women striving for the softer goals of civilization in the still raw state. But just as much as she grew in the eyes of those who admired her, she excited envy in those who might have challenged her. Her allies were generally faithful, but not surprisingly the first year was not entirely smooth.

Anne Martin had help in the early work in the person of Bird Wilson, an attorney in Goldfield, the only woman stockbroker in the state, who managed both a thriving practice in the communities of Goldfield and Tonopah and a ranch at Indian Springs as well. She was even-tempered, sensible, diplomatic, a fine foil to the sometimes impulsive, sometimes sensitive Martin. Wilson took primary responsibility for managing affairs in the southern part of the state and proved particularly diplomatic in smoothing out the complications that arose from a highly touted visit to the state by Charlotte Perkins Gilman, perhaps the most interesting figure of the entire suffrage movement, a woman able to look at large issues, a writer of note, and an accomplished lecturer.[23]

Gilman's services had been obtained with the help of Martin's influence in NAWSA's national headquarters. She was a national name—and she was a Socialist, a fact that split her loyalties when she visited Las Vegas, then a town small even by Nevada standards, and Tonopah. Perhaps because she understood the implications of the female vote more clearly—she knew how little it represented—she was insistent in placing her broader beliefs above the immediate question, even if NAWSA and the local groups were footing the bill.[24]

Although Gilman drew good crowds in Caliente, Pioche, and Goldfield, where Bird Wilson had raised funds by staging a performance of "How the Vote Was Won," Wilson objected to plans Martin had approved to allow Gilman to speak to the Socialists in Tonopah: "I do not think she has been quite fair, after making this little circuit especially for the suffrage clubs and at their expense, to fill in a date for any other organization while on that circuit." But she went on to arrange for Gilman to speak on the same platform with Nevada senator Francis Newlands and the visiting senator Champ Clark, who were to be in Las Vegas the same night, as "the whole town, of all political beliefs, would turn out to hear those two men."[25] Gilman would not cooperate, insisting on "speaking from her own platform or not at all." Her speech from an open car—a common suffrage platform—was booed, and the Las Vegas women were mortified by her stubborn refusal to cooperate and her uncompromising opposition to the Democrats.[26] It was Bird Wilson who finally soothed the Las Vegas women and brought them back to the organization.

Attorney Wilson contributed to the campaign as well with a successful pamphlet, *Women under Nevada Law,* a careful account of the limited rights of females in the state. In two years enough copies for every citizen of the state had been distributed.[27] While Bird Wilson did not hesitate to argue with Anne Martin, she respected the other's mind and work, sympathized with her, and understood her, as a 1912 letter shows: "I wish I could talk to you face to face for a few minutes, as I know just how weary you are with the work, how momentarily discouraged, and I am sure I could remove some of that load and brighten your spirits . . ." Wilson knew, too, how it mattered to Martin to receive the kind of praise Wilson would offer: "I could not but feel heartily thankful . . . that we have you at the head of our organization. For where is there another woman in the State who can do the work you are doing . . .?"[28] Her analyses of the political situation, too, were most frequently objective and right.

Whatever the organizational problems were, whatever slips may have occurred, the state society was considerably stronger at the end of the year than it had been at the start: in November Martin could boast in the *Woman's Journal* (the organ of NAWSA) that membership had grown twentyfold during the year;[29] she could claim support from major political figures and most of the major parties.[30] She could properly assert that women had as well made clear to political candidates for state offices that their views on suffrage counted, and women had turned out in large numbers to support those who agreed with them, handing out literature at fall elections, hoping to insure quick passage of the amendment a second time in the 1913 legislature.[31]

An undated speech Anne Martin preserved (usually she spoke extemporaneously from bare notes) suggests the tone speakers took as opposition surfaced:

We are heartened rather than disheartened by the signs of protest against
this long delayed measure of justice . . . Fear of the vested and vicious
interests has driven a few of our so-called supporters into the camp of the
antis, while our genuine supporters are staunch . . . No man deserving of
the name will be turned against a great principle of human rights because of
a personal petty reason. We are convinced there are enough broadminded
and courageous women, enough just men who want fair play to carry an
amendment through in Nevada.[32]

Both the concern for the "vested and vicious interests" and the appeal to
fair play are typical of suffrage arguments of the day, but much of the
effectiveness of early recruitment of women depended on personal
appeal, as Katherine Riegelhuth remembered many years later:

[We] were all so fond of Anne Martin because she was such a fine person
and so easy to talk to, and so impressive. You just wanted to do what she
wanted you to do. You knew it was a good thing because she said it was.
She could have convinced you to do anything because she was so likable.[33]

Not everyone agreed. In fact, such warm feelings had cooled, if they
had ever existed, in some Carson women by early 1913. It was Felice
Cohn, leader of the capital's sizable suffrage group, who took offense at
a reference Martin made to some members being jealous of the considerable attention she had been receiving as leader of the state campaign. At
least that was Minnie Blair's idea when she wrote to Anne Martin in
January about "some jealousy in the ranks" and urged Martin to act to
heal the breach.[34] If Martin reacted, whatever she did was not enough,
and Cohn became a potent adversary, a woman still dedicated to the
larger cause but determined to remove Anne Martin as state spokes-
woman.

Only a few years younger than Martin, also a graduate of Stanford,
Cohn had become an outstanding young woman by 1913. She had
passed the bar with "one of the best examinations of any applicant in
Nevada for years," to the great surprise of "many of her friends who did
not know that she was studying for the profession." Moreover, she could
boast of being the third woman in the nation to be admitted to practice
before the United States Supreme Court, and she had made her name as
the only woman land hearing attorney after service in the Goldfield land
office.[35] She had written the amendment for the state legislature in 1911
and had directed the lobbying that saw the amendment through the 1913
legislature with so little fuss that even the most confident of the suffragists were surprised.[36]

If the source of the problem between the two women was personal jealousy (or the mere imputation of it), the focus for the rebellion was the simple question of proxies for the state convention in February and the election of Martin to head the state campaign again. Such a battle was particularly surprising in the atmosphere of victory after the second passage, in the positive prospects that came from a rousing endorsement from Governor Tasker Oddie, and from Democratic, Progressive, and Socialist parties. Cohn did not, surprisingly, seek office for herself: her main concern was to defeat Martin. When that failed, she gathered numbers of women, particularly in Carson City and with less effect in Tonopah and Goldfield, and fomented a minor rebellion that delighted the Nevada press and gave ample opportunity for Martin's good and bad qualities of leadership to emerge.

Cohn called for dissidents to join a Non-Militant Suffrage Society, attacked Martin's English experiences as portents of trouble for the future, and claimed that Martin had tried to ram through the legislature a petition calling for a special election the coming fall to ratify the amendment. No such allegations were proved; such speedy action would not be consistent with Martin's tendency to exaggerate opposition and to prefer to believe that the struggle was fiercer than it really was. But cries of "gag rule" and betrayal surfaced in the *Tonopah Bonanza* in mid March. A delighted W. W. Booth, sworn opponent of suffrage, splashed his front page with a headline claiming "Tonopah Suffragists Declare War on Society President" and quoting the doubts of Mrs. P. E. Keeler, local president, about Martin's "high handed methods."[37]

Anne Martin had been a child half complimented by her ability to "take people down" and she had antagonized friends over the years and had lost allies when her sharp tongue sprang into action ahead of her thought. Her reaction, perhaps to be expected but exaggerated in response to the personal hurt, was to threaten both Booth and Mrs. Keeler with a libel suit. For a woman already in the public eye, Martin was, in 1913, particularly sensitive to criticism; but then, few women had such experience, and her reaction revealed a sensitivity she never overcame but learned to hide.

She demanded as a "moral duty" that the two see that the allegations be corrected with "prompt and equal publicity."[38] Far from frightened, Booth responded with a scathing editorial on 20 March, claiming "militant tactics are abhorable [*sic*]" and denying Martin's responses: "like every statement made by Miss Martin since her return," they were not to be taken as true. Insisting that there should be "no Hooliganism" in the campaign, Booth went even further: "If the record has been kept, it will undoubtedly prove that Miss Martin has been responsible for making more enemies for her cause than friends, and all that remains . . . for defeat . . . will be the continued activity of Miss Martin."[39] To Martin's horror, other papers throughout the state picked up the story and the editorial.

Allies responded in a variety of ways: Marjorie Brown, an influential member of Tonopah society who had been away in San Francisco during the ruckus, wrote to Martin to complain that "the suffrage quarrel has been used by others to augment other quarrels until I'm sick of every woman's organization."[40] Another Martin sympathizer echoed Mrs. Brown's sentiments, calling the squabbles only part of the "peculiar" conditions in the town where "one of the bitterest social fueds [sic] that I have ever seen in any small town" was raging.[41] Faithful Bird Wilson attempted to console her friend with the assurance that the *Bonanza* was "not read outside of Tonopah, and I have never heard a good word said of its editor . . . A knock from him is a compliment."[42] Her assurances were joined with those of Mrs. Brown, who had told the public (in the *Bonanza* itself) that "we do not want a politician, we want a reformer who is full of the justice of her cause, and this we have in Anne Martin."[43] While Mrs. Brown aimed to support, her words may have wounded Martin, who liked to see herself as a politician, strategist, and diplomat all in one. Quoting her favorite, Abraham Lincoln, Martin reminded suffrage presidents that "a house divided against itself cannot stand," and she asked that they not "be influenced by criticisms and false reports . . . With our hearts whole for the cause and with good team work we shall win."[44]

But Martin continued to distrust all of those involved in the nonmilitant faction, some of whom were old friends. Even a month later Bird Wilson felt obliged to reassure her and to hope they could "forget the more serious business of life and ride way into the mountains and catch the uplift that is there."[45] Months later, when Minnie Bray wrote that she was "serene as a summer day" about the situation in Carson and added that one of the Cohn faction had "spoken of [Martin] in the kindest and most loving manner" and had made no criticism of methods,[46] Martin remained concerned, in spite of assurances that when her enemy had appeared Cohn's speaking "was a fizzle . . . nobody crazy with enthusiasm."[47]

Martin did, however, continue to work, to follow advice to "get as close to your county organizations as possible, by visits, etc."[48] It is clear that she began to ask advice of others (not a regular habit of hers) and attempted to follow it. When Gail Loughlin, a feminist lawyer from Colorado known throughout the country, traveled to Nevada in October to speak in Reno, Winnemucca, and Elko, Anne Martin accompanied her, both of them speaking in each community.[49]

She had not, however, quite recovered from a tendency to overre-spond to opposition, as her reaction to the professional antisuffragist Minnie Bronson showed. Bronson, whom Carl Degler identifies as a special agent of the U.S. Labor Department, was general secretary of the National Association Opposed to Woman's Suffrage[50] and was an experienced public speaker who had appeared at California meetings. Dr. Anna Howard Shaw assured Martin that "Miss Bronson's appear-ance would do the cause good, rather than harm,"[51] and, although the antisuffragist drew good crowds, the equal franchise forces answered her arguments effectively, avoiding personal invective. Martin had not been so restrained in her press releases to local societies, one of which was gleefully reprinted from the *Western Nevada Miner* by the Reno paper.

In that document Martin had claimed that Bronson was in the pay of the familiar "vested and vicious interests," indicting the "saloon men and Mr. Wingfield,"[52] insisting they were in league with the National Liquor Dealers Association, which had openly fought suffrage else-where, and with the "red-light capitalists," clinching her argument with the claim that "anti-suffrage literature was given out over the bars in Cincinnati and Detroit."[53] However impolitic in its naming of names (George Wingfield was a wealthy banker and rancher, the acknowl-edged political boss of Nevada), the bulletin echoed those widely held beliefs of both opponents and proponents that enfranchised women would clean up the nation, especially its bars and brothels. The *Miner* used the accusations to resurrect the near-forgotten flap with the *Tono-pah Bonanza,* and added an argument *ad feminam* against Anne Martin that compared her with Bronson, "a real American girl." Bronson did not engage in "mud-slinging and wild eyed antics" and "never so far forgot her Americanism as to ape the cockneys of England by carrying a slinky little cane; neither was she arrested." While militancy had little to do with the argument, the *Miner* writer guessed correctly how defensive Martin was and questioned whether "this brand of female politician" could be compared with Bronson, who had worked for the working girl, while "female Hooliganism" had sent Martin to prison.[54]

Martin refrained from answering, either out of good political sense or, more likely, because she was headed to the convention of NAWSA in Washington, so she was demonstrating either a surprising slip of attention or a step in political maturity.[55] At any rate, she was busy in Washington when the attack surfaced, involved in the convention that would see the beginnings of a change in suffrage strategy. That annual gathering would hear the report of the new congressional committee of NAWSA headed by Alice Paul. Whether Anne Martin was already affiliated with the recently formed Congressional Union is unclear. The new group was headed by others who had WSPU experience in England. Cautious about adding any new militancy to her name, she may have belonged privately or delayed joining rather than be clearly affiliated with Alice Paul and Lucy Burns, leaders of the group.

Anne Martin already knew Paul and Burns, who had gone to England for graduate education and experience in social work and who had spearheaded the committee after 1912. Most suffrage activity until then had been directed at individual state campaigns, but more and more suffragists had come to believe that a federal amendment might provide prompter success for their efforts. Nevada's cumbersome process, requiring as it did a campaign of more than three years, was not too different from those of other states. Yet the yearly budget of the NAWSA congressional committee until 1912 was a mere ten dollars.[56] Elizabeth Kent, wife of a California congressman, had even given change from her budget. Alice Paul changed all that, and quickly, too.

Paul's plans for launching a federal campaign were many, but the NAWSA executive committee had agreed to a single initial request: to organize a suffrage parade in Washington the day before Woodrow Wilson's inauguration. This activity was acceptable to Dr. Shaw, who had seen such parades in England and New York. Granted authority to use NAWSA letterheads, the new committee was free to raise its own funds. Working from Washington headquarters, the committee, which became the Congressional Union in April, raised more than $27,000 in the first year. Its first public event in March 1913 drew eight thousand to ten thousand women and other gatherings followed. The Union also provided salaried organizers to state campaigns, initiated a nationwide press service, and demanded and got congressional hearings. Still, when NAWSA met late in 1913, delegates refused Union demands to move national headquarters to Washington, and although the organization agreed to provide money for the newcomers, after the convention NAWSA's board moved to separate the chair from the presidency of the Union.[57]

Anne Martin was with the Union in spirit, although she withheld public participation until after the state campaign was won, having seen how easy it was for her enemies to build on her militant activities. She did catch national attention at the Washington meeting. For her public part in the convention, Martin was clearly the author of the Nevada report, even though corresponding secretary Grace Bridges also signed it. It is a distinctly different document from the others offered; most reports were detailed lists of activities—who met where, what money was raised, who led what, how active the organization had been, what prospects were. Nevada's report was a performance, a rhetorical display, a defense of its president's action with few specifics about the program. Even the single fact cited—"an educational campaign . . . carried on for over two years . . . over two hundred columns or about 240,000 words (two good-sized books) of educational suffrage material in Nevada papers alone"—was offered as not having "protected us from the attack of our opponents," although no specific opponent is named beyond the ever present "vested and immoral interests." Much of the oration—report is too mild a word—was devoted to a comparison of the women's campaign with Lincoln's battle against slavery, "in no way comparable, save in one respect: the underlying principle of each struggle is the extension of human liberty." Both denying and insisting on comparison, she spent many words on a recitation—with variation— of Lincoln's famous letter to Horace Greeley, paraphrasing for her circumstances: "What we do or what we forbear about these interests opposed to suffrage, we do or forbear because we believe it will help to win the cause." Perhaps this line let her free the *Miner* and the *Gazette* from her wrath with a single noble gesture.

When she said "we" it is clear she meant "I" as she firmly defended "our sin of commission . . . of defending our cause when assailed by certain influences opposed to suffrage, and that of answering public misrepresentations of equal suffrage by an anti-suffragist." So much for Editor Booth. "We declare our policy to be never to attack, but to protect and defend our cause from misrepresentation." Perhaps she did answer the *Miner*'s attack, however circularly. "We shall," she continued, ". . . make every effort to keep the true and just view before the public, even as we deplore the necessity for doing it." Insisting that "justice for Nevada women was inevitable," she closed with yet another lesson of the master:

> As women consecrated to the emancipation of women, let us recall, and remember during the coming year, his words: In giving freedom to the slave, we assure freedom to the free—honorable alike in what we give and what we preserve. We shall nobly save or meanly lose the last, best hope of earth . . . the way is plain, peaceful, generous, and just."[58]

Whether she recognized the irony in such allusion before a group that found the problem of enfranchising women complicated by the possibility that many of them would be black is not recorded. She was a great success. No less a heroine than Jane Addams—the woman Martin always referred to as "the sainted Jane Addams"—rose, gave her a bouquet of flowers, and assured Martin that she would journey personally to Nevada and help with the campaign.[59]

Martin added to her national image with no fewer than fifteen addresses before she returned to Nevada, speaking in major cities in Connecticut, Kentucky, and Illinois, seeking support for the home battle, presenting a brighter picture of that homeland than she had seen in the 1911 article, as she wrote in 1914 to Agnes Ryan, editor of NAWSA's *Woman's Journal:*

> . . . the equal suffrage campaign has given Nevada more favorable advertising in the great cities of the East than it has ever before received from commercial clubs and boards of trade. Lantern slide lectures have been given . . . illustrating our chief industries and pointing out Nevada's services to the Union.[60]

Philip Earl concludes that she had "become something of a celebrity in her own right by this time and drew huge crowds. In her speeches she told of how many ranchers and their wives would ride for an entire day to get in to hear her speak." However the claim seems exaggerated for gullible eastern audiences, she flattered her home state, too. "She also told of the courtesy with which she was treated by miners and cowboys and of one particular wrangler who told her that he held meetings with his fellows at round-up time and had converted many to the suffrage cause."[61]

The final year of the campaign started, then, with national attention to the state president, attention that may have helped free the Nevada convention of factionalism and assure a unanimous election of Anne Martin in February. Outside speakers brought for open meetings drew large crowds that included, as the local press noted, "about one third men," a higher proportion than seen before at such meetings.[62] There were promises of support from NAWSA as well as personal pledges, one from Mrs. Alvah Belmont, later the generous source of funds for the Congressional Union and its successor, the National Woman's Party. Twenty men formed a Men's Suffrage League and state prospects seemed brighter than ever.[63]

Away from Nevada, developments were not so encouraging: President Woodrow Wilson had angered suffragists by failing to endorse their goals during a speech at their convention at the end of 1913,[64] and the determined efforts by the Congressional Union had brought a disappointing Senate vote of 34–35 for the amendment, failing the required two-thirds majority.[65] At home, the local papers carried regular accounts of the continued militancy of Mrs. Emmeline Pankhurst's WSPU, ever reminding Anne Martin of the unfortunate use her enemies could make of such action. To make matters worse, the most powerful man in Nevada, George Wingfield, the cowboy-gambler-mining millionaire who had firm economic control of the state and particularly of the already unfriendly *Reno Evening Gazette,* came out publicly against suffrage and threatened to leave Nevada and take his investments with him if the amendment carried.[66] Wingfield was a formidable adversary: he was the Republican National committeeman and one of his lawyers was Democratic National committeeman; he controlled banks, hotels, and cattle ranches all over the state. Although he claimed no real interest in politics and had turned down an appointment as senator upon the death of his partner, U.S. senator George Nixon, he was, as Gilman Ostrander has pointed out, "constantly drawn into politics by those personal friendships and animosities which so often overrode political considerations in a state where everybody knew everybody else and had strong opinions about each of them."[67]

Anne Martin made of Wingfield a particular, personified enemy, a convenient single figure on whom she could blame many of her troubles. Just as she had in her childhood understood Marie Bashkirtseff's "Breslau"—the rival that spurred her on—and had admitted that she had her own "Breslaus," she saw in Wingfield a point of focus. He embodied all the qualities of power that she envied; he had interests in all the institutions she held responsible for problems in the world; he was supremely confident (with good reason) that matters would generally go the way he wished them to. Later in 1914 she wrote to Margaret Foley about a dangerous ailment she called "Wingfield cold feet" that afflicted supporters and weakened their efforts for the cause when their husbands' jobs were dependent on Wingfield's good will.[68] She repeatedly insisted that Wingfield was tied to the threatening vicious interests and she seemed equally well convinced that he controlled the town. She was probably right on both counts, but it is also clear that Wingfield's threat to leave if suffrage passed was not particularly serious.

The immediate response to that threat seems to have been the circulation in suffrage bulletins and various newspapers of a bit of doggerel by an author both unnamed and undistinguished that went in part:

> We'll be sorry, George, to lose you,
> But where are you going to go
> Now that the women are voting
> From Florida to Idaho
>
> .   .   .   .
>
> Nevada's not the greatest state,
> And if it ever hopes
> To be among the best ones let
> The women have their votes.[69]

Perhaps she had reason to fear the singular influence, whatever party lines, for Nevada consistently had been—and still is—more inclined to vote for the personality over the party, to react to the power of individual men rather than larger issues. Still, the publication of humorous verse, not political polemic, was probably wise and may suggest some tempering of Martin's often rash response.

Although Martin continued to style her leadership after the authoritarian Mrs. Pankhurst, she had two experienced suffrage workers come to Nevada to help by April of 1914. One proved a lifelong friend, the other clashed with Martin and left. Maud McCreery arrived in March, sent by NAWSA but paid by the local society, and Mabel Vernon, a live contribution from the well-heeled Congressional Union, followed shortly. Martin introduced McCreery to suffrage presidents as state organizer and press director, noting her experience in campaigns in Wisconsin, Pennsylvania, and Nebraska.[70] Vernon had been asked for by name because of her "abilities to hold an audience in her hand."[71] A high school teacher and a Quaker who had met Alice Paul as a student at Swarthmore, Vernon had gone to work for the Union in 1913.[72]

From the first, Vernon proved the favored cohort, invited to live in the Martin house,[73] while McCreery saw her own tasks as speaker and press writer degenerate to dull office chores as public meetings faded and typing increased. Complaining that in spite of her willingness to work and her personal sacrifices (like many others she contributed a good portion of her wages to the cause), she was forced to do work that made little use of her experience. McCreery felt her reputation would be damaged if she continued, and, adding the familiar complaint of new Reno residents against the 4,500-foot altitude for good measure, she resigned.[74]

McCreery's departure excited the kind of action that demonstrated a vindictive streak in Martin's nature, that suggested that there was more than a small disagreement about expectations. When McCreery asked for references, Martin replied with a confidential letter to suffrage presidents that damned the organizer's performance and painted her as one who "invariably subordinated the State work to her own interests . . . a dangerous person to have in a campaign with election so near."[75]

Even Mabel Vernon, a lifelong friend and devoted supporter through ensuing campaigns, as close a companion as Martin seemed capable of having, found relations with her leader hard at the beginning, and she remembered problems in detail when she was interviewed sixty years later in the last years of a long, full life:

> . . . [Anne] was very able and quite a perfectionist . . . a rather rigid sort of person to start with. I can remember Sara Bard Field consoling me . . . She was a little more systematic than I, probably . . . but we got along all right. We became fast friends.[76]

Pressed for details, she remembered that although at times Anne Martin was "lively," she was a person "of great dignity" who made her friend unhappy with her "strict ideas of what I should do." But she also recalled happy times in the Martin house, where she lived in a beautiful room, "a front room," and that Dick, the temperamental Chinese cook, was "very good."[77]

Sara Bard Field, an experienced suffrage campaigner and freethinker, yet another occasional member of the Martin household, had met her hostess in 1913 when Field was in Goldfield seeking a divorce with Bird Wilson as her attorney. Disappointed in most of her acquaintances in Nevada during her long stay ("I didn't meet any people of culture in that long and painful period"), she was delighted with Martin's willingness to introduce her to old Reno families and with her help in getting one of Wingfield's lawyers to hurry her divorce. Oddly enough, the man had handled William O'Hara Martin's interests and still had remained a trusted ally in spite of his employment by the hated Wingfield.[78]

The inner circle in the Martin home would change from time to time as the campaign progressed, but relationships were never easy. Nor was Martin more diplomatic in her public life in the early months. Even after the restraint in response to Wingfield's threats, she made sharp and public criticism of Senator Key Pittman, a valuable state ally who had voted against suffrage on the national level while supporting it in Nevada. At first Martin wrote in private letters that traded on long acquaintance and recalled how the two had "talked on woman suffrage on several occasions in my mother's drawing room."[79] But she felt

moved to respond to Pittman's declared opposition to letting the "ignorant Negro have the vote,"[80] insisting that the senator should "vote for the
West." She argued that fears of Negro voting were ungrounded, since
"there are now 600,000 more white women than Negro men and women
together in the south . . . Woman suffrage means the establishment of
Anglo Saxon supremacy."[81] Politely, Pittman affirmed that he could
continue to support suffrage by the states, having as well an even deeper
fear of federal intervention in western states, and foreseeing white
citizens "being compelled to permit Japanese, Chinese and other Asiat-
ics to attend school with white children."[82] The pair of racists—certainly no worse than others of their times, but no supporters of a truly
representative electorate—traded correspondence for some time before
knowledge of the conflict surfaced. NAWSA president Shaw accused
Anne Martin of following Congressional Union tactics (that group was
by then opposing Democrats on principle as the party in power) and
damaging the campaign, capping her censure with the assertion "not
Miss Bronson and all the anti-suffragists together could have done more
harm to the campaign" than Martin's then public fight with Pittman.[83]
When Martin defended her actions and asked for more help, Dr. Shaw
took the occasion to lecture Martin and admonish her to learn from
experience.[84]

At the same time Martin was antagonizing Pittman, she tried to
publicize Wingfield's opposition beyond the Nevada border when the
university board of regents refused to allow the College Equal Suffrage
League to use the university name "when the Republican Club of young
men had freely done so." In a night letter to the *San Francisco Examiner*
to be used "only as unsigned telegraphic news" she claimed that "the city
of Reno is dominated by a Republican multimillionaire who threatened
to leave Nevada if woman suffrage carries next November," further
claiming that the state effort was "practically a battle for good government for people against a bad government of a few men desiring a wide
open state."[85]

Yet gradually, as more and more helpers came to travel the scattered
towns and as she herself became more active in the grinding chore of
canvassing the state, the frantic tone calmed, the explosions were
fewer—or less public. She expected total devotion from the women who
worked for her, even though their circumstances were very different
from hers, but she gave her entire attention, energy, and talent to the
cause, moving steadily from town to town, maintaining relations with
two national organizations, writing articles, sending out press releases,
and offering her physical presence and argumentative skills generously.

Although she had her problems with organizers from other states and regularly clashed with women not willing or able to give their entire attention to the struggle, she was clearly admired and respected by the majority of women who worked, and she pursued individual votes assiduously. Antoinette Funk, one member of the squadron of helpers dispatched by NAWSA, later reported with some wonder, "I believe she could address every voter by his first name."[86] In a two-week period in broiling July, Martin and Mabel Vernon traveled to Lovelock, Seven Troughs, Rochester, Imlay, Winnemucca, Paradise Valley, National, Battle Mountain, Golconda, Gold Creek, Tuscarora, Metropolis, Contact, Stillwater, Fallon, Wonder, Vya, Sheepshead, Buckhorn, Windfall, and San Jacinto, only three of which by the wildest stretch of the imagination could be called towns. Since few of these settlements had any kind of public gathering place except for saloons, they spoke in the street or in a church, local women gathering as much of a crowd as could be found.

Few of the organizers sent to assist had any experience with such arduous activity, although a few came to Nevada after train journeys to Montana. Learning from the California experience, Nevada's suffragists concentrated on rural votes even though that meant physical hardship, for railroads—built to service mines, not people—reached only a few communities. Martin wrote to Agnes Ryan of the *Woman's Journal* of that circuit:

> This [trip] was an object lesson as to the scattered condition of our electorate, and the difficulty of reaching voters personally. One would have to travel 100 miles all day from a county seat to a mountain camp . . . to reach seventy voters. In one case a three days trip was necessary to reach eighty voters. [Since] registration lists are now about 50% wrong . . . personal contact with the voters through public meeting is necessary, by means of these long trips taken by railway, automobile, stage, horseback, and sometimes by foot.[87]

Martin chose a picture of herself and Mabel Vernon gathered with farmworkers in a hayfield to print when victory came, and it was properly illustrative of the nature of the battle.[88]

Still, those women who came learned to adjust to new conditions. Margaret Foley came from Massachusetts, Maude Younger and Charlotte Whitney from California, Sara Bard Field from Oregon, Laura Gregg Cannon and Antoinette Funk from the East, Annie Kenney from England, and, finally, the stellar attractions, Dr. Shaw and Jane

Addams. Their letters catch the spirit of the campaign in detail—the complications of travel (Mabel Vernon thought that "all the trains left at midnight"),[89] the confusions of schedule, the hecklers, the dust, the heat, the small-town wranglings, the political skirmishes.

Margaret Foley kept a diary of her experiences that reflects the wonder and excitement of such a venture to an easterner who had never visited the West before. Tall, imposing, possessed of a strong voice that could be heard in the open, Foley had a past similar to Martin's in that she had been a part of the WSPU campaign and had worked for suffrage in her native state. Friends marveled at her excursion West: one wrote that Foley was "the first woman I have ever addressed with Reno, Nevada. I wish I could accidentally drift into one of your crowds and see how Eastern energy meets Western enterprise."[90] An unlabeled notebook indicates the individual approach of the speaker with the note "Ballot not the goal—only *a step for a Broader Social Service*" and reminds her that "simplicity and naturalness is the secret. Be serious, then tell funny story . . . at least four stories . . . begin with something local."[91]

Margaret Foley thoroughly enjoyed her new work in Elko, Battle Mountain, Golconda (where the meeting had to be canceled because of "dust and windstorm"), Montello, and other settlements. She thought the ranches wonderful and saw her first rodeo; when she told a meeting that all Nevada needed was "more people and plenty of water," a man yelled back, "That is all Hell needs," but she found that "all the men seemed to be in favor." She found the community of Montello, with no church and only a small school, "a beautiful spot," but she wrote on a postcard from there about "how very queer these towns look. The people are also very different from our people."[92] She was valuable enough to the cause, successful enough in her speeches that she was rushed from Goldfield to Austin in October to counteract antisuffragist Minnie Bronson, who made her promised return to the state. And although Anne Martin criticized her sharply when she missed a meeting in tiny Aurora after spending "all day on the road," she remained loyal.

Martin's angry demand that Foley should stick to her schedule, no matter what, "affected her so severely that [Bird Wilson] feared for a little time that she could not make a good speech" at the next town, but the easterner rallied and "regained command of herself, to the great delight of the audience." Regretting the censure, Wilson praised "these Eastern women unaccustomed to such conditions who made these trips . . . I don't believe we could find men who would do it. It makes me realize more and more the entire self sacrifice that women make for the cause."[93] Foley's own sacrifice was more than she intended in the end, for Martin's persistent closeness with money deprived her of a good portion of the expense money she was promised.[94]

But Mrs. F. A. Weeks of Searchlight reported the "glorious meeting" Foley held in the street, "crowded on each side . . . Everyone in this place turned out enmasse and after the meeting an ovation was tendered Miss Foley. [She] is the right woman in the *right* place."[95] Foley claimed in a newspaper interview on her return to have talked in the depths of eight mines, attended fifty dances, made one thousand speeches, and worn out three pairs of shoes in an odyssey that seemed in retrospect "like a dream, a dime novel, a moving picture."[96]

Although there were careful efforts to protect such speakers as Jane Addams and Dr. Shaw, even sixty-seven-year-old Shaw could report long days that started in Reno and moved to Washoe City, Carson City, and Virginia City, where she spoke at both a church and the opera house before regaining Reno at 11 P.M.[97] Sara Bard Field remembered the contrasts between spending a night in a luxurious Virginia City hotel followed by a return to Reno the next day down the hazardous Geiger Grade with a crowd of drunks, events only somewhat softened by the "nice welcoming committee" and what she called a "curious chivalry" on the part of Nevada men, who "really held women in the highest esteem . . . the rank and file of men believed that they would do a lot to help purify government."[98]

Both Wilson's account of Foley's efforts to bring men from the bars to hear her speak and Field's account of her return among drunks emphasize one reason for the great concern Nevada women felt about the saloon interests. The saloon was the center of male social life in the smaller towns, as it remained throughout the West until growth and respectability brought more and more stable men into households and other kinds of social intercourse. Especially in mining communities, temporary by their very nature, saloon life was all that the men saw, and that life was closed to respectable women. One organizer in Leadville charged with getting voters to sign pledges for suffrage explained her problems to Martin quite emphatically:

> It would be impossible for me to go among them with those blanks to be signed as there is no place for the men only the saloons to go after working hours and Mr. Bailey [her husband] would not approve of that.
>
> I have handed the blanks to the cook at the boardinghouse and he has had the men to sign them so am sending them to you in this letter.[99]

Canvassing by proxy was chancy and frustrating, but it was necessary.

Faced with a society that was still essentially male, frontierlike in its acceptance of what feminine nicety called vice, the women truly believed themselves battlers for virtue over evil, soldiers who sought power for the superior moral conscience of women in political life. Anne Martin and her supporters believed with Sara Bard Field that they were "trying to remake conditions," and understanding, perhaps wrongly, that the ballot would lead to the true emancipation of the sex[100] they would have agreed with Field's assertion that although there may have been "noise and confusion" in campaigns in the East, in Nevada "there is no confusion": "Everyone knows not only what women want, but why there is opposition and who represents it. The movement here has more the simplicity of a duel than the complexity of a battle."[101] Women saw themselves as battling for the right against a clear evil.

While Wingfield and the saloon men were easy sources of worry, Anne Martin did not underestimate the existence of women who did not believe in the vote: even the wife of her favorite cousin, Fred Stadtmuller, was an officer in the Nevada Association of Women Opposed to Equal Suffrage, a group headed by an old family friend, Mrs. Jewett Adams.[102] Martin made every effort, however, to separate the suffrage cause from other issues that might weaken their efforts, demanding that local presidents not "ally themselves" with a prohibition speaker making the rounds of the state. "We must keep the suffrage issue absolutely clear from the Women's Christian Temperance Union and every other issue but votes for women."[103] She publicly insisted that Socialist support of suffrage did not imply any reciprocal response from the women to a frightening new system,[104] and worried justifiably about Mrs. Gilman's appearance for the Socialists and about the women in Tonopah, whom Bird Wilson identified as "all Socialists."[105]

While the political connections of her speakers caused occasional problems, as often their beliefs spurred welcome new arguments. Maude Younger of California, a woman who had dedicated years of her life to supporting a waitresses' union, refused to go to towns where there was a boycott[106] and was able on request to "talk about the working girls and give first hand experience instead of the old suffrage arguments."[107] Laura Gregg Cannon, a national organizer particularly interested in labor problems and a proclaimed Socialist, refused to speak in Las Vegas where she had heard that the Socialists were working as scabs in a local strike, but observed that "all the miners [in Tonopah] who are helping me are socialists, as you can scarcely find a miner who has any energy who is not one."[108]

But when the votes were counted, suffrage had won decisively—10,936 for, 7,258 against. Not one ward in Reno had been in favor;

Carson City and Virginia City had turned the women down, too. As Anne Martin had expected, the small towns and the mining camps had supported the women, the cities—if they could be called that—had resisted.[109]

Anne Martin managed to orchestrate all these various voices into a not entirely harmonious campaign that perhaps sometimes produced a deafening clamor: Maude Younger advised her in October that members in tiny Golconda had complained of too many speakers.[110] Martin alone had what Sara Bard Field perhaps generously called "the efficiency, tact, and leisure" to lead the state.[111] If she was sometimes too quick to accuse and so embarrassed her cause, she did learn to listen, to refuse to be drawn into controversy as the campaign progressed. She could excite loyalty from her friends, and she could work with the best of them. At the end when the appearance of Jane Addams at two meetings crowned the Nevada campaign, Martin could point to the support of hundreds of Nevada women who had canvassed and raised funds by ingenious methods. She could see that she had been right about the nature and support of the opposition. Perhaps it was suitable that at the victory party three days after election A. Grant Miller, a Socialist leader, painted out the black Nevada on the suffrage map of the West.[112]

The campaign had called forth her best qualities: a dogged determination, a single-minded dedication to the matter at hand, an ability to mix well with most other women and with men of all sorts, and a willingness to give all that she had to give—time, energy, thought, money for a worthy cause. She proved to be a methodical leader who expected and won support from many different sorts of women. But perhaps because she so valued their work in the campaign she had also come to believe in a myth: that the women for whom she and others had labored so hard would soon be eager to use the vote to advance particular causes and particular women. She really believed that suffrage had come directly from her efforts as commander in chief of a faithful army of female recruits against enemies perceived as somewhat larger than they were.

Martin's squabbles with her fellow workers and her fussing over money were less important than that she was a model for women to emulate—a woman acting for her cause with all of her abilities. She had demonstrated her leadership; she had come to think of herself as a woman of abilities that had a valid public use; she had come to see her world as wider by far than Nevada. Her life had a meaning and she had a new place in which to try her skills. The first of her many campaigns was the most successful, and she was ready to seek wide opportunities in the national battle for political power.

CHAPTER 7

CLAMOR IN THE STREETS

Leader of the New Militancy

Mr. President, how long must women wait for liberty?
—Inez Milholland

So long as you send women to prison for asking for justice, so long will women be willing to go in such a cause.
—Anne Martin, 1917

DURING THE YEARS between the Nevada suffrage victory and 1918 when Anne Martin embarked on a personal political mission, she served yet another political and organizational apprenticeship. She worked on the national level for the federal amendment; she achieved national prominence and national notoriety; she learned new skills and grew new ambitions. Yet she also tried hard to retain her hard-won leadership of Nevada women even as her national activities became more daring. And she made yet another canvass through Nevada for a different cause.

Anne Martin cherished the moment in December 1914, only a month after the victory in Nevada, when she met President Woodrow Wilson for the first time. She remembered his words for many years, repeating them proudly in the autobiography she reworked in 1940: "that is the way suffrage should be won, by the states."[1] Yet even before that proud occasion, less than a month after Nevada women had won the right to vote, she had already joined a struggle that would make Wilson the prime enemy and federal action on the vote a prime goal. Even during the Nevada campaign Martin had argued with NAWSA president Anna Howard Shaw about the Congressional Union (CU) and its tactics.[2] Later she remembered 1916 as the year when she decided ". . . with a clear choice still before me, whether to 'go' with the powerful old national . . . or whether to 'go' with the young and untried Congressional Union—and I chose the latter because I thought . . . the Susan B. Anthony amendment a quicker and more effective way of winning suffrage for all American women."[3]

The decision was one that affected her subsequent political life far more than she could have suspected then, a decision based on both previous experience with the British militants and personal acquaintance with CU's founders. By 1914 the Union had become a separate organization employing the publicity-seeking tactics of the English Women's Social and Political Union. In 1913, its first effort on Wilson's inauguration day had drawn eight thousand women down Pennsylvania Avenue and, in militant tradition, brought violent episodes that required troops to be called, even though the march was orderly and peaceful.[4]

Although the CU worked with NAWSA to bring the federal amendment to a vote in the spring of 1914, by summer Paul's organization was irritating state campaigners by mounting drives in nine western states to defeat Democrats, claiming that party responsible as the "party in power" for the failure of Congress to pass the amendment.[5] Since Nevada Democrats supported state suffrage, Martin dared not have public ties to the women campaigning in New Mexico, Arizona, and California against her own allies. As news reached Nevada, Bird Wilson worried that the CU stand could cost "equal suffrage at least 150 votes in Goldfield alone."[6]

After the Nevada victory, Martin joined a ticket of younger women who ran for office in NAWSA, hoping to replace Dr. Shaw and her associates, who had done little since CU split away to advance the federal amendment. The younger women lost, and Martin and the others committed themselves to the new group.[7]

If such a change demonstrated some personal pique, it also reflected Martin's earlier interest in the WSPU in England. Martin did not emphasize her new affiliation immediately, however much she sympathized with that faction from the beginning. Although the CU activity had been limited to lobbying intensively in Congress and to staging colorful demonstrations, Martin had worked hard to erase the mark of militancy struck by her English ventures. Her firsthand experience with the three-year battle in Nevada argued against state-by-state effort. Her first move was to enjoy that national attention that the victory had brought by appearing throughout the East before women's groups, even though, as she wrote a Nevada friend, she was "not very well."[8]

Her time in the national spotlight was short this time, for by February she was back in Nevada, involved with turning the Equal Franchise Society into a civic league to combat "evil interests."[9] With the legislature in session, Martin and others hoped to carry enough influence as leaders of the newly enfranchised women to fight a new and liberalized divorce law that provided for only six months' residence in the state and to oppose new gambling laws. One immediate response from nearby Gerlach must have discouraged her:

> Now the ladies here are not in favor of opposing the divorce laws or gambling. They seem to think that Nevada should have thoses [*sic*] laws as it brings money into the state where otherwise it would go elsewhere. The Ladies here are very plain spoken, and it does no good to try and change their opinion. This is what they tell me. We have our votes and that is all we want and all we care for.[10]

But in Carson City, Bird Wilson and others cared for more and worked with legislators for a number of reforms: raising the age of consent to eighteen, limiting the workday to eight hours for men and women, clarifying community property rules, repealing capital punishment. But as Wilson reported, she was "too impatient to be a good reformer. I want to accomplish everything in a moment." Even before the reforms failed and the new gambling and divorce laws passed, Wilson had "about decided that this is going to be a good state to raise hogs in, but not families, so am going to ranching."[11] Still, she stayed with the lobbying effort long enough to see passage of a public kindergarten bill before the family problems took her away from her Nevada interests for good.[12]

Martin's ambitions for a strong state organization of women to back such demands for legislation were dampened by factional problems with the Equal Franchise Society. In January, while Martin was still in the East, a Woman Citizens Club organized, made up of various members of the suffrage group who wanted to use some of the leftover treasury for their purposes. Accusations flew between the two groups, and until new stationery could be printed, the name of one defector from the Civic League—Martin's group—was boldly lined out in red; Martin was at war with longtime supporters and with new Reno proposals for limiting saloons at the same time.

By April, Mabel Vernon wrote her friend, worrying about a "breakdown" and asking if Martin was working herself "to death again" in the struggles.[13] Although she had had several bouts of illness during the year, Martin managed to last through the May city election when the reform effort to halve the number of saloons—from eighty to forty for a population of twelve thousand—failed to pass. While she tried to claim that the "issue was not a clear 'wet' or 'dry' issue but one of method, rather,"[14] she was clearly disappointed. Finding comfort in naming a familiar enemy, she blamed political power George Wingfield in a letter to Anna Howard Shaw:

> He could only get his gambling bill by a system of trading votes . . . this split the governor and other politicians followed . . . they fear my influence in the state against "wide-open" conditions . . . They fear me because woman suffrage is absolutely the only thing that has beaten Wingfield and his machine.[15]

Although Martin was expected in New Jersey to participate with the Women's Campaign Alliance in an effort to win suffrage there, she could not leave until late summer. In June she was too ill to work, and by July she was still in Palo Alto recuperating from what a friend described as a "critical surgical operation for an intestinal trouble of very complicated character."[16] But before she met her obligations to the eastern suffragists, she turned her attention back to Nevada, where first efforts had begun to form a state branch of the Congressional Union, and to an article urging women to attend the September conference the CU had planned for women voters in conjunction with the Panama Pacific Exhibition in San Francisco.

In spite of illness, she put her pen to work in defense of the Union in an article she hoped would bring followers. "Nevada Women and National Freedom" was published in *Everywoman,* a general circulation publication tied to neither NAWSA nor the Union. Martin's battles with Dr. Shaw, long waged by private letter, erupted publicly in the piece, and Martin spared little in her attack on NAWSA and its leaders. Playing on the predominance of western women as voters, she urged the cause of the September gathering, countering Shaw's claim that the convention would be used for "consolidating the women voters of the west against the Democratic party because that party has not passed suffrage legislation." Martin surely knew the ultimate purpose of the Union was just exactly that, but she wrote persuasively that the convention would have an opportunity to discuss and decide its policies and honestly quoted the Union's appeal to women who would work "without considering the interest of any national political party." She further insisted that if women voters "do not regard the winning of suffrage for all the women of America [as] the paramount . . . issue . . . they can reject this principle," neatly sidestepping the question of means, ignoring the "party in power" stand of the Union, and pushing the desired ideal— national suffrage.[17]

Considering her defeat for NAWSA office the previous December, Martin's accusation that NAWSA had rejected the western women, "these children it has forgotten or never knew," seems somewhat personal; the board, she complained, did not "contain a single name of practical suffrage achievement, tested by . . . winning campaign states . . . Is the national association avoiding that efficiency which may win campaigns in too precipitate a manner, or does it prefer to have no alien blood near the throne to jeopardize the security of the present dynasty?" Warming to her subject, she defended the "expeditious and spirited methods" of the Union, blamed NAWSA for having an "instinctive repugnance" to the very name "West," which stood for effectiveness and suffrage accomplishment.[18]

The long discouraging months of illness, disappointment, factions, and challenge had swelled her anger at her defeat to both rage and new action, rage that ignored the long support of NAWSA in the state campaign, Dr. Shaw's personal efforts, and her own indecision. She challenged the Union to offer her more. Perhaps the ballots of December 1914 had helped her decide, but after such a tirade, her break from NAWSA was complete, if not very clean.

Whatever its announced intention, the Women Voters' Convention in San Francisco offered little public opportunity for discussing policies and procedures: business sessions were packed with speakers, and even the luncheon reception and tea offered a full roster of addresses—and very little chance for delegates to speak. The program included impressive names: Alvah Belmont, the Union's richest contributor; Maria Montessori, the educator from Italy; Phoebe Hearst of California. Both Bird Wilson and Anne Martin spoke, as did Sara Bard Field and Elizabeth Kent, wife of a wealthy California congressman and later a steady supporter and contributor to Anne Martin's many campaigns. As if in keeping with Martin's accusations about NAWSA, most of the eastern women who dominated the Union's board were absent, except for Belmont and, of course, Alice Paul.[19]

At the close of the convention, Sara Bard Field, accompanied by two Swedish women drivers, set out across the nation, carrying to Washington a petition signed by 500,000 western women voters. In a live demonstration of the Union's publicity-seeking skills, the three left in a flurry of speeches and banners to stop at cities all the way across the country, gathering support for the amendment as they went.[20] Anne Martin emerged from the convention solidly accepted by the inner circle of the Union legislative department, committed to organize lobbying in Congress.[21] Her clear public affiliation with the CU, accomplished over the length of several months and carrying with it a commitment to public, national participation, was an important turning point.

In the Union she found allies who remained close the rest of her life; more important, she chose a radical, generally younger group of women pledged to a feminism that was larger than the vote, a group that included women of a different sort from those in NAWSA—educated, vigorous, brave women who had established themselves as workers for social change. Some, like Crystal Eastman, had achieved some public status before they joined: Eastman, an attorney, was a central member of the Greenwich Village feminists that included Socialists Henrietta Rodman and Susan Glaspell. She had written New York's workmen's compensation law, campaigned for industrial safety, and, with her brother Max, supported the efforts of the IWW and knew John Reed and Claude McKay and Emma Goldman. Like Paul and Lucy Burns, she had been a social worker, too, running a recreation center and spending her evenings at Greenwich House Settlement while she attended law school.[22]

Another member of the early executive committee was Mary Beard, historian in later years, at that time specializing in the history of labor and devoted to its goals, who wanted to mould a "big and glorious link in the C.U.'s role of a real woman's movement."[23] Florence Kelley, another attorney, had worked in settlement houses and as a consumer advocate, and, like Martin, had worked with NAWSA, moving to the CU when the young organization offered more vigorous action.[24] These women had many common interests beyond suffrage: most were Socialists and pacifists as well. Eastman split her efforts between the CU and the Women's Peace Party for many years.[25] One scholar has noted that most of the participants were white middle-class women with exceptional educations (M. Carey Thomas, president of Bryn Mawr College, for example)—"strong women, independent women." They were drawn together by Alice Paul, a Quaker settlement worker and sociologist, a tiny woman with a big will who ran the Union and later the National Woman's Party with the same kind of authoritarian style Emmeline Pankhurst had shown in the WSPU. Margery Nelson called her a "charismatic leader [who] knew how to mobilize people." Paul's special qualities impressed Nelson many years later when Nelson met her in

1971: "The magic of Alice Paul is not in her personal charm—but in her impersonality—in her incredible mind—mass of data—and devotion to the cause—the fact that she will expect anyone else to work as she does."[26] Inez Haynes Irwin called the Paul manner "the quiet of the spinning top," adding that with one accord members agreed, "She is the party. They regard her with an admiration that verges on awe."[27] Later, the appeal of the group verged on the romantic, as Irwin recalled in later life, remembering her own response to the WSPU's increased militancy in 1910:

> . . . when in England the first militant of Mrs. Pankhurst's forces threw her first stone, my heart went with it. I watched . . . with an avid and profound interest. At last the tradition of female patience, of feminine taste in deportment, had gone by the board.[28]

While many members of what Paul called her "little band" left the party as the years passed and others drifted into separate endeavors, all remained interested throughout the twenties when splits within the movement weakened its thrust and the mass of women forgot their quest for equality. They were lifetime feminists, not mere suffragists. Although they later divided in their efforts—particularly over protective laws—throughout long lives, none lost interest in woman's state, woman's progress, woman's special world. Martin clearly had the respect of these women during her time with the party.

Anne Martin's political career was no doubt shadowed for the rest of her public life by the three years she gave to the national movement, her parlor socialism strengthened in some ways. Carried along by the enthusiasm of the brash, ambitious party and its members, she could forget the caution that had controlled her actions during the Nevada battle, even though both the militancy she later tried to forget and the pacifism she smothered during her Senate campaigns interfered with her drive for political office. Apparently she foresaw no such campaigns in 1915 when she responded to the new party's energy and ambition.

Back in Nevada after the conference, first Alice Paul and then Mabel Vernon and Florence Wise tried to direct Nevada women into the Union, only to find that such organizing was far different from getting women together for their own immediate suffrage. A majority in Reno still accepted Martin's leadership, but a noisy minority protested against her, her agents, and her friends. While the spring factional battles had turned many women against Martin, the more difficult problem was that the conflict had made her supporters so defensive that Wise found it impossible to present her plan to form both groups into a neutral organization with another woman in charge. Martin had agreed to lead the Nevada Congressional Union before she went back to the New Jersey campaign and her supporters would hear of no change, her enemies make no compromise. Wise saw a "very mistaken view of the CU and its militancy" in Reno, but could do little to counteract it. The "unreasonableness of these women," she wrote, "their extreme and shortsighted hero-worship of A.M., whom all of us admire and respect tremendously . . . did prevent our active work."[29] Martin evoked the same intense reactions throughout her public life: her admirers could be her enemies, and few women held mild opinions about her. Still, the conflict did not prevent her from being elected in December as a member of the Union executive board, one of only two women from the West in leadership—to the extent that it could exist in Alice Paul's little army.[30]

In Washington, Martin had meanwhile begun her work as chair of the legislative department. Irwin praised her as "a born general" with an instinct for the strategy and tactics of politics. Martin supervised all the lobbyists, sending them to both houses with specific instructions, received and collated reports, and developed close relations with the constituents of each congressman. Maud Younger recalled her lobbyist's work as following a "path of white marble":

> And white marble, though beautiful, is hard . . . and when you have walked around each of the five floors [of the House] you have walked a mile on white marble. When you have gone this morning and afternoon through several sessions of Congress you have walked more miles on white marble than a lobbyist has time to count.[31]

In the early days, in addition to public demonstrations with many women marching, the Union women tried a number of feminine approaches to the members of Congress. They sent them birthday cakes and valentines, hung a May basket for the President, and produced verse on various occasions. One congressman found a basket filled with forget-me-nots to remind him:

> "Forget-me-not" is the message
> I bring in gladsome blue;
> Forget not the fifty-six years that have gone
> And the work there is still to do;
> Forget not the Suffrage Amendment
> That waits in committee for you.[32]

When the cross-country automobile travelers arrived finally with their petition in Washington, Mary Austin directed a reception for them that set the tone for later public performances of the Union. More than forty mounted women, representing most of the states, led the group and "great numbers of flag and banner bearers, wearing long purple capes with deep yellow collars and white stoles, hundreds of women carrying purple, white and gold pennants" welcomed the envoys. A band played "Dixie" and the "Marseillaise" while the petition bearing half a million names was unrolled its full one hundred feet by twenty bearers. Anne Martin introduced the women, Sara Bard Field and Frances Joliffe, to President Wilson, asking him what his response would be. Not prepared for a speech, Wilson hedged on the central issue and declared he had an "open mind" but was not yet willing to agree to help the women to "a new freedom and a larger liberty."[33]

The English women had slowly developed the public demonstration into a wonderful performance, and the Union found many occasions to copy the Pankhursts' art. Inez Milholland Boissevain came to be the regular "woman on a white horse" to lead the parades. A fine horsewoman and a beauty by any standard, she was a living demonstration of the spirit of the Union—and a sprightly answer to the cartoon caricatures of feminists as ugly harpies who hated men. She reflected that spirit as well in her training as a lawyer. Behind her in the processions silken banners waved and fine horses pranced down the avenues; martial music brought the crowds. Such "militancy" was still within the bounds of propriety, such display a fine attraction.

When NAWSA met in December of 1915, members first showed real interest in enlivening the pursuit of the federal amendment, for state campaigns had gone badly that year. New Jersey, Massachusetts, Pennsylvania, and New York—states that had produced sixty years of leaders in the suffrage movement—refused the vote to their women, in spite of intensive campaigning. Conscious of how little progress they were making, NAWSA's leadership persuaded Carrie Chapman Catt, president of the New York society, to replace Dr. Shaw. Catt came, bringing with her a two-million-dollar legacy from Mrs. Frank Leslie, publisher of *Leslie's Weekly*, a legacy to be expended "to the furtherance of woman suffrage."[34] The board had dropped its support for the Shafroth-Palmer Amendment, which had called for state referenda to hasten suffrage; it had responded to the CU activity with a new interest in lobbying in Washington, in joining its massive forces for federal action. Catt insisted that her new board be made of women who served more than decorative purposes: she insisted that when a woman's family responsibilities interfered with her full-time service, she must step aside. Just as the CU demanded total devotion, the new NAWSA board sought the same, for, as Flexner concluded, "the day for the amateur reformer had given way to the professional organizer, just as was becoming the case in the labor movement."[35]

Professional was an apt term for the CU members who worked under Anne Martin in 1915, trying to wrest the amendment out of a House committee for a vote before the fall elections. Most House members wanted to postpone so that there would be no recent vote against suffrage to damage their re-election chances in the fall. Martin's deputation of six badgered one representative steadily, demonstrated their knowledge of how each member of his committee stood on the votes, and insisted on a vote before summer. Paul's publication, *The Suffragist,* reported the entire encounter, as it regularly did.[36] Not only was the pressure kept steady, but publication as soon as possible of commitments or half promises kept the constituents informed so that letters from home could support the lobbying effort. There is no question that the federal woman suffrage bill "first became a live issue in Congress because of the activity of the Congressional Union . . . They took up the issue when it seemed dead and brought it very much to life."[37] And Anne Martin directed that congressional effort.

By April of 1916, Alice Paul had proposed a plan to "terrify the men in Congress," to charge CU women to organize "an independent political Party that will be ready for the elections in November," adding that if the women prepared diligently enough, "they won't have to go into them. The threat will be enough." And she asked for a convention of the party in June in Chicago, the time chosen to coincide with Republican and Progressive party conventions there. Such a meeting, Paul claimed, would "decide how to use these four million votes that women have."[38] Anne Martin became chair of the new party, picked by Paul but officially chosen by the delegates to enforce a policy "to secure the passage of the Susan B. Anthony amendment, irrespective of the interests of any national political party." The party pledged as well "its unceasing opposition to all who oppose this amendment."[39] Opponents clearly included President Wilson and, by CU and Woman's Party reasoning, candidates of the Democratic party for Congress.[40]

The new party's interpretation of "nonpartisan" had changed; while other suffrage groups opposed individuals who did not support suffrage, the Congressional Union and the Woman's Party (they remained separate for some months) were firm against the party in power, echoing the Pankhurst attack on the rather different political system of Britain.

While a Democratic senator may have voted for suffrage, he might be an enemy simply because he was a Democrat, while a Republican who had not voted for suffrage might be ignored simply because of his party. Since from 1913 on the Democrats controlled the government in Washington while Republicans maintained power in most of the states, the approach was, as one scholar puts it, "absurdly unrealistic."[41] However shaky the thinking behind Woman's Party purposes, Anne Martin took her new position seriously, asserting the party's aim was not "to create sex antagonism; it has no fantastic vision of sex solidarity; it is simply an organization of woman voters of the twelve free states of America whose bond of union is suffrage first."[42]

The stand against the Democrats cost the party some supporters at once: Dudley Field Malone, their finest male speaker, an attorney who was particularly useful, refused to work against Wilson in spite of the total involvement of his wife, Doris Stevens; Sara Bard Field and Charles Erskine Wood, a leader in western liberal circles, shared a home and plans for the future, but split simply and agreeably on Wilson.[43] Mabel Vernon recalled many years later how difficult it was "campaigning against Nevada Senator Key Pittman, our friend."[44] But Anne Martin relished the public attention she won in news stories throughout the country; she pronounced on the future of woman for the *San Francisco Chronicle,* for example, asserting that, no, feminism would not make women masculine and yes, it would drive out the social parasite.[45] She claimed that the "parasite woman who practices alimony as a trade," tired of marriage "conceived in lukewarm scheming love," would give way to working women who would not "choose men for the support men could give them" and would marry on "a common plane of independence and self respect." While the language does not sound much like Martin's, the idealism does suggest hers.

In Nevada her absence had been noted, and she felt pushed to send personal letters to Congressional Union chairs (it was hard for the state groups to keep up with the party changes), Civic League leaders, and others. Many of the women were confused about what they belonged to at a given moment, but most were Martin supporters. She urged them not to affiliate with the State Federation of Women's Clubs, a body she believed unconcerned with political action. Despite the complications of moving to a new headquarters for the party in Chicago and of organizing a state convention (she was still leader in Reno), she still managed to visit suffrage conferences in the Midwest and pull together an April state meeting of the faithful in Nevada. Planned to correspond with the arrival of the "Suffrage Special" train (another Paul-created publicity effort), the convention drew one thousand women to hear Inez Milholland and Lucy Burns. Martin's two-week return to Nevada had, she hoped, healed the organization.[46] But when the purpose of the party to work against Wilson was understood and when the news of a WP policy conference at Colorado Springs that detailed the approach reached Reno, some of the most faithful ran from both the league and Martin's influence.

At Colorado Springs Martin had reiterated the stand: "Our single plank is suffrage first; the political freedom of women before the interest of any national party."[47] No record suggests that the members of the various Congressional Union or Woman's Party clubs had been consulted about decisions, and it is clear that Martin simply decided on the course of action that lost her some of her staunch supporters, workers she could have used in future campaigns. Before the Colorado Springs executive conference she wired Minnie Flanigan to "have the state board by proper motion withdraw affiliation from national association." Obviously she was assured that the board would follow her wishes, that Flanigan would accomplish such a basic and drastic change in the same obedient way that she would comply with the last request: "Please have my long dark green riding coat and trousers sent to me here collect." Typically, she also asked Flanigan to "wire Hughes as representative of thousand Nevada women," not deceived that she represented them precisely, but certain that there would be no competing wires.[48]

While Martin apparently saw no contradiction between thanking Nevada senator Key Pittman for his announced intention to vote for suffrage[49] and then launching a campaign against him, three members of the Women's Civic League did. In a public letter supporting Pittman and President Wilson and carefully reminding Nevada women that the senator and president and certain other candidates had worked to get them the vote, they praised Wilson, "who has accomplished two of the really great things for which all women stand. He has maintained peace in the midst of a world's conflagration and he has thrown the protection of legislation around the toiling children of the land. What mother can fail to call him blessed!" Speaking perhaps for many others, they swore "the Woman's Party can never, under these conditions, receive our support, nor do we believe the cause of equal suffrage will ever be advanced by striking down its friends." Leading the signers was Helen Belford, a suffragist from the early days, an influential woman married to a judge so strongly for the cause he was known as "Suffragist Sam" in the community.[50]

Back in Washington, Carrie Chapman Catt called a special meeting of NAWSA to face what she called "a crisis in the suffrage movement." Whether she was responding to WP tactics or merely asserting her new leadership, she faced questions raised by an increasingly impertinent CU.[51] She announced a "three cornered debate" to offer the delegates a chance to decide whether to concentrate on the federal amendment, continue to work in the states, or "continue . . . present policy" and work for both. While NAWSA's congressional work had been expanded after the expulsion of the CU, Catt herself knew that more concentration was necessary. If the CU had done nothing else, it had drawn everyone's attention to the importance of federal action. But she took the younger organization to task for "the audacity and novelty of [their] claims that have piqued the curiosity of some and aroused the angry indignation of others." After all, she reminded her delegates, NAWSA had first introduced the federal amendment in 1875, and it already knew the dangers of partisan action. She attacked the party-in-power concept specifically:

> There are splendid, big-souled Democrats and Republicans in Congress who want to put the Federal amendment through, and there are other stubborn, narrow-minded, tradition bound Republicans and Democrats who will block the amendment as long as they serve . . . I refuse to believe that party power, sordid as it undoubtedly is, has so far lapsed into autocracy that men of brains will bend the knee and vote the way the president orders . . . the non partisan appeal in the long run, though less spectacular, is more compelling, and quite as quick.[52]

President Wilson spoke as well, insisting that suffrage would come eventually, their cause would be triumphant, that he had come not to "fight anybody, but with somebody." Nevertheless, he warned, "You can afford a little while to wait."[53] The suffragists applauded politely, the Woman's Party was impatient.

All Wilson had to do, the Woman's Party reasoned and Anne Martin said, was to induce Congress to pass the amendment and all efforts to work against him and other Democrats would cease, for "women first, party second" was the entire doctrine of her party. But they began plans immediately to organize separate parties to fight Democrats, since Wilson did not seem either willing or able to comply with their demands. Martin herself was back in Nevada by late September, not entirely comfortable with the change. She explained it all to Sara Bard Field: "It was necessary for me to come out to take an active part in the Nevada campaign, as the fight is going to be very close."[54] In the East,

Alice Paul took over Martin's work along with her own. Martin faced another season of heat and dust in a campaign far less popular than her last, with reduced forces, little money, and the same huge area to cover in the too-familiar desert sun.

Many Nevada women must have agreed with Mae Packer, a teacher at Manhattan, who insisted her WP officer had made a mistake, for Packer was a Wilson Democrat, not a "pure feminist," and she was convinced that Wilson had really kept the nation out of war: "I have made myself responsible for every man that dies and every boy and man that comes home a helpless sufferer and cripple from war."[55] Wilson gathered a great deal of support in the state from his claim to have kept the country out of war, support that did not change when the nation entered the conflict, an irony Woman's Party workers never noted. Martin was aware that personal loyalty to her would not transcend such convictions, but she keenly felt the implications when Bird Wilson withdrew not only from the Nevada party but from the national advisory board as well, an act that caught the attention of the *San Francisco Call*, Fremont Older's paper, which had generally supported Martin in the past. Wilson regretted the publicity—"I would have written you so that you might have been advised of my motion personally"—but she explained it carefully, reminding Martin that she had taken the position on the board for a single year, "*provided* they were not going to use the tactics formerly adopted, of trying to defeat Congressional candidates merely because they belonged to the party in power":

> . . . the year has expired. They have adopted the objectional tactics . . . It is a matter of great regret to me that you, my dear friend, and Sara Bard Field, both of whom I admire so much and hold in such fond regard, should be persuaded to follow the dictates of Miss Paul and her associates in this regard. It seems to me a departure from the straight and honorable road to the object we have in view. It may be politics, but I can't see how it is *good* politics. And surely women want to be good politicians . . . I cannot work side by side with you in this campaign as it has been my pride to do before.[56]

Martin responded sorrowfully, recalling that "the work we did together on the Nevada Suffrage campaign will always be one of the best memories I have," but insisting that the battle against Wilson was "the only thing to do if the party in power continued to block our amendment and denied justice."[57]

Just as her workers had done in 1914, organizers journeyed across the state, gathering women together for small meetings, stopping in the street to draw men and women, presenting in person the point to be made. Anne Martin had plenty of problems with them. A Mrs. Latimer, supposedly a veteran campaigner from Kansas, "collapsed" mysteriously in Eureka and was in a few days induced to go to San Francisco "under the care of [the Martin] family physician."[58] But by the end of October, Martin wired that Latimer "broke parole and returned here. Dreadful situation. Husband on way."[59] Mabel Vernon took care of the headquarters in Reno while Martin traveled, and five or six organizers shared the too-familiar routine of town to town, camp to camp experiences, always counting on a personal visit from Martin to help their argument. Although minor violence broke out in Elko when the party banner was torn down, Martin drew good crowds everywhere while Vernon wrote to recalcitrant women explaining the party stand and begging for help in setting up meetings.[60] Martin persuaded Maud Younger to come to sway the labor vote, and the California woman who had headed women's unionizing in New York paid her own expenses. Even Louise Martin, Anne's mother, was pressed into service and spoke from a street corner, standing on a chair. If Mrs. Martin had collided with her determined daughter when Anne was young, she had become convinced by 1916 of the justice of her daughter's cause—or causes. Mabel Vernon recalled that Mrs. Martin was heckled by a drunk and by a woman with a Wilson banner, but bravely continued until a policeman escorted her home.[61]

A highlight of the campaign was the appearance of the star of the Woman's Party show, Inez Milholland, then touring the twelve suffrage states in the anti-Wilson, anti-Democrat campaign. Although she was not well, Milholland kept a schedule that included four appearances in three days in Winnemucca, Virginia City, Carson City, and Reno, the last a big event in a large theater that Vernon remembered sixty years later:

> Just Anne and Inez on the stage . . . dressed in white. And some of our Reno women had arranged a beautiful bouquet of American Beauty roses. After the meeting, Senator [Francis] Newlands said . . . "I see there are reasons for having women, besides the political reasons. They add beauty to the scene" . . . she and Inez were both charming and beautiful . . . It was very simple.[62]

The beautiful Milholland became the party's first martyr when she collapsed a few days later while speaking in Los Angeles. The *Suffragist* described the tragedy: "In the middle of an intense sentence she crumpled like a wilted white rose and lay stark upon the platform." That "intense sentence"—"Mr. President, how long must women wait for liberty?"—became a rallying cry for the new party when Milholland died some weeks later.[63]

In Tonopah, Martin's old enemy Felice Cohn claimed that "the Woman's Party had one plank, that one plank covered with a carpet of gold from the coffers of the Trusts and Morgan."[64] Had she found the time, Martin might have argued with that, for she could have used a carpet of gold: she had fallen behind on payments on a land investment, she could not trace what was due her from the family estate, and she was besieged with letters from creditors while a family lawsuit dragged on in Carson City.[65]

The election results hardly cheered her. Although the campaign had been a close one, Wilson and Senator Pittman had won in spite of the Woman's Party efforts; the contest was, however, the closest of several between Republican Samuel Platt and Pittman. While one scholar termed the campaign a "disaster" for the Paul camp,[66] another believed that "the fury of woman scorned was fully demonstrated."[67] More cautiously, Aileen Kraditor points out that the election was "fought on other issues, particularly questions of peace and preparedness,"[68] and the correspondence with Martin from her former supporters would seem to confirm this. Moreover, when Illinois, where women had presidential suffrage only, counted its votes, Hughes ran ahead of the Republican majority in the state.[69] Not surprisingly, the Congressional Union and the Woman's Party—still officially separate—called the new policy successful and Anne Martin guessed that women's votes in Nevada had been split between the Republican and Socialist candidates, basing her statement on no perceivable evidence.[70] The *Suffragist* was sure a protest vote had been recorded, quoting Ray Baker, then an ambassador, as calling the Democratic victory in Nevada complete, "notwithstanding the bitter opposition of the women who voted almost solidly against the President."[71] The *New York Times* assumed that the election had proved that "members of both houses will not be thrown into a state approaching hysterics by the rustle of a skirt; fear to meet militant advocates face to face; or sidestep every time a member of the female species arises at a public meeting."[72]

In Nevada, some were less kind: the *Carson Daily Appeal* observed that "it is evident that the egotistical germ that took possession of Ann's [*sic*] nut a couple of years ago has not been dissipated and it will probably require another walloping such as it got last Tuesday to finish the job. We are ready whenever she is."[73] But Martin's *Woman's Party*

Bulletin of the next week found that "we [the WP] are now a factor to be reckoned with. Our work is going on until the amendment, the political freedom of women of America, is won."[74] Privately, she responded to George Wingfield's secretary about the campaign, noting that the Republicans did little for Hughes or for their Senate candidate, nor did they attempt to answer the "Wilson kept us out of war" claim, sure that Oregon and Illinois had proved the party's effectiveness in electing Democrats.[75]

At Christmas, Anne Martin staged a last ceremony as head of the party, gathering the women for a memorial service in the capitol rotunda for Inez Milholland. She gave the central address, drew testimony from the faithful, and topped it all with a chorus of young boys.

By 1917, Martin was spending more of her time in Washington and traveling for the Woman's Party than in Nevada. She remained chair until March, even though during the Nevada campaign Paul had run the party, answered mail directed to Martin, and made most of the important decisions. It must have been no great surprise to Martin when the two units—the Congressional Union and the Woman's Party—were formally joined into a single group. Alice Paul thought many years later that Martin "didn't think it was quite right that she was replaced, but it was done without any apparent friction." Paul favored a single chair and Martin turned down the job, agreeing to be vice-chair in charge of lobbying.[76] Martin may have frequently been unrealistic, but she also knew Paul's power and had the good sense not to charge against her.

Up until 1917, the tag of "militant" had perhaps been misused for the Congressional Union, had derived as much from the common English experience of many of the leaders as from any overt activity. While the members were impatient and outspoken, eager for action and noisier than the more restrained women of NAWSA, very little overt action had earned them the term. Foreshadowing what was to come had been a quiet demonstration in the final sessions of Congress in 1916, an act that echoed similar ones in England by the WSPU. Five women let down a banner from the visitor's gallery as the president spoke. Although pages removed the banner, the women were not asked to leave.[77] On January 17, the first of the pickets stood outside the White House with banners based on Milholland's last public words: "Mr. President, What Will You Do for Woman Suffrage?" and "How Long Must Women Wait for Liberty?" Picketing the White House was novel; the women were polite; "the President courteously raised his hat to the motionless women who stood on either side of the gates with unfailing regularity day after day regardless of the weather."[78]

On 4 March, as if to celebrate the combining of the two more militant organizations, Anne Martin organized one of the largest White House demonstrations the party ever mounted. One thousand women stepped out in a driving rain to move slowly around the presidential residence for more than two hours, hoping to present a petition to the president. Two bands provided music in spite of the weather, and Vida Milholland, sister of the lamented Inez, led the parade. Doris Stevens remembered that "there were almost as many police officers as marchers," the Washington force augmented by officers from Baltimore and plain-clothesmen. When the column approached the entry, Anne Martin spoke to the guard: "We have come to present some important resolutions to the President of the United States," she began. "I have orders to keep the gates locked, Ma'am." Around the gates they went, refused at each one.[79] For Anne Martin, the ritual must have seemed very familiar, for it repeated the pattern of all those trips to Parliament the WSPU had made. Now she was the leader, still respectful, offering to send in her card if the president would not accept resolutions.[80]

The women won what they wanted: attention from the national press, publicity for the amendment. From that day on, one NWP officer spent her entire time recruiting pickets of all sorts. Paul showed no mercy in expecting women to participate. Sara Bard Field had fought tuberculosis for years, but when she protested that picketing for a person with her health record "would mean a very possible death," Paul answered, "Well, that would be very good for the cause."[81]

By 1917 the ranks of the party had broadened somewhat. Inez Milholland had long urged bringing women in from the labor movement, and Mary Beard argued that the party should "develop some Annie Kenneys," referring to the millworker who had joined the Pankhursts.[82] Polish immigrant Rose Winslow, who had begun work at age eleven in a Philadelphia hosiery factory, traveled across the West speaking to working men and women "about the conditions of exploited women workers."[83] And while such women as anarchist Ernestine Hara Kettler journeyed all the way from Everett, Washington, to join the picketing,[84] aggressive working women who liked militancy and college graduates from the settlement houses poured in; Alice Paul courted others. She made a particular effort to find women to bring prestige or money. For the most part, however, the Woman's Party attracted big city, sophisticated young women quite different from the middle-class and middle-aged matrons of NAWSA.[85] When Jeannette Rankin took her seat in Congress in 1917, the first woman ever to do so, she was flanked at a celebratory luncheon by Carrie Chapman Catt on her right and Alice Paul, suitably, on her left in a grouping that seemed truly symbolic. The occasion was almost the last instance of cooperation between the two and Rankin's place in the middle proved awkward in ensuing months.[86] Both organizations felt they had helped her to office, both expected help, and they were clearly separate. While Catt had accepted the goal of the federal amendment as the speediest way to suffrage, she had no use for militancy in its newest form. Wilson's demand for a declaration of war from the special session of Congress widened the gap and provoked the intensified picketing that brought confrontation and jail to the pickets.

Alice Paul and a good many of her followers were Quakers, not easily swayed by the nationalist fervor the war excited. Many were also members of the Women's Peace Party Jane Addams had organized in 1915 and later, like Martin, spent their lives working for the Women's International League for Peace and Freedom. Unlike their English counterparts, who disbanded as soon as the war began and became ardent patriots, NWP used events of the war to provoke government and mob action. Sidney Bland wrote that Paul knew that "alternating periods of violence and suffering, intertwined with deep, if brief, enjoyment of partial victories, had advanced the suffragette cause and might provide the spark needed for the American movement." As recent studies of violence suggest, "the greatest value to be gained from confrontation . . . is provoking it."[87] Neither the silent sentinels nor the moving pickets provoked attack, but when the banners began to protest the quality of American democracy the violence and arrests began.

NWP militance never approached the English brand, which had included arson, window breaking, and personal assault: American militants "threw no rocks and broke no windows," they did not engage in arson or physical attack on public officials. They did picket, they burned Wilson's words, they embarrassed the government with accusations that America was a democracy in name only, a protest that brought the first mob reaction from servicemen and hoodlums. The only charge ever made against them was obstructing sidewalk traffic. But they went to jail and once there protested conditions and responded to brutality by hunger strikes. And the American government, having learned nothing from the English experience, like the English resorted to forced feeding and "made martyrs wholesale."[88]

As Eleanor Flexner makes clear, "they were among the earliest victims of the abrogation of civil liberties in wartime." Police arrested the pickets, not the men who destroyed banners and mistreated the women. Sentences gradually grew from a few days to six months.

Although not all the women arrested were jailed, most of the leaders, including Martin, Paul, and Burns, served some time.[89]

By the time Anne Martin was arrested on 14 July and charged with obstructing traffic, the provocation was slight: there had been no violence, she was carrying the purple, white, and gold banner of the party that displayed no message at all. The charge was obstructing the public highway.

At her trial, Martin claimed that while the sidewalk was "unusually spacious," her body occupied a space in the "vast area perhaps one foot square." She did admit that a crowd had assembled, brought there, she suggested, by the published declaration of police that they would arrest demonstrators. It was the crowd, she said, that had obstructed traffic, not she. She demanded a separate trial by jury and a chance to face her accusers.[90] The judge found her guilty, but she found an opening to announce—and the party loved to repeat her words—that "so long as you send women to prison for asking for justice, so long will women be willing to go in such a cause."[91] Other women in the delegation made their protestations of innocence, and as if to underline Martin's claim that "persecution has always advanced the cause of justice," the judge sentenced each of them to sixty days in the workhouse.[92]

In every detail the protest, the response, and the sentencing followed the pattern of the treatment of England's suffragettes. The women, of course, refused the option of a fine. "You had better decide to pay your fines . . . you will not find jail a pleasant place to be," the judge argued. But it was little surprise to anyone that the women refused the fines. Jail was a necessary crowning to the ritual.[93] Mabel Vernon wired Minnie Flanigan in Nevada that "Anne was splendid" and urged Flanigan to have "hundreds of telegrams sent President Wilson immediately protesting unjust sentence."[94] The Nevada press published bulletins about the imprisonment, most of which appeared only after Martin's three-day stay in Occoquan workhouse was over, an appeal having freed the women. In less than a year all the charges were dropped against the women, a fact seldom noted by either the national or the Nevada press.

Martin never wrote about her experience there, although she did recall the English trial of 1910. But Doris Stevens and other women who went to Occoquan remembered those days for the rest of their lives. If their accounts reflect a kind of class snobbery that seems distasteful now, they mirror the sense those women had of their status as ladies, as women to be properly protected. Stevens remembered being taken "side by side with drunks and disorderlies, prostitutes and thieves," first to the railroad station and then by train and blacked wagons, "blacker than the dusk," to the workhouse where most of the women rejected the "minute piece of dirty soap" offered with the required shower and tried to sleep "side by side with negro prostitutes." Stevens protested, "Not that we shrank away from these women on account of their color, but how terrible to know that the institution had gone out of its way to humiliate us. There was plenty of room in the negro wing."[95] In their carefully segregated society the women saw such placement as intended insult.

Later, the authorities used class and racial conflicts even more effectively. As Ernestine Hara Kettler recalled, Occoquan was "a real workhouse—you worked or else . . . you were 'or elsed.' . . ." When the women demanded to be considered political prisoners and protested the moving of one of their number to a mental ward, "that's the time [the superintendent] called in deputies . . . he called in Negro girls to come in there and—I'm telling you—they beat hell out of us . . . The Negro girls . . . considering how badly they were treated—got the most intense joy out of beating the hell out of the white women. The superintendent had to call in men deputies to haul the Negro girls off of us and get them outside." And the women, most of whom had never been arrested before, had to share quarters with drug addicts, eat food full of worms.[96] To make matters worse, the *Suffragist* noted, the sixty-day sentence was three times that given three-time prostitutes.[97]

Anne Martin was released, along with others from the same deputation, after three days, pardoned by the president.[98] The episode for her was brief. She went back to work recruiting new members and lobbying. Much as the picketing and the arrests and the clamor in the streets attracted the press (and kept the amendment in the public scene), the steady work in Congress continued, helped as the year went along by renewed attention from NAWSA. Martin's association with the picketing was a distinctly minor part of her service to the Woman's Party, yet that minor incident became the focus of attacks on her throughout her 1918 campaign for the Senate, just as her limited participation with the WSPU was blown out of proportion during the suffrage campaign. Martin did not participate in what became the most notorious incident in August (she was gone, recruiting) when a banner accused "Kaiser Wilson" of betraying American women. The battle of the banners shocked the nation.

Martin earned her position as vice-chair of the party, traveling much of the time: she toured congressional districts with Maud Younger, she spoke at the Tennessee Suffrage Convention, she traveled to Kansas and Oregon, inspiring young women to join the work in Washington, and she closed the tour with an address in California. In Los Angeles, the

Suffragist complained that "the Department of Justice attempted to cancel the meeting at which she appeared and hecklers proposed 'a vote of confidence in the president,' " but the meeting ended with the raising of $500 for the suffrage cause instead. In San Diego, Martin was warned again, supposedly by the Secret Service, but she told the agent to "follow me and arrest me any time he wished to, but to stop speaking to me." Nothing, she told her audiences, was "to be won by treading the path of submission." When at one meeting antagonists accused her of attacking the president, she replied that she thought they should "think of the indignity the President is heaping on the twenty million women of this nation."[99]

Just as she had lost the support but not the friendship of Bird Wilson in 1916, she endured censure over the picketing from those she admired. Lou Henry Hoover, a close friend from Stanford days and wife of Herbert Hoover, tried to soften her criticism, suggesting that Martin was not really responsible for the NWP's "naughty baby play":

> [We] recognize you can't be responsible for all your friends' acts, especial-
> ly in an organization . . . But do your effective work along your own
> legitimate line. You accomplish infinitely more. And try staying with the
> persuasive rather than the bullying mood. *Because* it's more effective. Tho
> I'll acknowledge the latter comes to one's mind at times . . . And keep your
> friends in the same line as far as possible . . . I wish I could repeat to you all
> the conversation I hear on sense versus nonsense in . . . your campaign.[100]

Bird Wilson wrote again, remaining silent on the issues but complimenting her friend on her development "in the line of public speaking . . ." Martin, she wrote, was "forceful and effective."[101]

Anne Martin's experience with the Congressional Union and the National Woman's Party, in its beginnings and during the three years she worked openly for it, gave her confidence to launch a more individual and daring campaign in the following year. The functioning of the NWP in 1918, however, may have been an impetus as well, for there were limitations everywhere she turned.

Officially, she was vice-chair of the organization and chair of the legislative committee, but with Alice Paul as chair, Martin's title was distinctly decorative. Her second responsibility was diluted by Maud Younger's recognized leadership as head of lobbying. The resultant conflict—"they weren't particularly congenial," Mabel Vernon remembered[102]—may have helped Martin decide to leave or at least to move on to other things. Younger's ties to Congress were sharply different from Martin's. While Anne Martin worked doggedly, took pains to organize, studiously maintained lists and appointments, and stubbornly labored to meet and persuade the right people, Younger knew most of them personally through her intensely political family; while Martin worked out systems and scrupulously kept a personal file on each member,[103] Younger had direct and easy access to many of them. Martin would be sure to see that difference, almost sure to resent it.

But whether she was unhappy with her position in the party or not (she later accused the NWP of preferring "political cleverness to integrity"),[104] two events helped her decide on a new direction. On 24 December 1917 Senator Francis G. Newlands died; on 10 January the United States House of Representatives passed the suffrage amendment by a single vote over the required two-thirds margin. The first event provided an opportunity for a new course; the second gave ample excuse for a change, for both NWP and NAWSA were optimistic. Wilson himself finally helped put the amendment across as a "war measure" in token of the work women were doing for the war effort. Even Senate passage looked possible; in fact, the Senate had issued a favorable report on the very day after one of its members had visited the Occoquan workhouse. Surely, the suffragists reasoned, the amendment was certain.[105] Anne Martin could freely leave the suffrage cause for a personal campaign.

The years from 1914 to 1918, when she finally declared her intention to run, had given Martin a great deal of experience: her work in Washington had demonstrated to her both how the Congress really worked and how entirely male it was; her rise to public prominence in the National Woman's Party had shown her personally that she could demand respect and expect support from other women in Nevada and beyond; her contact with the kind of women she had met in the NWP— women with ideas, women with purpose, women willing to act boldly— had strengthened her feminism. Practically speaking, she had mastered a public personality and presence that never left her and she could see a way to use her new skills in service to her state and to her sex.

She determined to run for the Senate, encouraged by her friends, excited by the chance to be a "first," and eager to try her hand in practical politics on a national scale.

CHAPTER 8

THE SENATE CAMPAIGNS

"A Forerunner and a Pathfinder"

I want to knock the fear out of the hearts of women.
> —Anne Martin

I want to see what women can do to this busted old system before I plunge into r-r-red revolution.
> —Lola Maverick Lloyd

WHEN ANNE MARTIN declared her candidacy for the Senate in March 1918, she had some cause to believe that she might succeed: Jeannette Rankin had gone from suffrage leadership to political success in 1916. Like Montana, Nevada was sparsely populated, boasting no real city where concentrated populations might be swayed by tightly organized political machines. Convinced as she was that she had "beaten" Wingfield's forces, she believed that the concentrated canvassing that she and her supporters had done and the careful and systematic organizing rather than any other factors had won the suffrage. If a considered, planned, orderly approach to the voters had won that battle, she thought, the same techniques perhaps might win public office for another woman. Like many others, she believed women had sought the vote so that they could change the world.

Unlike many Nevada office seekers and officeholders, she was a native; like many who had sought the seat, she was after her first public office, aiming high. The difference of gender was a point of principle and became an issue in the campaigns. She did not dodge the issue of a woman in office; rather, she hoped that there would be many women who would vote for her merely on the basis of her womanhood and the moral superiority that implied in a nation new to the idea of a woman in the political world. As Kathryn Anderson wrote in her thorough study of Martin's two campaigns, Martin "could have chosen to confront whatever resistance to a female senatorial candidate that existed in the attitudes of the Nevada voter by minimizing her sex and preparing a platform otherwise undistinguishable from that of a male candidate. Instead, she constructed her campaigns around the issue of woman's more direct participation in government, making gender not only a central factor but also a central issue."[1] She announced a rationale for woman's participation in government on two levels: "the level of justice and the level of necessity"; those same lofty abstracts that had explained United States entry into the war served to demand political recognition for women by both vote and voice.[2] If she was deluded in believing women were ready for her, she offered herself as candidate sincerely.

Before she left Washington, she offered her resignation to the National Woman's Party, not insisting it be accepted. She needed the help of the party, both for money and for organizers, but she also knew that her party membership could be a political liability. She could not, however, publicly admit that. In a letter to Elizabeth Kent she claimed she would never have offered it "on the ground that it would be to my advantage."[3] The party accepted the resignation and sent her off, apparently with its blessing. Much later, Alice Paul remembered that "the Woman's Party put a great deal of power and effort into getting her into the Senate . . . We raised money for it, and we gave her a large farewell luncheon at which Julia Lathrop, I remember, opened with a speech . . . I know it was a very expensive campaign."[4]

After the March announcement, on her way back to Nevada again under NWP auspices, she addressed a gathering in Denver and presented the central ideas that were to inform her campaign. Although she later sharpened the details, the spirit remained the same. The progress of the federal amendment was "more important than my campaign" but she would run on "just principles and vital principles by going over the heads of party organization . . . I think I have a good fighting chance to get a majority of the votes. If I do not . . . I will have been a forerunner or a pathfinder for other women to make a fight." But she was quick to add that she could not run if she did not represent something else besides women. She firmly backed the president on the war, she stood for improved treatment of labor, for distribution and development of government-owned land, for conservation of food, for concern with the nature of the peace to follow the assumed victory. Women, she claimed, were "natural conservators," women's skills a national need. German women were not enfranchised; giving American women a voice in government affairs would strengthen the nation.[5]

In declaring her nonpartisanship, she expressed the long-established concerns of a suffrage movement that saw party politics as morally questionable, a movement whose horror at NWP tactics had been based as much on an unwillingness to connect with either party as on the publicity-seeking antics.

To help her, Mabel Vernon, a familiar ally, left the NWP to become campaign manager, apparently against the advice of the leaders who, she recalled, "wanted me to retain my relationship with the party and to do whatever was necessary for the *national* campaign. Actually, Anne felt she would be aiding the cause of women by being elected." Still, Vernon recalled that her decision was "very personal." "I liked Anne. I wanted to do the thing that would help her."[6]

Press response in Nevada was varied and prompt: the *Reno Evening Gazette,* never particularly helpful in the suffrage campaign, gave news space on the front page and a few days later reprinted a positive response from the *Churchill County Standard* that admitted that Martin's announcement

> takes what has heretofore been considered somewhat of a joke out of the realm of pleasantry and banter and places it on a plane where it must be considered seriously . . . Miss Martin has the undoubted right and privilege to aspire to any position in the gift of the people, and, as she states in her announcement, is entitled to the same consideration accorded to a man under similar circumstances, without reference to sex—no more and no less. So be it.[7]

The *Standard* proved fairer than some of the state press. From the very beginning the *Carson Daily Appeal* made highly personal attacks, marking Martin out quite distinctly from the male candidates about whom it had little to say. First irritated by the excessive claims of the earliest dispatches and by the gushing accents of the eastern press, the *Appeal* (and several other Nevada newspapers whose comments the *Appeal* steadily reprinted) tossed any restraint aside. At first the writers were content to question the veracity of press releases, but within a few days the *Appeal* was sniping more personally: "How Old Is Anne?" read a headline that discussed an "old puzzling problem,"[8] a question teased into "how old will she be when she gets to the Senate?" the next month.[9]

No less personal was the *Elko Independent's* labeling of her as "Ann the Ancient, the Plug Ugly of Female Politics," who had, the writer insisted, "rung her own curfew" and urged that women do almost anything else, "put a woman in the President's chair if possible and you think best, but in the name of the blatherskite fate that directs Ann's destiny, keep her out of all your activities. The people of Nevada will keep her out of everything else."[10]

Making an issue out of age was rude rather than realistic: both Martin's major opponents were older than she; had she been elected, she would have been the youngest member of the Senate. More politely, the *Tonopah Times* soberly suggested that the event should not be regarded as sensational, in spite of the wide national publicity. On the contrary, "Miss Martin's candidacy is most logical, and the very natural consequence of special training and fitness and extensive public activities in connection with many of the most important economic and social problems."[11]

National reaction was more positive: scores of stories hailed the idea of a woman running for the Senate in accounts that exaggerated what newsmen and women saw as her unique qualities: her western birth, her campaigns in the desert, her ladylike demeanor that contrasted with stereotypical views of the feminist. In fact, the Nevada press reaction suggests a resentment of such vast attention. The *Carson Daily Appeal* observed early that "Miss Martin has not overlooked the necessity of securing the services of a good press agent and whether inspired or not, he tells some things that Nevadans, who have known Anne all her life, are profoundly ignorant."[12] Like the *Reno Evening Gazette*, it reprinted as well from the *Nevada Miner* a complaint about "junk and bellywash being sent out to keep the titian haired 'maiden' in the calcium glow."

> We fed it to the office goat and he swelled up from too much gas on the stomach and died. We tried it next on a prospector's burro and it only got far enough down the burro's throat to choke him to death.[13]

However cruel the taunts of the Nevada editors about her age—she was forty-two and had never concealed the fact—and the inaccuracies about her appearance and experience, the national press wrote glowingly—and accurately. Winnifred Mallon's releases from National Woman's Party headquarters were factual enough: she emphasized Martin's athletic prowess, her tennis and mountain climbing, her wide travel and foreign schooling, her efforts for suffrage. Nevada editors may have found these features disturbing in a number of ways: state pride discouraged thinking of travel in Nevada as grueling, although it was; foreign travel and advanced study for women were uppity and eastern and thus suspicious. Although important men in Nevada politics and business life spent long periods of time away from the home state, when Martin did the absences were noted. The same editors who had delighted in reporting the White House picketing gleefully reminded their readers of the events in Washington, of "female hooligans cavorting around the White House and harassing the president."[14]

Many of the national papers made headlines of Martin's poise and womanliness, as if a woman politician should be, as the *San Francisco Examiner's* report put it, "large, imposing, august—a personage who would be entering . . . as a battleship enters the harbor, full steam ahead." To find a small woman—she was little more than five feet tall—with a "low, sweet voice, the 'excellent thing in woman,'" and "masses of black hair that shaded blue eyes, which were now keen and intent, now twinkling with humor," was to find a contradiction to the stereotype.[15] That the eastern dispatches made much of her "youth" particularly upset the Nevada newspapermen. The comments about her age only opened the way for state papers to offer more insults. To her credit, Martin never responded to the personal attacks, which certainly distinguished her unfairly: no other political candidate for any office or any party in the 1918 campaign was treated so badly. Whether the press attacked her as woman or as the particular woman she was, she bore it bravely. None of Martin's enemies—and she had a good many—ever denied that her personal behavior was above reproach.

Nevada editors regularly reminded their readers that Martin had a press agent, organizers, and money—all from out of state. The *Mason Valley News* complained about the "Belmont money bags," and yet another metaphorical sally claimed Martin's "political money barrel has no bottom,"[16] clearly assuming that the money expended in the campaign came from the NWP, an unwarranted assumption that Martin must have wished were true, for money was a serious problem in both 1918 and 1920.

Although Martin asserted that $3,000 had been raised from mostly eastern sources before she returned to Nevada,[17] such a claim may have been wishful thinking: individual letters in the months of March and April indicate that disappointment was regular. Elizabeth Kent worked vigorously from Massachusetts but she was unable to tap some of the expected sources: the Hoovers never contributed, nor did Mrs. Belmont, who claimed to have spent too much on the National Woman's

Party. After Kent took much trouble to reach the wife of wealthy Adolf Sutro, who had made his fortune on the Comstock, that wealthy woman finally gave ten dollars.[18] Mary Austin, ever amused by Martin's ambitions, expressed some doubts, but she sent ten dollars—for a hat, she insisted, not the campaign fund.[19] Nevada women did help, but all of their gifts were small, usually only five dollars. Although Minnie Flanigan of the Reno Women's Civic League acted as treasurer and the league officially functioned much as a political party might to pay some campaign expenses, most of the money came from Mrs. Kent, from Dr. Margaret Long, and from Martin's own resources. Martin's older brother and all of her sisters helped, but the charge of heavy support from the NWP was wrong. When Alice Paul called the campaign "expensive" for the party, she had to have meant the cost in womanpower normally working for Paul and the federal amendment, the cost of time from Mabel Vernon, from Mrs. Kent, and from the other organizers whom Martin paid.[20]

Vernon served from mid June as campaign manager, and Martin paid a secretary from April on; seven or eight organizers received small salaries and expenses from the campaign fund, operating in much the same manner as they had in suffrage and NWP drives. While several of the workers returned part of their salaries to the cause, Dr. Long, who left her Denver medical practice from June to November to help her friend, not only gave her time and paid her own expenses but also brought her own car and drove Martin and others throughout the state during the last two months.

Although Anne Martin used Nevada women to help her organizers circulate nominating petitions (as an Independent she needed three thousand signatures to qualify), the NWP inner circle did most of the work. As Anderson has shown in her study, if Anne Martin did not clearly perceive how her privileged position—her income and her freedom from family responsibility and the compelling need to support herself—allowed her to run for office, the other participants did. These women, Anderson argued, had "more than a casual stake in [the campaign's] success."

> Although they were not the candidate, they saw the campaigns in some ways as their own. Each had made a difficult decision to interrupt her work with the NWP on the federal amendment. Their reasons varied: some believed in Anne Martin and wanted to help her, some saw the campaigns as an opportunity to help other women, and some acted out of a sense of self-interest.[21]

Most of the organizers had felt pressure from Alice Paul to stay with the fight for the amendment, but Paul finally left the decisions to the individual workers. For Mabel Vernon the choice was even more difficult, for her entire public experience had grown from long acquaintance with Alice Paul starting in undergraduate days at Swarthmore. Vernon denied appeals to work in other campaigns and worked for Martin in 1918 and 1920, she thought later, because Martin's effort "was interesting, much more than the suffragists were or some of them are today."[22] As Anderson noted, such cases "suggest that Anne Martin was capable of competing with Alice Paul for the allegiance of star organizers."

> Securing more direct participation in politics for women, as a cause, was not clearly competitive with suffrage. But then, given that the suffrage movement was at its peak, with the smell of success tantalizingly close, and the idea of women as direct participants in politics was only beginning to surface, with all the implications only vaguely formulated, we have no reason to expect otherwise.[23]

Certainly the correspondence from the other organizers indicates the feeling that the campaign was a joint effort of some symbolic import for women, as part of what Margaret Whittemore called "this big movement," one that clearly meant more than the passage of the amendment, one that included actions like Martin's knocking at the men-only door of the Senate.[24]

Anne Martin tried hard to persuade Bird Wilson, her ally from 1914, to become her campaign manager, seeking her not only for the Nevada experience but also because Wilson had remained a strong friend in spite of many personal differences. Wilson's final decision rested on the need for money; responsible for an ailing mother, she needed $200 a month, four times the amount paid the others, and Martin could not afford that expenditure.[25]

Whether Bird Wilson's presence would have changed anything is doubtful, for the Nevada perception of the campaign as an eastern one supported by eastern money was not likely to change. Outside funding was commonplace in Nevada, but the money usually came from California, a suitable source, perhaps, since Nevada silver had so enriched its larger neighbor. Emphasizing the foreignness of Martin's workers ignored the scores of Nevada women who helped gather names for the nominating petitions, arranged for meetings, opened their homes to workers, watched polls on election day. The eastern women were visible and strange; the western women the editors ignored. With no party organization to assist her, Martin created her own corps, treating her organizers as officers and the local women as soldiers in what she and the others saw as a fight for women's possibilities in the political world.

And a battle it was from the very beginning, a battle generally ignored by the other two parties, who seemed to fear very little. If Martin seldom confronted her opposition candidates, she had to struggle steadily against the press. The Democrats had the advantage in running an incumbent: Charles B. Henderson, a California lawyer who had served as a district attorney and later as a university regent, had been appointed late in 1917 to the vacancy created by Newlands' death. He would be running for the remainder of Newlands' term. Running against him on the Republican ticket was E. E. Roberts, Nevada's sole member of the House.

Shortly after her announcement, Anne Martin had written—but not mailed—a letter to prominent Republicans asking them to try to persuade Roberts not to run, claiming that Roberts believed her running as an Independent would "cost his own election and perhaps elect Mr. Henderson." Hoping for an endorsement before the primary, she claimed such support would "strengthen the Republican party, not only in Nevada but in eleven other suffrage states in the country."[26] Socialist Martin Scanlon did little campaigning, nor, for that matter, to judge by newspaper coverage, did either Henderson or Roberts until October, both confident in their nominations. Martin, on the other hand, endured months of hard labor: the campaign for funds began in March and the drive for signatures for her petition of nomination in June, the search for support thus constant for many months.

Senator Henderson was careful to make a public stand for suffrage when the Senate considered the amendment in September and to have his remarks printed for state distribution. The senator's remarks may have seemed ironic to Anne Martin, trying as she was to change woman's social role and show that women could act in politics, arguing for change. Senator Henderson, on the other hand, maintained that voting would not change women, but in a sense his remarks praised female fortitude. The western woman was a "real mate" for modern man. He insisted that "the best type of western men owed their power of endurance, their incentive for creative work, to the quickening influence of woman's greatest charm—her understanding sympathy." The senator concluded that the "truly mated" westerners had therefore given their women the vote first.[27]

Henderson's speech reveals attitudes common to the men of his period—that woman's participation was more helpful in terms of sympathy than in action, in supporting male endeavors than in speaking for women for themselves—and handily suggests that southern senators might keep the vote white, keeping "order" just as the southerners had succeeded after Reconstruction in preventing black males from voting.[28]

From the start, Anne Martin faced a tremendous task. Aside from the difficulties of running without a party structure and party funds to help her, she had to find those three thousand Nevadans to sign a petition favoring her candidacy, a task made more difficult by the women's newness to political activity. Scores of signatures had to be sought twice because women signed their husbands' names, not their own. She had to overcome the animosity raised by the 1916 campaign and by the internal battles among Nevada women. Most of all, she had to persuade women to vote as women, not as Democrats, Republicans, or Socialists. In spite of an official platform that marked her concern with land distribution, railway rates, water, and the war, her real goal as she saw it and as her supporters presented it was making a first step for women's active participation in politics, for women voting for women's concerns and for reform.

There was little evidence that women would vote as a group, but Martin was not alone in suspecting it might happen. Those who opposed suffrage fought it because of that very suspicion. As one scholar has observed, "The few instances in which women had played an active role in politics provided some basis for speculation about the development of a political constituency," for women in Illinois had clearly voted against a machine candidate, and Massachusetts and Ohio women had been credited with defeating mayoral candidates already.[29] Nevada women, however, had failed their first test when Reno's new female voters had not seen women's issues in the divorce laws, gambling laws, or the control over the number of bars. If the state's women were strongly behind prohibition, this single issue did not help Martin, for Henderson was counted as a "dry," too.

That she understood the magnitude of her battle is clear from an interview with Freda Kirchwey published in April: "Chiefly I'll be running against traditions and prejudices that have a long if not an admirable history to back them up."[30] As the months passed, she spent more time running against her own past and the NWP's current picketing than against either Henderson or Roberts. Her 1917 statement that she would not knit for the war until the national amendment was passed returned to haunt her; petty issues assumed monumental size to the state press in a fever of patriotism over the war.

Anne Martin had spent two months touring the state in June and July; her campaign in general was more strenuous than that of either opponent. Convinced that if a little voter contact was a good thing, more must be a better one and reminded of the suffrage strategy of constant small meetings and steady individual effort, she insisted that a stream of organizers keep moving about the state arranging meetings and gathering groups for speakers who might be one organizer, then another, then Martin again. Within her own corps, the women complained—although not directly to the candidate. Ella Riegel wrote Mabel Vernon in August that "Miss [Jessica Granville] Smith and I feel this tour had been badly planned and a great waste of time, energy, and money," pointing out that the opposition had done no canvassing, while both Anne Martin and Margaret Whittemore, for example, had spoken in little Pioche before Riegel arrived: "In spite of the fact that every house in Pioche was circularized, we could get only 40 people at the street meeting last night (5 women and 5 drunks, who applauded prohibition) . . . The committees will resign in despair.[31] Martin herself, remembering that the small communities had passed suffrage in 1914, put in long days of speaking and weary hours of travel while seven staff members went town to town, ranch to ranch. The towns were still as far apart, the transportation still as rudimentary as it had been in 1914 when the campaign had been for suffrage, but the helpers were fewer, the reception, if not the weather, cooler. In towns boasting such luxuries the Martin forces arranged talks after the movies and saw to it that when Martin's campaign slide was shown women would be present to applaud. Although most of the group moved by train or automobile stage, Dr. Long drove various workers and, on the final tour, Martin herself at a time when, as she recalled later, "fifteen miles an hour was good time."[32]

News releases made much of the difficulties, although Nevada papers seldom printed them in full. Accounts offered by the various women affirm that the work was exhausting in the hot Nevada summer, perhaps much as Martin's press agent described it in an article about the organizers, whom he named the GATs, for "Get Anne There":

> They have invaded barrooms and "joined us" in something light. They have danced with cowboys in country school houses, dropped down mine shafts and climbed up reefs in search of the elusive vote. They have broken down on the open desert, only the alkali in sight, when motoring with their

canteens and their lunch box. They have slept out in their blankets in the lee
of a sage brush and listened to the howling of the coyotes.[33]

Dr. Long recorded October snow in Ely and reported some problems
with the car—"I think it was due to the strain of putting her up the wash
at Armagosa where I broke the muffler"—and although she longed for a
bath, offered "to stay out as long as I can and go to Hell or anywhere
else—according to orders."[34]

Jessica Smith reported a "wild sort of week, out of the world in
Mormon land where the flies are so thick and the people so dirty and the
food so abominable that Las Vegas seems like heaven."[35] Still, the
organizers enjoyed much of the rugged campaigning. Dr. Long described the techniques by which an open air meeting began in Eureka,
where she brought part of the audience ". . . from the brink of the saloons
. . . by the process generally known as 'gathering in the crowd.' It is
accomplished thusly, a quick rip up and down the street with a lassoo, a
quick jerk, a quicker mount to the soap box and the application of a Mike
and Patter, a general laugh and you have them—the regular performance
begins." And she remembered from an outdoor meeting in Caliente "the
cigaretts glowing in the dark, the yelling babies, the inevitable dog
fight, while engines roared up and down the railroad track."[36] But the
Nevada papers resented Kathryn Lincoln's all too colorful published
letter and when the *Wells Herald* picked it up from the eastern suffrage
publication where it appeared and reprinted it with sarcastic parentheti-
cal comments throughout, several other newspapers followed suit.[37]

Anne Martin did not spare herself in the campaign: she made as many
as five speeches in a day, traveling from settlement to mine to open air
meeting at the slow pace the desert roads required. Not surprisingly, the
antagonistic press paid little attention unless an opportunity offered for
criticism. Unimpressed at the campaigners taking on hardships that
were everyday matters for Nevada women (who had the sense most of
the time to stay put), Nevada newsmen saw nothing quaint in the
campaign and refused to take Martin seriously. They would not respond
to issues at all. Organizers were primed with political arguments; they
met the same questions about picketing the White House over and over
again. As the *New York Post* correspondent put it, what figure Martin
would cut in the campaign was "somewhat problematical: She has been
made the butt of concerted attacks on the part of the Democratic press of
the state . . . particularly because of the picketing of the White House
[but] while no one believes she has even an outside chance of winning,
she is showing more strength than was at first anticipated." The corre-

spondent, perhaps one of the few nearly objective observers on record, characterized her as "not a brilliant speaker, but a vigorous one who depends on ideas rather than eloquence," but he noted she lacked "readiness to mix with the people" and had no "facility for catering to the crowd." He guessed that she might win "the big end of the women's vote anyhow."[38]

Occasionally a Nevada paper would attempt a straightforward account. In Tonopah, where the all too familiar *Bonanza* that had attacked Martin in 1914 and 1916 continued with a barrage of personal slamming, the opposing paper, the *Times,* offered an account that listed her platform and quoted her at length. Once again her primary concerns, rather than the published platform, took first claim. Echoing the spirit of her slogan ("I am pledged to no party, but to the interests of the whole people"), she considered herself an Independent, "free to serve all groups," but she made a particular appeal to justice for women:

> It is fairness not just to myself nor just to women but fairness to the state and to the nation. Patriotism demands that our country have the full benefit of woman's experience . . . In the food administration, for instance, woman's experience in household economics would have averted the profiteering in wheat.[39]

Still, even the *Times'* apparent sympathy might have had other sources, for the story appears next to her paid advertisements and Mollie Condon, reporting the price of printing in a similar paper, noted that the price "includes a flattering write up."[40]

Still seen as a White House picket opposed to Wilson, Martin had to contend with other claims as well. Condon reported that opposition elements in Ely claimed that "she is opposed to the Red Cross . . . she supports the IWW [Industrial Workers of the World]."[41] Martin's months-old statement that she was "intensely interested in legislation in behalf of labor, even the I.W.W., who had never been particularly a problem in Nevada," enraged the *Carson Daily Appeal.* Days before the election, the *Appeal* resurrected the story, long circulated in smaller communities, as an example of

> her absolute ignorance of Nevada history. But it can be recalled that Ann has only lived at brief times in Nevada in the past twelve or fifteen years, the balance of the time being spent in other places where the opportunity presented itself and enabled her to satisfy her intense appetite for notoriety. Evidently she knows nothing [of the years between 1905 and 1908] when

I.W.W. activities were quieted and ended . . . only when . . . authorities
were compelled to call in federal troops.[42]

It mattered little in 1918 that the Nevada problems with the IWW had
been exaggerated, the conflict magnified by management to kill union
activity.[43] Martin's statement was hardly an endorsement of the Wobblies, nor was her remark about knitting "opposition to the Red Cross."
Only eastern papers reported that her two younger brothers and two
brothers-in-law were in service, and when her brother Karl wrote from
the front, the Reno paper printed his letter, identifying him only as "the
son of Mrs. W. O. Martin."[44]

While the *Appeal* was a small paper with limited circulation (Nevada
had nothing like a metropolitan daily), it was the custom for small
papers to pick up each other's editorials, and the *Reno Evening Gazette*
regularly reprinted the attacks in its column on the state press. The
Carson paper gave very little space to political news or political comment (most of its first page was boilerplate and the back was almost solid
with advertisements), but a week seldom passed without a comment on
Martin and the *Tonopah Bonanza* did the same.

Whether the attacks came from personal animosity or opposition to
women in general is hard to determine. Certainly male candidates for
office received respectful treatment for the most part. Other women
running for office—and there were several—may have been ignored,
but they were not attacked, either. When Republican E. E. Roberts
opened his campaign in October with a fist fight, no editorial comment
followed, and Roberts was the state's sole congressman.[45] Nevadans
understood the rules were different for men and for women. In spite of
protestations of fairness, Nevada newsmen treated Martin unkindly,
marking her out with insults and innuendos not directed at her male
opponents, different in kind and in quantity from comments made about
men.

Martin's expensive press agent was not much help either, and it
would appear that he aggravated the problems created by national
attention and excessive zeal in the early months. First press dispatches
had come from NWP headquarters in Washington where staff continued
to place articles in the eastern press, but by September Anne Martin was
pleading with Sara Bard Field to find an agent, "preferably a man," to
deal with the state press.[46] W. M. Rannells of San Francisco demanded
and got $100 a week, four times the salary paid to organizers, but he
offended the locals immediately by introducing himself as "a brother
newspaper man under the press agent's curse."[47] While he argued that

editors would get "nothing but straight news from Anne Martin head-quarters," his stories would have done a sob sister proud. When the IWW flap developed he dwelt on a "little woman in a drab raincoat and a flat sailor hat . . . at the gates of the great railway shops at Sparks, speaking very earnestly to throngs of men in oil stained overalls pouring back to the round house and shops after lunch hour."[48] His effort to create clever and colorful stories became a joke throughout the state. In a rather odd way, the ineptness of Rannells and the general nastiness of the press kept Martin in the public eye, but hardly in the way she might have wished.

Hiring Rannells, insisting on a male, presented other problems. Her Stanford classmate, Winnifred Harper Cooley, daughter of the women's movement's faithful historian Ida Husted Harper, had offered her services earlier. In Reno for a divorce, Cooley had placed a complimentary article in *Sunset*, a California-based magazine of wide circulation. When Cooley learned of Rannells' appointment, she fired off a furious accusation at Martin for having "hired a man after telling me you had neither need nor money for one!! One is used to these political dodges from men—but does not expect them from women!" And to top off her anger, she enclosed a copy of a letter from *Sunset* editors who had asked for a "London atmosphere anecdote" playing on the suffragette experience and who added that their "indifference to Anne's aspirations is colossal."[49] That indifference to her aspirations found its match in Nevada editors.

Wearied with the long months of campaigning, no doubt frustrated at the response of the press, Martin found new obstacles in the last month. By October, Nevada citizens felt the first attacks of the epidemic influenza that had spread across the nation, killing thousands in 1918 and 1919. While many communities simply canceled all public meetings, others did not. Jessica Granville Smith reported from Las Vegas that "they don't quarantine the houses and if you canvass you are apt to run right into it." Smith also reported that "they"—unidentified further—were "circulating all sorts of stories about A.M. making the rounds of the cafes in Reno, being an utterly abandoned creature . . . I can't trace the stories—but isn't that a rotten way of trying to destroy a candidate?"[50]

In Anne Martin's own eyes she was being deserted by the people she counted on, too. Still convinced that big, liberal national names would help her cause as they had apparently helped suffrage, she tried through summer and fall to persuade them to help. She begged Dudley Field Malone, defender of the pickets and nationally known as an attorney, to come to speak, sending telegram after telegram to him and to his wife, Doris Stevens, an old friend from NWP. She tried as hard to persuade Jane Addams, ill in Colorado, to come again. In spite of warnings from her organizers, she brought Charlotte Perkins Gilman for a brief tour, hoping to woo Socialist voters. Sara Bard Field and her friend, Charles Erskine Scott Wood, appeared briefly, but when Field returned to California she was injured in an automobile accident that killed her son. Elizabeth Kent, still in the East, functioned as fund raiser but could not leave a son ill with flu-induced pneumonia.[51] The campaign balance was $9.00 in late October.

A last flurry of printed materials was sent through the state, lauding Martin's "ability, training, character, courage for principle and fight for people." One handbill signed by Martin bore the mark of Rannells in its lavish prose, which called on the memory of Inez Milholland and the words of President Wilson and urged the use of "woman in the winning of the World War" to ensure democracy, "true democracy that like a cross is held before the eyes of our dying soldiers." Woman, so the handbill went, was to do her share:

> So the Heart of Woman, as she sits Folding and Folding Bandages soon to be Dyed Red, must cry out—"It isn't enough to Sacrifice; in the New World that Their Deaths will have made Possible I must lead, not Follow Blindly; when the Nations of the Earth Meet in the Adjustment that Must Come, side by side with Man, Free and Equal, I must HELP REBUILD THE WORLD."[52]

A more rational and restrained appeal, "Why You'll Vote for Anne Martin," claimed that it was part of "War Democracy that Nevadans elect the First Woman Senator." The detailed appeals were to mining men and "You Who Labor" and advocated special railroad rates, subsidies for mines, government ownership of utilities, "fair hours, good wages, healthful working conditions, equal pay for equal work for women, abolition of child labor," and all the generalized goods of political paradise. Most of all she demanded that "woman be made a part of the government."[53]

Martin's other printed materials and the seldom published press releases show an effort to make a number of political points: Democrats were "wet" in spirit, in spite of public protestations of being "dry"; Henderson represented big business; Roberts was a mere politician; land should be made available to all and the government should irrigate it.[54] While her own appeals to voters sprang from these principles, none was

particularly revolutionary in a period of rapid change. Most important to
Martin and her workers was the effort to establish the right of woman to
function in the political sphere, one to which she had been newly
admitted.

Making no pretense of chivalry, the Nevada press responded with
treatment that was highly personal, continually directed at her militant
activities and her opposition to the president in time of war. That Wilson
had come out for suffrage that fall and that Anne Martin could, as Mabel
Vernon told a supporter, "work in complete accord with him"[55] did not
matter. To suggest that entrenched male thinking could not accept a
woman as an officeholder would be wrong, yet it may be that Martin's
particular character—rebellious rather than submissive, assertive rather
than subdued, abrasive rather than accommodating—was her strength
as a candidate, her doom as a public woman at that particular time. Her
organizational experience, her campaign acquaintances with many
Nevadans, her position as symbolic female contestant on the political
field should have been marks in her favor. She was no longer an
uncertain dilettante but a woman with a mission.

Martin's status as an Independent made the campaign continuous and
difficult, but she compensated with wide mailings to particular groups,
with paid advertising explaining her platform, with literature distributed
by cooperating women throughout the state, but most of all with constant personal contact by her organizers and herself. She stressed the last
so strongly that some reacted against it: in October, Ann Penn Aston of
Goldfield complained that "this canvassing is creating antagonism and
alienating the committee."[56] Yet that personal contact seems to have
been the most successful of all the campaign strategies.

Women responded to Martin's appearances. "Your talk to the people
made me proud I am a woman," one wrote.[57] Letters from organizers
reported regularly on Martin's personal effect. A Reno labor leader
observed that she "easily won nearly everyone with whom [she] was
able to meet this way."[58] The president of the Machinists' Union wrote
that "the majority of men in this shop seam [sic] to think that Miss
Martin is a wonderful woman."[59] And the *Oakland Tribune,* after the
election, noted that Martin had won the attention of "men and women
who had never before given the woman's viewpoint much thought. . . ."
"So if Anne didn't win, she didn't lose. Her campaign talks were little
classics, in the sense that she talked of real things and real issues, shorn
of the 'bunk' of most political talk."[60]

When the votes were counted, Anne Martin came in third with 4,603
votes, with the winning Henderson taking 12,197, almost half of those

cast, Republican Roberts well behind with 8,053, and Socialist Martin Scanlon with a mere 710.[61] As Anderson observed, "Martin's strategy not only failed to elect her, it may not even have been responsible for the votes she won," suggesting that Martin's votes may have come from Socialists because "her platform was sympathetic to labor and because she campaigned more vigorously than her Socialist opponent."[62] Martin herself told her workers that the state was "not ready to accept a woman senator," but claimed that she had "cut into both parties."[63] Her repeated assertions to the press that she had indeed won by showing that a woman could gain votes—wherever they came from—were sincere, in the light of her own statements at the opening of the campaign about her reasons for entering. She promised at the end of it all to run again in 1920, for all of her efforts had been in pursuit of the time remaining to the late Senator Newlands at the time of his death.

While a successful woman candidate for university regent had run unopposed, ironically, a woman was elected to legislative office in 1918—Sadie Hurst, a member of the Reno Woman Citizens Club, that splinter group that had broken with Martin's Civic League years before. The press wrote almost nothing about her, nor did she campaign much at all. She announced herself as "Endorsed by the Club Women of Reno" and advertised that she was "Not a Member of the Woman's Party." Her success demonstrated mistakes Martin had made and would make again. Hurst ran, she claimed, at the behest of the numerous organizations (civic groups and women's groups) to which she belonged.[64] If that is so, then her election was indeed an example of a women's bloc. Martin, ever impressed by national figures and national names, had done little to mend any Nevada fences broken during her campaign in 1916. She did not realize that she was no longer the woman who led the state to suffrage; she was the anti-Wilson White House picket.

Anne Martin's victory was one of being a woman publicly, daringly in action against the male world in one sense; it was more specifically one of demonstrating how suffrage techniques and woman speakers could work. The method of the small church or home gathering had been borrowed from NAWSA and from the NWP, just as the speakers had learned their skills working with those groups. Although typical Nevada campaigning by men featured large gatherings and set speeches arranged by party officials, still, as one historian remarked, "a senatorial candidate could shake hands with most voters in those years. Furthermore, Nevada's citizens usually expected him to do so."[65] The intense personal contact in Martin's campaign showed ways women could work for candidates, for change.

No matter how much the press raged about the fact, Nevada women seemed unconcerned that Martin's organizers were outsiders; they were impressed by the speakers' oratorical skills, however uncomfortable they were with canvassing themselves.[66] But the locals learned to work individually in their own ways. From Luning, a woman wrote with pride that ". . . we have done some quiet, dignified, effective work in our own way and know that we have *converted* some strong thinkers to her side and they in turn have some influence."[67] By observing, by participating actively, Nevada women came to new views of themselves and their possibilities. As Pearl Karaus of Yerington phrased her hopes for the 1920 campaign, "my heart is in it for much more than Miss Martin, much as I admire her."[68] As Anne Martin had predicted at the beginning of the campaign, when she expressed her need to "knock the fear out of the hearts of women" with political ambitions, "even if I should not win, it will never seem so strange when a woman tries it."[69]

Anne Martin proved that her own heart was in the struggle for much more than the office with her activities between the two campaigns. Her loss came only six days before the end of the war, a conflict that had distinctly affected her efforts for the Senate. Certainly the press reaction could be traced for the most part to her opposition to President Wilson in 1916 and to the unpopular activities of the NWP that continued through the fall. Like many other groups, Nevada editors saw the picketing, the burning of "Kaiser Wilson's" speeches, the constant harping on democracy beginning at home as unpatriotic, almost seditious activities. The *Carson Daily Appeal* approvingly printed an impassioned bit of verse, written by "a lady who has championed the cause of suffrage all her life," that echoed the attitudes of suffragists and patriots alike:

> There are just two kinds of women in this dear land of the free
> Who fail to give the president their utmost loyalty.
> The women of the nation march beneath Old Glory's fold,
> But the Woman's Party bears a flag that makes the heart run cold.
> For when before have women flung a banner to the skies
> And made their flag a flaunting rag—a thing of shameless lies?
> There are just two kinds of women by whom this might be done—
> There's the limelight Woman's Party—and the daughters of the Hun.[70]

After 11 November, the war done and the nation calmer, women could be optimistic about change. If the constant demonstration in Washington brought the federal amendment to the public's eye, as both Flexner and Andrew Sinclair have claimed,[71] it is also true that their militancy "only emphasized the reasonableness of NAWSA's position."[72] Whichever the cause, suffrage won important battles during the war: New York, North Dakota, Indiana, Nebraska, Michigan, and Rhode Island granted suffrage, and historians agree that the activity of the women in the war effort was a major factor in the changed attitudes of American men.[73]

During Martin's first campaign, the majority of suffragists supported the war in traditional fashion: Anna Howard Shaw directed the Woman's Committee of the U.S. Council of National Defense, joined on that group by several NAWSA officers; NAWSA supported hospitals in France; one officer headed the Women's Land Army; throughout the country suffragists were public in their contributions even though NAWSA president Carrie Chapman Catt had opposed intervention and wanted to put suffrage first, just as Alice Paul continued to do. But whatever her attitude, Catt served on the U.S. Council of National Defense at the same time that NWP women toured the country with a prison special, exploiting the government's injustice to women.[74] Even in the NWP, Harriot Stanton Blatch was excited by the conflict: "War!—it does make the blood course through the veins," she wrote. But she saw the possibilities for women in a warlike metaphor: "American women have begun to go over the top. They are going up the scaling ladder and out into All Men's Land . . . The rapidly increasing employment of women today, then, is the usual and happy accompaniment of war."[75]

Indeed, a number of slowly developing changes were accelerated by the demands of war: the first of the equal pay laws was passed in 1918; wider employment of women in industry brought the Women's Bureau of the Department of Labor into existence by 1919. The suffrage amendment itself passed the Senate in June of 1919, although ratification dragged on until the next August.[76]

Anne Martin may have followed the struggle closely, and she surely kept in close touch with her friends in the NWP, but she did not actively appear with the party or return to NAWSA, either because the end seemed in sight or because she could not comfortably work with either group. She had learned that her NWP connections had hurt her in 1918. She spent some time in Nevada in early 1919, regularly attending legislative sessions and actively testifying for an irrigation bill she had drafted with Sardis Summerfield, legislator, attorney, and long-time friend. The bill provided for irrigation districts in water hungry areas. Based on a California act that had proved successful, it competed with another that Martin condemned as unworkable.[77] When the bill was tabled in favor of the opposing plan, the ever venomous *Appeal* tagged it the "Anne Martin irrigation bill" when it lost.[78] Martin stayed only a few weeks in her native state. Her eye on the 1920 election, she left and set up an office in Washington. Such a choice seemed reasonable to her and she spent little time in her native state, true to Nevada political tradition.

Although she had hoped to work with her old acquaintance Herbert Hoover during the recovery period, he rejected her offer of help as he had a previous one to assist in the "Food Will Win the War" campaign. Various handwritten notes for the never-finished autobiography accuse him of ignoring her offers to help, but there is no correspondence in the files to clarify just what offers she made nor did she remember in 1932 or 1940 just exactly when those offers were made. In later years she explained the refusal in various ways: he had disapproved of the picketing, he feared association with her because she was "a dangerous person."[79] But she did not allow Hoover's refusal to interfere with her preparation. Assuming that Senator Henderson would be her opponent in 1920, in January she had filed charges that he had overspent and had accepted contributions from "several appointive officers" in violation of federal law.[80] By April she learned that the Senate committee to which she had appealed claimed to have "no authority" to act on the charges.[81] Whether she could have proved anything remains questionable, but a letter from prominent California Republican William C. Ralston suggests there may have been some concern about the charges and reveals that her firm belief in a "bi-partisan machine" effort may have had basis in fact. Ralston wrote to fellow Nevadan George Bartlett with a warning in early 1919:

> Anne Martin is in Washington and her representatives are trying to make all the trouble they can for Henderson. They are going to contest his seat at the next session and claim undue use of money . . . She is in damn fine biz, but I want you to know this, tell your friends and prepare ground for it is coming. I got this from a very high Republican source, they thinking I would help out after getting all the data I said *NO*. Not in a million years. That Republicans had helped elect Henderson and me for him.

The question of the charges was a public one that belied the "*Confidential*" of Ralston's letter; perhaps the label hoped to conceal an open statement about the "bi-partisan fusion candidate" that Martin believed Henderson to be. Still, the attempt to contest the 1918 vote failed.[82]

Anne Martin responded eagerly to J. A. H. Hopkins of the Committee of 48 to End Privilege, a loosely organized liberal group making plans for a third party in the 1920 elections: "It would be a wonderful thing if the liberal forces of the country could be united and a political party formed that would forestall Bolshevism and prevent a revolution." She offered to organize Nevada for such a group.[83] But she devoted most of her time to writing, trading on her political experience and her writing skills to publish a number of articles, both to help finance her coming campaign and to explore issues she found important. That she was invited to write them suggests she had made some impression on the editors as one to speak for women and emphasizes her steady efforts at maintaining her national feminist contacts for the future. She was working on material that was current and related to her particular concerns, material she knew well from her days lobbying with the NWP. She courted the Republicans, too, for the senatorial nomination. She had appeared at a Republican party conference in Washington to impress upon that party the certainty of twenty million female votes by the time of the next election.

When she published the first of her 1919 articles, she identified herself as a candidate for nomination.[84] She was certain, she told the Republicans, "that party will win the election which offers the most sincere and appealing issues to the minds and hearts of women."[85] "What Women Should Vote For," published in *Good Housekeeping* in November of 1919, sought to persuade women voters in 1920 to place other vital women's issues above the interest of any party by demanding certain reforms: care for maternity and infancy, the removal of children from industry, the feeding of undernourished children, no discrimination in Civil Service, and "the elimination of all remaining barriers in law and custom which perpetuate inequality, and prevent [women's] equal participation in government."[86] Martin argued with voluminous evidence for the proposed program and included as well the other points that became her 1920 platform; she attacked the economic conditions of inflation and profiteering; she hoped for a secure peace. In subsequent articles she specifically expanded on maternity and infancy care, the favorite goal of a large coalition of women embodied in the proposed Sheppard-Towner Act, "the first venture of the federal government into social welfare . . . the first major dividend of the full enfranchisement of women."[87]

Little discussed by historians of the Progressive movement, almost forgotten in the following flood of social legislation, the Sheppard-Towner Act sought to establish a modest nationwide program of pre- and postnatal care, maternal education, and minimal medical attention for infants through federal grants to states. It became a prime issue for the new woman voter, drawing support from the ever increasing women's organizations, uniting disparate elements of the feminist movement in much the same way suffrage had before and the Equal Rights Amendment did forty years later. Not surprisingly, opposition came from many of the same sources—die-hard antisuffragists. The bill had been written by Julia Lathrop, head of the Children's Bureau, and was first introduced, quite suitably, by Jeannette Rankin during her single term in Congress. Defeated in 1917, it was revived as a joint measure, but in 1919 it was jammed in committee.[88]

As more and more states gave women the right to vote, a Women's Joint Congressional Committee headed by former NWP member Florence Kelley united the new voters in an impressive campaign that included articles like Martin's in mass circulation magazines and lobbying by women's groups throughout the nation. Martin's articles formed a central part of *Good Housekeeping*'s contribution to the battles for a measure that would involve both state and local governments. The magazine supported Martin's arguments with editorial comment and published forms for women to use to influence Congress.[89]

An assortment of forces opposed the bill. Most formidable was the American Medical Association, but there were others: "medical liberty" groups who opposed vaccination, quarantine, and the Wasserman test; nonmedical practitioners of the American Drugless Association; the antisuffrage women who saw the bill as a Communist plot. Medical Women, a group separate from the AMA, stood strongly for the bill, as did prominent physicians. When it passed, just before the 1920 elections, that success seemed to prove that Congress had responded to those twenty million women voters, united once and perhaps for the last time on a single issue.[90]

With this effort Anne Martin had briefly found her way back to the mainstream of American feminism. Her articles show thorough research into the problems of maternal care and protection of infancy; the thoroughly documented "Everywoman's Chance to Serve Humanity: An Everlasting Benefit You Can Win in a Week" cites comparative health figures throughout the world to present the need, while "We Couldn't Afford a Doctor" dramatizes the problems of cost and the difficulties of women in sparsely settled states.[91] Although Martin later reflected the NWP's objection to special legislation, in 1920 she argued for maternal protection. Most of all she repeated her insistent demand that women should vote as women for social reform. More objective than her previous writing, the articles inform without attacking.

Two other articles more specifically address broader issues for the coming campaign. In *Reconstruction* she outlined water problems of the small homesteader in Nevada and urged passage of a federal bill to help returning soldiers develop marginal land.[92]

More sweeping aims emerged in "If I Were Senator," printed in the *Independent* for May 1920. Martin announced her plan if elected to "humanize our government and make it a genuine servant of the people's interests." Attacking Congress as obviously incompetent, she compared it unfavorably with the Russian Soviet, arguing that the Russian body was "nothing more than occupational representation worked out in practical politics." The American counterpart, she complained, was stuffed with lawyers—60 percent of the House, two-thirds of the Senate. "If our Senators are by any chance not lawyers, they are chiefly bankers and capitalists." She called for replacing the privileged groups with a fair share of representatives including "both men and women" so that the nation would have a Congress "representing the various occupations and needs of the people." Such a body would not have passed the Cummins-Esch railroad bill that returned transportation to private interests. For that matter, she was for nationalizing basic industries, for limiting the power of the president, for amending the constitution to bring American government to resemble the British parliamentary system, for limiting powers of the Supreme Court, and for popular election and recall of its judges. For good measure, she suggested reorganization of governmental departments into "natural agencies springing from the living needs of the people."[93]

Martin had changed her views on the League of Nations and directed her aims at the postwar world. She relegated her woman's program— exactly that of the Everywoman's Platform advanced in *Good Housekeeping*—to the last two points, conflating the issues into two items. She called as well for restoration of free speech, improved pay for soldiers, establishing collective bargaining and the right to strike, controlling the cost of living by government ownership, taxing "16,000 war millionaires," enacting the woman's program, and—this proved the main problem for her campaign—"release of political prisoners and conscientious objectors, following the humane example of our associates in the war."[94] These ideas were consistent with third-party views suggested by the Committee of 48.

Although she had announced in 1918 that she would try again, Martin made an official announcement 2 April 1920 by press release from her Washington office, offering herself as the Republican nominee if the party would accept her platform.[95] The second campaign was a smaller version, no less trying, than the first.

Why did she try again? Perhaps only because she had promised to, perhaps because she hoped for party endorsement. At the start of a second campaign, Martin knew too well the trials of independent candidacy—the petition signing, the organizing, the financing by an ever shrinking group of supporters to do battle with better-organized, comfortably financed campaigns mounted by state parties. Yet she also worried about the traditional parties for reasons that had made the entire suffrage movement strive for nonpartisan status, that had driven the NWP to insist that a campaign against Democrats was not a partisan matter, however odd that seemed. Perhaps, too, she remembered her battles with George Wingfield over suffrage. Wingfield was still the political power in Nevada. Her major Republican competition for the Senate was a former governor, Tasker Oddie, already a part of the state party organization. Had any of the new Republican women voters read the *Independent Woman* they might easily remember that Martin had accused leading politicians of trying to persuade women to do "the necessary drudgery to elect a full national ticket" of men by making "an impassioned tribute to the nobleness and unselfishness of womanhood."[96]

Nevertheless, she assured Will Hays, who chaired the Republican National Committee, that she "would be sorry to run as an Independent, thus once more splitting the Republican vote."[97] Clearly, she wanted to enter the primaries as the favored candidate, as she wrote to a leading Republican woman in Las Vegas:

> . . . if the Republican leaders refuse to give me the nomination, as they gave Judge Downer the nomination for Congress in 1918, and as the Democrats gave it to Senator Henderson, and if the Republican leaders insist on running a Republican candidate in opposition to me in the primary, on their shoulders alone will rest the responsibility for a split in the Republican vote . . . Under no circumstances will I enter the primary against a candidate backed by the big business bipartisan fusion machine.[98]

How she could imagine that she could be a Republican candidate on her platform puzzled at least one supporter, who wrote, "I think you have a good platform, but I can't understand why you call it Republican as it hasn't the remotest resemblance to the platform they fixed up in Chicago."[99] Martin even discussed her chances with the hated Wingfield, who, she reported, "tried to convince me that I have a good chance of winning the Republican primary . . . He promised to back me to the full extent of his power if I received the nomination."[100]

Martin's hopes of being "given" the Republican nomination demonstrate either an odd naiveté about party politics or completely unrealistic wishful thinking; even if Ralston's suggestions that Republicans had elected Henderson were not true, the climate was quite different from that of 1918. The Democratic success in 1918 was heavily influenced by support for Wilson and the war; by 1920 division had returned. Even the *Carson Daily Appeal,* sturdy Wilson backer throughout the war, felt the Democratic party was a sinking ship and later in the campaign thought it might be sunk—as perhaps it was, by "the Anne Martin, an Independent fighting craft."[101] Martin was surely more likely to take votes from Henderson if he ran than from any Republican candidate. Moreover, Republicans from all over the state declared themselves interested in the nomination. With such an open battle, Wingfield could easily tell Martin he would support her if she won the primary, but he knew quite well that she had little chance of winning if she did enter. Her platform, based so strongly on third-party principles, was far from Republican in spirit, even in a state where party labels meant less than personality and support from the right people. Her belief that she would "split the Republican vote" seemed based on some memory of the then moribund Republican progressivism that had once been a vital party force.

She may have known how unreasonable her wish was to have Republicans accept her. Yet having felt the brunt of independent campaigning, she longed for party help, both to keep the support of those who might finance her and to make her second battle more plausible to herself. Just as she had courted Prohibition party support in 1918, she kept the possibility open for the third party until midsummer when progressive elements of the two major parties gathered in Chicago for convention. One 1918 slogan had been "Over the heads of the party machines straight to the hearts of the people." Even if she should win the primary and Wingfield's backing, would not she be the "big business fusion candidate"?

Just to be secure, she began a petition campaign for independent nomination in early summer, perhaps as much to show strength to the Republicans as to assure herself a place on the ballot. Committed to another try, she finally chose to run on her own ticket, not in the primary, probably because she knew she had little chance; as a nominated Independent, she could at least make the whole distance. She did not decide until the last minute before the primary and that decision did not please her supporters. Katherine Mullen had refused to come in June, writing that she could not "face again the buffeting of campaigning for an Independent and for such a long time," even though she had first agreed when it appeared Martin would be running for the Republican primaries in September.[102] But Mullen finally did participate, along with familiar co-workers: Mabel Vernon as campaign manager, Dr. Long as chauffeur and organizer, Mollie Condon, Jessica Granville Smith, Ella Riegel, and, again as star lecturer, Charlotte Perkins Gilman. Two new organizers joined the staff as well as did Martin's niece Edna, who helped gather names for the petition.

Money was an even greater problem the second time around, partially because the amendment was still creaking toward ratification, but also because the 1920 platform was less attractive to the moneyed women Martin sought as backers. Elizabeth Kent continued to serve as fund raiser but her time was limited for her husband was seeking election in California. Mrs. Kent wrote Martin that "many of your most loyal friends are members of the Woman's Party and will feel its work the larger work."[103] Mrs. H. O. Havemeyer, a longtime friend and a wealthy woman fully capable of supporting the campaign, objected to Martin's ideas of public ownership and refused to contribute in June,[104] although in the fall she sent a large check, forgetting the platform, on the basis of Martin's "fine determined character and indomitable pluck."[105] Alvah Belmont, treasurer of NWP, was afraid of "radicalism," Doris Stevens wrote, "more class conscious than she ever has been . . . and imagining she's poor."[106] Helen Clegg Winters was more blunt. Still wishing "very much that we might have had many such women [as Martin] in the Senate," she agreed that Anne Martin was "distinctly on the side of the working man," and Winters was "not inclined to feel kindly toward all or any of you who are forcing the poor rich to pay it all."[107] Mrs. Victor DuPont found the platform "too bolshevistic to merit support."[108]

The novelty had worn off Martin's ambitions and the inherent contradictions in her position emerged ironically in such responses from wealthy women. Because she was herself a woman of independent means, she was free to pursue political office, but her ideas alienated others of her class and acquaintance. In the end, the money came from Dr. Long and Mrs. Kent and, of course, from Martin's own sources. Once again there were contributions from Nevada women, still small, still few; once again the organizers contributed part of their salaries to help the cause.[109]

Working with less money, the Martin forces found nothing easier: the *Tonopah Times,* for example, took a news release, treated it as advertising, and charged for it. Mabel Vernon paid the bill, protesting all the time.[110] On the whole, the press paid little attention to Martin beyond simple news stories announcing she was in town. True to form, the *Carson Daily Appeal* could not resist a personal dig. Quoting a *Washington Herald* story that Martin was "a pretty little thing," the *Daily Appeal* had to add ". . . to the reporter who penned the above a mud fence would undoubtedly appeal as a work of art."[111] While national attention was less, an interview about Martin's platform started the major conflict of the early months, a conflict that nagged her throughout and that brought her dubious publicity—almost the only attention that she got in some places without paying for it.

Even before Anne Martin had returned to Nevada in late May, the Darrel Dunkle Post of the American Legion had passed a resolution against her position on amnesty for "political prisoners and conscientious objectors." The resolution received wide publicity in the state where editors managed to twist its general statement to mean support for slackers, draft evaders, and—fighting words in Nevada—members of the Industrial Workers of the World. The same editors who seized on her vague comments on the IWW in 1918 and had tied her more closely with the Wobblies by calling NWP "the IWW of the Woman's movement" again questioned her patriotism.[112] Reacting immediately, Martin tried to clarify her stand in a wire to the *Reno Evening Gazette,* claiming she wanted amnesty for "all political prisoners and conscientious objectors imprisoned under the espionage act for political opinions as distinguished from direct incitement to violence, acts of violence, or overt actions of violence against the government." But she firmly maintained her position: "I would rather be defeated because of my stand for the constitutional rights of the people than elected because of cowardly silence about them."[113]

By June the accusations had spread throughout the state, and Margaret Long wired frantically to Martin, "your platform release of conscientious objectors is misinterpreted as Unamerican and as protecting slackers and spys [sic] you cannot send too strong a statement denying this."[114] Martin responded in letters to the *Gazette,* which printed them not as news but as letters; the paper printed the responses but editorially attacked her. Her first letter tried to defend the action on broad principles, calling on Abraham Lincoln and the Constitution both and insisting she meant those "imprisoned for mere expression of opinion."[115] When that approach only provoked another attack on 25 June, she cited specific cases and righteously and rightfully accused the Legion of singling her out:

> It is not recorded that the Darrel Dunkle post has accused President Wilson of treason and lack of patriotism for these piecemeal releases [of prison-

ers]. The post reserves its attacks for me. However, the man who got twenty years for saying that "President Wilson is the greatest president England ever had" is still serving his time and Rose Pastor Stokes is still under a ten year sentence for saying "since government is for the profiteers, I am against the government."

She accused the "Reno boys" of ignoring the distinctions, adding she opposed releasing those convicted of "contemptible crimes," bolstering her case with reference to her two brothers, "both volunteers, both members of the American Legion." To close her defense, she quoted her own commitment to "uphold and defend the constitution," reaffirming her brand of "1776% Americanism."[116]

Dr. Long, usually the calmest of the crew, feared the flap would kill the campaign and suggested writing Judge Patrick McCarran, who Long said had influence over the *Appeal.*[117] Considering that paper's record of petty personal attack, such an effort might have seemed a waste of time to Martin.

Finally, Martin urged newspaper editors to print her reply as they had printed the accusations; the *Appeal,* to its credit, did, but many other editors refused.[118] Hoping for support, she wrote to her brother Karl. Far from supporting her view, he answered that it was his impression that the only conscientious objectors still in jail were "the vilest of cowards."[119] The questions continued to appear, even though she twice elicited evidence from Roger Baldwin and the American Civil Liberties Union supporting her own point of view.[120] Baldwin's evidence came after the Reno post had reaffirmed its stand, even after Martin had spoken before them,[121] and the rest of the press had tired of the whole question.

In August, when Tennessee finally ratified the federal suffrage amendment, climaxing the years of struggle, Anne Martin was unable to attend the celebration Reno women mounted. She was trying to produce practical political results.

Just as she had tried to discuss issues in 1918 and wound up defending picketing, Martin found it nearly impossible to discuss issues in 1920. Just as she had done in 1918, she used paid advertising and flyers to offer her ideas to the people. The major effort of the campaign remained what it had been in the past—personal contact. The second campaign saw some basic changes in method and personnel: more Nevadans participated, particularly men with ties to labor; fewer organizers moved about the state; fewer large meetings occurred, for the rental of halls was beyond the tighter budget that stretched to include small payments for each name on petitions to those who circulated them.

Mollie Condon sent a letter naming possible male helpers, concentrating on what she termed "radicals," and correspondence shows that help came from those men: Steven Collins in Goldfield, Frank Costello in Tonopah, Donald Wilson in Virginia City, Elbert Howard in Las Vegas, Thomas Hamer in Round Mountain. They canvassed, collected signatures, organized meetings. But many of the men who first offered to help were not even in the state by election time. Howard, for example, had moved to Doyle, California, by November, and George Johnson of Ruth explained how "50 men has [sic] left . . . in the last 10 days and some has been layed off in the pit."[122] Earlier, Walter C. Clark of Goldfield told how "they are laying off men . . . and putting them on the hike so they will lose their vote on election day," adding that such action showed how "men have sold us everytime." Clark wanted a woman "whom I can trust to look after the interests of the people."[123]

As Anne Martin had observed in 1914, Nevada's population shifted regularly. Heavily dependent on mining, the state had lost voters both from depletion of mines and from the slackening of railroad construction to serve those mines. D. S. McFarlane wrote from copper-mining Ruth that "votes are going to be scarce in this vicinity owing to laying off so many men here and at McGill and I guess all over the country which compels them to leave and lose their vote. I would like to see a law passed that would allow a Registered voter to vote any place in the U.S."[124]

Other towns had changed, too, since 1918. Long reported that "Thompson and Wabuska are dead—too small for a meeting for you— Mason is going down fast. Three to six families in Ludwig."[125] J. D. Lorraine of Beatty offered to get the votes for "our beloved Daughter of Nevada Anne Martin," even though "our precinct Rhyolite is bust up . . . and from 5000 inhabitants only 4 left . . . few's the people yet left . . . in the county."[126] Yet some places grew: Long wrote from tiny Broken Hill that "in a month or two there may be one or two thousand."[127] Martin remembered that her strength had come from the mines and the small towns in 1918, and in September she launched once more into the country after the September primaries had decided her opponents: former governor Tasker Oddie for the Republicans, Senator Charles Henderson for the Democrats. She remained optimistic, but Katharine Mullen, discouraged in sweltering southern Nevada, wrote she could have little enthusiasm "when I know that Anne Martin knows that only a miracle will elect her!"[128]

Martin may have been listening in the spring to the railroad labor men who expected support of her candidacy in "a state like Nevada where the labor vote practically ensures success,"[129] for she continued a barrage of flyers directed to labor, a stream of letters and more and more personal contact. One of her major arguments was that Senator Henderson, assumed to have much labor support, had "dodged the issue" on the Esch-Cummins bill that returned the railways to private control at what she claimed would be a cost to the buyers of "75 dollars a year," and she boasted of her endorsement by laboring men in Sparks and Ely.[130] Mullen saw a need to "kill Henderson with the Laborites," even though in August she found the Las Vegas men "railroad *boobs*" and "terrible Democrats . . . horrid toward women."[131] Perhaps cooled off a little later in the milder clime of Fallon in the north, however, she used a "pathetic tale" to persuade the "overall men" on the grounds of the county fair after George Wingfield had objected to posters.[132]

Anne Martin's appeals to women to vote for her as a woman continued, and there were more women who responded to it, women, like Lola Maverick Lloyd, who went beyond feminism. Offering a small contribution, she wrote, "Goodness knows, I hope Miss Martin will go in! I want to see what women can do to this busted old system before I plunge into r-r-red revolution."[133] Women from Yerington and Ione wrote, making gender an issue.

Once again, the canvassing presented constant physical challenge to the women, even the hardy women of the sort who had done it all before. Dr. Long, who years later teamed with Anne Martin to drive all over the West, wrote long letters to friends and to headquarters about the problems on sometimes literally a campaign trail. Martin preserved a dim photograph of Jack Rabbit Pass "where we broke the fan belt," an otherwise unidentifiable patch of dust and sagebrush surrounding a rutted road,[134] and Long wrote to a friend about a day that was more routine than the women might have hoped when they came across the desert

> . . . [after rain] had been just enough to wash out all the automobile tracks so one road looked just as much travelled as another. There were no sign boards so we followed a wagon track, which gave us a sense of security, as in all probability it would lead to somewhere. The roads were the roughest I have ever travelled over, except for one fine stretch of ten miles across a dry lake.

When the two women finally arrived at a supply depot for shepherds, the "man in charge gave us a fine supper of ham and eggs . . . pleased to meet Miss Martin." Long noted that the day had been "a drive of eighty miles between ranches and we saw no other automobile, in fact no other living thing except a herd of wild horses."[135] On the same trip, Martin wired Vernon that they had "lost their way" between Coal Valley and Ely in the blistering desert heat.[136]

Returning to more comfortable Reno for the end of the campaign, Martin staged a closing meeting at the smaller Rialto theater in Reno, speaking herself about the major points of her program, and letting the final and climactic speech come from Parley Parker Christensen, presidential candidate for the Farmer Labor party. Christensen claimed to be for her, "strong as horseradish," and had carried on a long correspondence with her over the months between the April opening and November end of the campaign. He was willing enough: he canceled two other meetings to appear for her, only to arrive minutes before the Reno meeting.[137]

The last few days were hectic ones. One man wrote to claim that Henderson men were "combing the tenderloin," gathering up voters in "gambling houses, pool rooms, and questionable resorts." He wondered how, if Reno had 12,000 people, there could be 8,000 voters, "with 3,000 schoolchildren, 300 Indians, 3,000 aliens, 1,000 divorcees subtracted" and urged careful poll watching, a habit feminists had learned in the suffrage campaigns.[138] The ever faithful Charlotte Perkins Gilman made several appearances, cutting her price for Martin.

When the results were in, the total for Martin was only 378 votes greater than in 1918, but the other results and their significance were quite different. Oddie won with 11,550 over Henderson's 10,402, Martin's 4,603, and 710 for the Socialist candidate Martin Scanlon. Martin's 1918 votes were hard to assign to either party, and she only guessed when she claimed to have cut into both parties. But in 1920, as Loren Chan, biographer of Republican Tasker Oddie explained, her vote may have helped defeat Henderson and elect Oddie, who was backed by Wingfield. "Her most impressive showings," Chan wrote, "were in Washoe [Reno] and Nye [Tonopah] counties, where she garnered 1057 and 686 votes, respectively. Had Henderson been able to capture the Martin votes in those two counties, he would have been re-elected and Oddie's political fate probably would have been finalized." Chan quoted in support of his views the *Pioche Record,* which characterized Martin's followers as "die-hard, thinking progressives in the state who were deceived neither by Oddie's racism and reactionary superpatriotism nor by Henderson's campaigning on the virtues of Wilson's Fourteen Points."[139] While Martin made clear to the press that Oddie ran far behind Coolidge in the election,[140] she gave credit to her support from labor in Washoe County for splitting Henderson's vote.[141] *Labor,* national publication of the Plumb Plan league for nationalized railroads, agreed. In spite of it all, Martin claimed, labor groups in those counties, miners and railway craft workers, "split Henderson's vote."[142] She also considered the "Republican landslide" important in defeating the "democratic reactionary" rather than the "Republican reactionary." Still, ever the lady, she told her Washington friend, "You will undoubtedly meet Senator Elect Oddie and his wife when they come to Washington. They are very pleasant people."[143]

The *San Francisco Call,* once a supporter of her aims, grumbled that she had "defeated an incumbent and put a reactionary in his place . . . an action as simple as that of the mice who elected a white cat after being persuaded that all that was wrong was the color of the incumbent black cat as king."[144]

Some agreement, then, exists on the effect of Martin's 1920 effort, so much like the 1918 one, but perhaps more important in its results in that she possibly did affect the outcome of the election, though not exactly in the way she expected to. Her techniques remained essentially the same in both campaigns, although the second involved more men as active workers and a more determined approach to labor, both in platform and in the direct appeals of the literature.

As before, the Nevada press managed to connect her with radical elements. With a few exceptions, however, the attack was less personal. In place of allegations of being "an abandoned creature" (claims spread orally then), questions of her "masculine" nature began to circulate enough that a friendly editor felt called upon to defend her and her associates. Charles Dick of the *Fernley Enterprise* answered those rumors carefully, asserting she was "an unassuming woman whose whole soul and earnest sympathy were with the home and fireside . . . the *Enterprise* glories in her nerve and untiring effort . . . Anne Martin, Dr. Long, Mabel Vernon and others are the highest types of American womanhood, regardless of insidious insinuations."[145]

The platform in 1920 presented new problems. While few seemed particularly concerned about what Martin said she believed in 1918 (that try had the newness of a woman's boldness to pass over all other obstacles), the moneyed women on whom she relied for support shied away from so radical a program. Martin's call for blanket legislation to remove all discrimination against women contained the seeds of the Equal Rights Amendment, which split feminists into two warring camps in the decade to follow. Some women, like Mary Dreier, fearing the loss of protective laws, refused support on that account, even though Martin insisted, "We are really standing for the same things, welfare and equal opportunity for women."[146] While Martin's attacks on vaguely defined forces of "big business" and land interests appealed to labor, she did not find a clear point of difference with Henderson; her more sharply progressive proposals offended some possible supporters among the wealthy.

But her support of the Sheppard-Towner Act became one of her most effective appeals. Because she had received national publicity when she testified for it and had published articles that supported it, she had shown something stronger than talk, something more acceptable than brave if misguided picketing of the White House. Form letters to heads of women's groups emphasized the demand that women save the mothers and babies and caught attention with a comparison of the requested four million dollars for Sheppard-Towner and "47 million appropriated for the protection of cattle, hogs, and plants."[147] She drove home the unwillingness of men to assume responsibility when she reminded Nevada women that when she and others had testified to a committee that included thirty members, "we spoke to half a dozen elderly men that were clearly bored."[148]

In 1920 she made more specific appeals to women, taking a new direction once suffrage had been ratified. "Women are half the people," a paid newspaper article argued. "Their unpaid labor in the home earns half their family's support. Women create half the wealth, yet only men govern us and make the conditions under which we live and work." She asked women of both parties, "women first," to use their political power for "women and children rather than for the success of any party."[149]

Anne Martin assumed that women would support her as a woman and that both men and women would find her a champion of certain principles. In this assumption were certain basic contradictions, both in the way Martin and her supporters viewed women and in the ways the majority of men and women did. Both groups agreed that women were inherently, biologically, essentially different; they agreed that woman's skills were the protective, nurturant, maternal qualities that had sent them into those acceptable occupations that were extensions of the motherly work—teaching, social work, nursing. In fact, suffrage arguments insisted the effect of woman's vote upon the electorate would be to restrain vice, clean up the country, reform the masculine world. Both opponents and proponents of the vote for women accepted the view that politics was a male preserve that, to suffragists, was in need of ordering; to antisuffragists, politics was a jungle that would coarsen the female who entered. What women called "vicious interests"—liquor dealers, for example—combated the vote because they, too, agreed on what female intentions would be, what female moral leadership would demand.[150] They were all wrong.

Sheppard-Towner slipped by because politicians still believed in a woman vote that was to be tried for the first time in 1921. Experience in Reno had hinted that women would not necessarily vote when the new voters had not banded together to fight gambling, liquor, and divorce laws in 1915, but such a demonstration could easily be discounted by someone like Martin when it had come so shortly after suffrage in a state with such limited sources of income that it was beginning to develop vice as its livelihood. The same women who felt their right to the vote quite sincerely and worked for it steadily had to make great advances in thinking to be as strongly persuaded as Anne Martin that electing a woman was an important next step.

The women who had listened to her in 1919 at the Republican conference had given her some warning when they had responded more vigorously and enthusiastically to a male speaker's call for them to support the party program than to her charge to use their new power to "frame and force" a woman's program of their own.[151] Then she had called such a reaction "instinctive," expecting that women's "political humility and subjection [would] continue as long as their economic subjection."[152] Yet she expected Nevada women to vote for her on the basis of her gender when women already defined as politically minded were only politely interested in the idea of female action in politics.

She had to persuade both men and women to accept both the idea of her candidacy—that a woman was more capable than a man of tending to women's business—and herself as the particular woman who could act for them as the political representative of her state. But she had as well to convince both that she was something more than a woman, that she was a politician who could move effectively in the Washington world. Woman politician, or more precisely in the language of the day, lady politician, may have seemed a contradiction in terms.

Anne Martin needed to sell herself as well as her program. In 1918 she was hesitant to do this, in view of the Nevada editors' objection to her militant suffrage background and their insistence on making that an issue while conveniently ignoring her leadership in 1914. While her lobbying experience seemed important to her, whatever accomplishments she had shown as an organizer were eclipsed by the association, unfortunate for the political atmosphere when she ran, with the National Woman's Party. In 1918, the superpatriotism of the noisy small town editors, rankled by the 1916 campaign against President Wilson, found her an easy target. In 1920, when the state and the nation as well had made an abrupt about-face on the Democrats, she did not manage to break the gender barrier or appeal with issues to attract more than a few voters. Speculation about who those five thousand voters were is just that—speculation. She could not have done so well in White Pine County and in Reno without labor support; she could not have attracted the body of women voters without doing better. The tiny showing for the Socialist candidate, who campaigned hardly at all, suggests her votes came from working men, if the sense of her workers was anywhere near correct.[153]

Certain kinds of women clearly supported her. Those who wrote to Mabel Vernon or to Martin herself repeatedly asserted their faith in Martin as a representative of women and as a particularly able woman. Most were women of some means, married to prominent men. But others were like Theresa Carlson of Tonopah, a Socialist and a miner's wife, who worked steadily and wrote early in the campaign:

> The strike last year opened our eyes to conditions in this state, and the same forces that defeated you are arrayed against us . . . the miners are with us women and we will help you, provided of course that you are on our side. Some of us were on the "soap box" last summer, and are willing to stump the state for you.[154]

While Carlson's support of Martin both as woman and friend of the working class is exceptional, other women clearly saw Martin as their chosen delegate to speak for women and women's concerns. Pearl Karaus, a teacher, was typical of those; employed women generally backed her as well. Some supporters were professional like Dr. Nellie Hascall and Dr. Marie Michel. The latter identified closely with the candidate, and, asking Martin to overlook her poor English, wrote with more feeling than grammar:

> . . . your labor will not be lost, it is an education to the general public for tomorrow—I am certain of it . . . inspite of it all, I feel mentally serren as a gloriouse morning of june, so, keep up your nerves, and someday see you ambition realized, with an army of old soldiers just like me behind you . . . keep yourself always on redeness . . .[155]

Clearly drawn to Martin as a fellow fighter, Michel supported Martin as a champion of changing conditions that had marked her own life. Others saw her as willing and capable of correcting wrongs. A Mrs. Simmons of Caliente, worried about "depraved children" in her town, about the thriving red-light district, complaining that there "isn't a man that holds a job that will do his duty . . . I want to do it so doggone dry that they can spit cotton."[156] These particular correspondents reflect concerns that may have attracted women to vote for her, but it is clear that the mass of Nevada women did not feel the same.

Anne Martin, probably not as serene as a glorious morning after her defeat, understood to some degree what had happened in the campaign and wrote an article, never published, to explain it. She offered a number of reasons for her defeat: only twelve thousand women were eligible to vote and not all of them voted; she "started at scratch" while opponents had a head start; she needed $2,000 more; the transient character of the working population cost her votes. Much of this was true. But her major explanation rested on women not voting for her. Did anyone expect, she asked, the women "to vote for me simply because they find a woman's name on ballot?" Yet she wrote that women would "vote for women and principle if we can only help them *see* it," and insisted that her sex was "less controlled by party discipline, less subject to 'gang' or party rule." She saw her efforts as a test, finally admitting that "it would have been a miracle if I had been elected in view of the handicaps of the campaign." Although she made fewer claims in 1920 to any sort of victory, she saw the next task as one to educate and organize women for the kind of political participation she thought essential, for the "sex solidarity" that became her goal in the years after suffrage.[157] She had come to believe that women would have to learn to vote as a bloc to be effective equals in the political world.

Martin would probably have agreed with Harriot Stanton Blatch, who had warned that "we must make our minds up that altho all sorts and conditions of women were united for suffrage, that political end has been gained, and they are not at one in their attitude towards other questions in life."[158] Blatch's reaction to this perception was to put all of her efforts into the work of the Socialist party; Martin's was to run for office a second time, perhaps aware that her candidacy was doomed, but stubborn enough to keep her promise to try again, naive enough to hope that she could secure the Republican nomination in a state notorious for its political chicanery.[159]

Anne Martin's determination and ambition to pursue not just one but two challenges to entrenched power may well have resulted from the conflict of the two worlds in which she lived during the years between suffrage and her first campaign and between the first and the second. She spent very little time in Nevada from 1914 on, a fact not particularly

distinctive for a Nevada politician. But while such men as Senator
Francis Newlands, Senator Key Pittman, and Senator Charles Henderson spent little time at home, when they returned they were accepted
members of a male community of politicians, one that had its internal
rivalries or interparty conflicts, but one that knew its initiates. Anne
Martin's Nevada world was a female one that included the small number
of professional women, most of the women who were organized into
clubs of some sort, longtime family acquaintances, and a few male labor
leaders—not one of whom was in any way qualified to offer sound
political advice, provided Martin had sought it. She had managed by
1918 to lose many of the women who had supported her in the suffrage
effort in the petty battles between the Women's Civic League and the
Woman Citizens Club, and the 1916 campaign against Wilson had
alienated even more of the women she needed. Senator Henderson could
afford to start his campaign well into October; Martin needed far more
than the head start she gave herself to win Nevada voters. She had some
contact with Nevada officeholders, but correspondence suggests she
asked few for advice beyond clarifying legal technicalities for her filing
of petitions or legislative advice on the irrigation bill. She relied on her
female Nevada world that was still young at politics, removed from
men's councils.

Anne Martin's other world centered around Washington, around the
widening circles of American feminists, a very different world that she
found new and daring. Especially in the NWP, but in other contacts as
well, she moved among women with large visions of what women could
do, women eager to see themselves as independent movers in a new
world that would offer equal opportunity if they worked hard for it.
Crystal Eastman and Inez Milholland were attorneys, Alice Paul and
Lucy Burns educated sociologists, Charlotte Perkins Gilman a self-
educated powerhouse of a woman with a vision well ahead of the times.
Through writer Mary Austin, her longtime friend from days in England,
Martin expanded her acquaintance to the fringes of Greenwich Village
Bohemia. Inez Irwin, the NWP's dedicated historian, and Doris
Stevens, a member of the NWP lobbying team, gave Martin entry into
the small but noisy community of New York and Washington liberals
where Martin became friendly with Dudley Field Malone and with
Roger Baldwin, both powers in the American Civil Liberties Union in
later years, who respected her enough to invite her to join the first
national board. Through Mrs. J. A. H. Hopkins she met and joined the
Committee of 48 in its 1920 effort to organize a third party. In the
Women's Peace party, later the Women's International League for

Peace and Freedom, she associated with the most respected woman in America, Jane Addams. Her personal acquaintance included women at the front of social reform in unions, consumer protection, welfare, and journalism. That was an intoxicating air to breathe in such company where women full of hope saw a new world just beyond their grasp.

The eastern world told her that change was imminent and that women could bring it faster, that the cause was the center of an existence. The Nevada world was distressingly familiar after suffrage: women accepted the vote as they accepted the automobile—a new contraption yet to prove itself indispensable. To move beyond that acceptance to united action, to see themselves immediately as a power group separate from the protection of the male was beyond their power, either in Nevada or elsewhere. While the eastern women of the vigorous feminist circles hoped idealistically for a new age, the vast majority of women continued business as usual.

Rose Schniederman, a union leader and a friend of Martin, echoed Martin's own grudging explanation some years after when questioned about the voting record of women:

> I am just as disappointed in women's suffrage as I am in men's suffrage . . . Women have done very little in four years of voting, but men have done tragically little in a hundred and fifty years. Why suddenly demand that women do the outstanding thing which we've given up expecting from men?[160]

To suggest that Martin might have done any better in either campaign if she had spent all of her time in her home state until she ran for office is to assume that Nevada women would have acted as few women do now. Caught up in the excitement of progress and hope in the East, Anne Martin hoped for more than Nevada women or other American women could give.

At the beginning of her first campaign, Anne Martin announced that she wanted to "knock the fear out of the hearts of women. Even if I should not win, it will never seem so strange again when a woman tries it."[161] She perhaps overclaimed her goal: Jeannette Rankin had won national office in 1916 and had run for the Senate herself in 1918, declaring some weeks after Martin had. What happened to Martin may have had the opposite effect: she endured highly personal attacks that might have daunted others.

Anne Martin's courage is unquestioned; her motives are less certain. The courage is documented in the record; the motives must remain conjectural only. Perhaps she was deluded to hope for victory, especially during the second try. Whatever her intentions, her delusions, her mistakes, she made two sincere and stubborn efforts to rally women around a woman candidate; she dared and she gave all of her energies to a decade of campaigns, including state suffrage and the federal amendment, two hardy pursuits of the Senate. If she failed as a politician, she succeeded as a valiant battler against the odds. The second campaign was not the end of her life in politics, but it was the end of its most active phase, the last act on the national scene. That she continued to work for principles, to support her loved causes, most of all to continue to strive for the advancement of women in small ways and large support the sincerity of her lost venture in the male world of political action.

CHAPTER 9

DR. ANNE MARTIN

Persistent Feminist, Worker for Peace

She has done more for the women of Nevada than any other person.
—Nevada legislator, 1947

AFTER THE VOTES were in, after the concessions were made, after the supporters left Reno, Anne Martin might well have felt her political life was ended. Her second effort to enter the Senate had exhausted her funds and her friends' patience. Even the most hopeful of candidates must have seen long before the end that the story would not change the second time, must have realized that while the impact of her support could perhaps be measured in Tasker Oddie's election in a rarely close contest, she would not succeed. If stubbornness and a sense of obligation had reinforced her second decision to run, no similar forces could draw from her an offer to try again. But the long campaigning had not weakened her belief in the need for women in politics and if suffrage was accomplished there were other directions for her energies. No one knew quite what to expect from the new woman voters and Martin, like many others, was eager to see what might happen next to influence the choices. She went to work promptly as a writer, first to respond to the forces she felt had hampered her own efforts, later to push the concept of sex solidarity that became her goal for the rest of her life. And she turned to the cause of peace that she had found too dangerous for public embrace in her time as a candidate.

Martin left Nevada after the 1920 defeat, a defeat no less disappointing because it seemed to have had more political effect on the state. Republican Oddie and many more of his party headed for Washington; Anne Martin moved with her mother to Carmel, California, the seaside city that had been a favored vacation spot for years.

Both public and private records suggest that it was Louise Martin who determined the move should be made, Anne having little part in the decision. Vague references in the notes for the autobiography refer to a "collapse," understandable enough after so long a strain; an article written many years later recalls that "shortly after her defeat Miss Martin was taken to Carmel-by-the-Sea" by her mother[1] and Martin suggested a passive role in a 1938 diary entry: "Why did Clara [a younger sister] allow me to be taken from my life work in 1921 when the Reno home was sold and be exiled in Carmel?" Her always autobiographical poetry included a frequently reworked quatrain addressed to her mother:

> I told her I must go or die,
> Must leave this lonely valley
> That took and gave me nothing back
> My Life a gray blind alley.[2]

Whether Nevada was a "life work" or a "gray blind alley," Martin left, but she never moved her voter registration and she returned with the regularity of an unwilling child duty bound to a stern parent.

If there was a collapse it was a short one: by March Martin had published a first article in the *Nation* and a second one followed in the *New Republic* in July. While the first was a defensive complaint about the divided reaction of Nevada labor to her candidacy, the second blamed "woman's inferiority complex" for the failure of the sex to seize its new power to advance, to demand the political power it could own.[3] Martin took pains in the first to refute the claims of *Labor* magazine that she had been the tool of Republicans who had accomplished "what the reactionaries hoped for—the defeat of Henderson." *Labor*'s support of Henderson, in contrast to Nevada union support of Martin, seemed to Martin to indicate not, as the publication claimed, that "workers [should not] permit their gallantry to override their common sense," but that, as Martin asserted, "they cannot trust their leaders."[4] But while her interest in labor remained, her lasting concerns with political power emerged most strongly in the first of a series of articles she wrote to advance yet another long campaign to urge women to elect women, to take the power of the vote in hand and go against the male bastions, leaving behind the "woman's inferiority complex" of her title.

"If we could only change our opinion of ourselves," she argued, "our shackles would drop off instantly." Woman's lack of faith in herself lets her endure double standards that demean her. After a spate of the ever present personal references, Martin urged sex solidarity among women who had learned as much from life as men had "in the muddy pool of party politics." The iron had entered women's souls, she thought, and they were shaking off the complex, preparing to remove remaining discriminations and participate equally in government.[5]

No matter how Martin longed for change, the minds of women were not unified around any single purpose, even though no one was quite sure about that in 1921. Alice Paul and the National Woman's Party had opened the first decade of American women's enfranchisement with a massive meeting to which they had invited representatives of all the major women's organizations to present their ideas for unified action. That meeting proved as clearly as any gathering could that there was no equal temper of feminine minds, but rather a widening abyss between the NWP and the larger NAWSA group, already formed into a nonpartisan, educational organization, the League of Women Voters.[6] While Sara Bard Field spoke with hope of revolution, nothing happened. Instead, three "full days of dull meetings" avoided all doubtful subjects, "like birth control and the rights of negro women," Crystal Eastman complained.[7]

The NWP, already convinced that a second amendment to remove all discrimination was the correct course, remained a single-issue feminist organization; the other women's groups went their separate ways, pursuing separate goals. In its singlemindedness, the NWP stepped with its traditional vigor from the mainstream of organized women to remain outside for many years until the revitalized women's movement brought the women back to the ERA, not the party back to the women.[8]

Anne Martin found herself cut off from both the purist feminism of the NWP and from the conservative, nonpartisan policies of the League of Women Voters, transformed from NAWSA with very little change in policy. She did not support ERA until well into the forties, for she felt that women should grasp equality themselves, not ask it of men; women should organize to take political power, not seek a favor as they had been forced to beg suffrage. She could accept neither the restrained tone of the LWV nor the more strident demands of the NWP. She hoped for a united voting force of determined women, united to reform, to clean up the nation. She worked, then, essentially alone. Even though she kept in touch with the NWP and on occasion would offer it her aid, she spoke for most of the decade as a separate voice with a single aim—sex solidarity.

In the first months following ratification, the Congress of the United States feared and Martin hoped that women would think and vote together. No one knew that women would not (as so many had assumed they might) clean up vice and corruption, take over moral leadership, and polish up the nation in short order, like a harried, hurried housewife impatient with the mess left by men. Many believed, as William Chafe put it, that "pure in spirit, selfless in motivation, and dedicated to the preservation of human society, female voters would remake society and turn government from war and corruption." To do this, Chafe continued, "they had to vote together, organize on the basis of sex, and demonstrate a collective allegiance to common ideals and programs."[9]

At first the kind of cooperation demonstrated in the Women's Joint Congressional Committee promised true female unity in pressuring Congress for reform. The Sheppard-Towner Act, passed by a worried male Congress and signed into law in 1921, drew support from women of all persuasions and produced the first victory. A modest effort to reduce infant and maternal mortality, the act provided small sums to states to encourage prenatal and postnatal care, open consultation centers, provide visiting nurses, and, in some cases, pay for hospital care. Some days as many as fifty congressmen met determined women in their offices for interviews encouraging action on the bill. According to Stanley Lemons, "fear of being punished at the polls" was the principal force moving for passage, for the women's vote "was an unknown quantity at the time." Not surprisingly, the only woman in Congress during the session, antisuffragist Alice Robertson, voted against it and claimed that most women would oppose it if they were well informed.[10]

When the bill passed, everyone wanted credit for it. Anne Martin always boasted she had been a prime mover, even though her articles in 1919 were the last apparent contribution she made and others did the final lobbying. Carrie Chapman Catt claimed success for the League of Women Voters. But the coalition of the WJCC and the efforts of top women on national committees of both political parties had mattered considerably. Both Maud Wood Park and Florence Kelley of the WJCC resented Catt's claim. Quibbles erupted into squabbles. The Sheppard-Towner Act did not last out the decade; indeed, for a while it became the focus of Red baiters who saw in it the "beginning of Communism in Medicine."[11] But women's potential power, for a very short time, had shaken Congress into action.

As the men on the Hill soon learned, they had little to fear. Although there were small victories through the WJCC in consumer protection, citizenship laws, child labor and civil service legislation, the unified power women needed and Congress feared never materialized. What did come was a growing rift between feminists and the social reformers.[12]

Feminists argued that logic demanded equality, which, once achieved, would improve the lot of everyone; there would be no need for piece-meal, special legislation; men and women and children would all be protected in a truly egalitarian society; protections won for women would be extended to men. Not so, argued the reformers: women needed the protections they had won; special legislation could not be sacrificed to an ideal of equality. Such NWP stalwarts as Florence Kelley of the Women's Trade Union League and the WJCC left the party over the issue; others followed suit.[13]

Anne Martin took her own stand, neither supporting NWP's federal amendment nor rejecting it out of hand, but pushing for women to take power through election at all levels. Suitably, "Feminine Solidarity" was the title for her talk early in 1921 to the National Association of Bank Women[14] and she pursued her argument in a number of publications. But just as her own goals changed, so did those of the woman voter. Martin never deserted the cause of sex solidarity, but her audiences dissolved as professional women pursued more specific issues. The very bank women who heard her in 1921 had begun to concentrate on shop talk by the end of the decade; Martin herself found more use for her energies in the Women's International League for Peace and Freedom as the years passed. At the beginning, however, peace and feminism seemed comfortable partners for her mind and energy.

When she left the country in 1921 with Mabel Vernon, she went with dual intentions: to visit other women throughout Europe to talk about peace and to reestablish her publishing contacts and write more articles for the English and American press. Vernon emphasized the nature of the trip (one financed by the sale of some of Martin's stocks) as one to meet Alida Heyman and Anita Augsburg, leaders of WILPF, and Gertrude Bauer, a member of the Reichstag.[15] Jane Addams' letters had introduced her to those women who led the peace cause in Europe.[16] Whatever the dual intentions of the trip, Martin's greatest success in publishing came from other topics. Only one article, "Jane Addams' Work for Peace" in *Time and Tide*,[17] responded to the trip.

But 1922 was a successful year for her as a writer, perhaps the best she had, with multiple publications on both sides of the Atlantic. Most of the work dealt with the sex solidarity theme; one was part of a series collected in a book. While the first made clear her feminist stand, the last effectively cut her off from Nevada politics for many years to come, for

it was seen as a libel on the state. Ironically, her success as a writer only
served to isolate her from the comfort of groups she had enjoyed before:
feminist organizations and Nevadans. While the appeals for sex solidarity did not antagonize other groups, they clearly reflected a separate
view from those other women expressed, however much they may have
agreed.

Recognizing the direction taken by the League of Women Voters to
"train for citizenship" and the NWP for a "blanket bill" to remove
discrimination, Martin insisted that "equality laws will not and cannot
equalize, any more than declaring the earth flat can make it flat. But the
process of winning a half share in government will go a long way toward
developing a sense of equality in the minds and hearts of women." And
then, she believed, "the laws will take care of themselves." It was time
for women's organizations to endorse candidates, to unify, to "march
together toward Government itself, bastioned and buttressed against
them."[18] Those bastions and buttresses shielded what she called in
another piece "sex aristocracy." Writing in the *English Review,* a
respected organ that published in the same month works by H. G. Wells
and D. H. Lawrence, Martin sought a legal system that would be
"humanised . . . when women as legislators remake laws, as lawyers
interpret them, as judges apply them, as jurors render verdicts."[19] To
bolster her argument, she offered examples of continuing discrimination
against women that had sturdily survived the granting of suffrage: loss
of citizenship upon marriage to a foreigner, a double standard for sex
offenses that saw "women punished heavily, while the men with them
suffered light penalties or none at all," acceptance of inferior status in
the professions. Joining men's political parties did no good if women
believed themselves inferior: "They do not see that when swallowed up
in parties they are powerless." Only direct action—actual and equal
participation in government—would end discrimination.[20]

Ideas in this article and in a slightly different version of it published in
Sunset magazine are very close. Martin was referring to this piece when
she claimed in another work, "Women and Their Magazines," that
editors refused to print serious feminist thinking.

As Martin saw American feminism, it was headed in the wrong
direction or, perhaps, two wrong directions. English women had seized
their opportunities better. Although history proved that neither nation
was ready for female equality, Martin thought the British course more
encouraging. The Woman's Freedom League had as its goal three
hundred women in Parliament, she noted, and various factions of the
English suffragist force had forgotten their differences.[21] In a longer

article in the *New York Times Magazine,* she offered more evidence of English cooperation as example for American separation, arguing for the direct action, the direct support of candidates that she saw as the surest and fastest way to equality.

England's Consultative Committee of Women's Organizations headed by American-born Lady Astor was showing the way; that coalition could in no way be compared to the WJCC with its "conservative" insistence on legislation rather than legislators. Observing the differences, Martin found herself feeling that "England is the 'new' world and America the 'old.' " Englishwomen's efforts made no great impact on British parliamentary government, but to Martin they represented the kind of response she saw as essential if American women were ever to gain power in the political world. Englishwomen, she wrote, were not theorizing about equality but were "going out and taking it, backed by the power, the organizers and the funds of their societies."[22] While England's women worked for election, American women's groups were "comparatively so short sighted and dull in action that it is difficult to discuss them without prejudice . . . [for] both apparently still believe that equality can be legislated."[23]

Martin hoped to find new audiences for her beliefs in a book-length manuscript she tentatively called "Woman Today and Woman Tomorrow." Typically, however, her aspirations outran her application. While she proposed a few new articles, the bulk of the proposed work would come from reprints of articles and from speeches already composed. She did write some new material, but most of what she offered publishers came from pieces she had written but not placed before. Still, the ideas were few and frequently repeated, the examples all too similar, the personal bitterness often apparent, always latent. Her sincere belief in woman's potential was strongly tied to her waning faith in her own, for she saw herself as exemplar of women's plight in some ways, as one of a small body of advanced women at other times. Most women, she wrote, saw the world through blinders, self-imposed blindfolds; their minds were bound with manacles forged by their own man-influenced thinking: "when women know and feel their real status (laws or no laws), then and not until then will they *take equality* and secure a half share in government and the affairs of life."[24]

Most women, she believed, were easily led by the press. Perhaps goaded by the lack of interest women's magazines had shown in the articles she tried to sell them, she charged that such publications talked down to women and treated feminists unfairly. The fiction in them was "soothing syrup" to augment the "raw narcotics" of editorial policy determined by men. "It is the policy," she wrote, "of the 'home' magazines to keep women, or a majority of them where they are." Even basic interests were ignored, she claimed, by a magazine who "soft-pedalled in its columns the importance of breast feeding . . . Perhaps because of the lucrative advertisements of prepared milk and baby foods the magazine was carrying?" While Martin longed for a "generation of woman engineers to tackle the job of household engineering," men who controlled the magazines offered repeated images of women in a single role—housewife. Constant hammering on the homemaker role aimed to keep women satisfied with their inferior status as housewives, as "brakes and parasites on the woman's movement."[25] Yet she had sympathy with the young wives of University of California professors, women who could not afford babies because their husbands' salaries were too low.[26]

Only one article in the year moved to a subject other than feminism. That one may have removed any chances she may have had to re-enter Nevada politics, for she managed to antagonize just about everyone in conservative Nevada with her contribution to the *Nation* series, *These United States*. Martin was in good company for the series: H. L. Mencken, William Allen White, Edmund Wilson, and Dorothy Canfield Fisher were among those contributing articles on their home states. Although some Nevadans must have agreed that the Silver State was the "Beautiful Desert of Buried Hopes" she called it in her title, she spoke candidly of the state's position. Nevada was "the ugly duckling, the disappointment, the neglected step-child, the weakling in the family of States, despite her charm and beauty and great natural advantages." Like the heroine from the nineties ballad, however, Nevada was more to be pitied than censured and, the author argued, men were the cause of all her troubles.[27]

Echoing words from her suffrage campaigns, Martin deplored the maleness of the state and the state of those males: she deprecated the legalized prostitution and the proportionately high population of jails and prisons. Admitting that exploitation by mining interests might explain much of the sorry state of her state, Martin insisted angrily that the monopoly of the livestock industry and its control over the water supply was the source of most of the evil. Nevada's legal prostitution was flaunted in "redlight districts surrounded by high-board fences, to the children of the town," while homeless men "wandered to spread the social canker." Pointing to Utah as a state that had shown how the desert could bloom with the right sort of leadership, Martin was saddened that Nevada lay victim of "servile legislatures, migratory lawmakers, adventurers in high office." To endure, she argued, Nevada had to develop "natural resources for the good of all, instead of gutting them for the enrichment of a few, to the ultimate injury of all." If not, Nevada would continue to lie "inert and hopeless, like an exhausted Titan in the sun—a beautiful desert of homeseekers' buried hopes."[28]

If her language was extreme, most of her facts were straight; the inferences, the implications may have had less foundation. Few could deny that Nevada's great wealth had gone elsewhere, that Comstock silver had built fortunes and factories in far cities and in San Francisco while but little remained in the land of the source. Little effort seemed directed to making that desert bloom. And as madame of the country's back room, the national mecca for divorcees and gamblers, Nevada was no lady. Still, the locals howled in response—once they found out what she had written.

Not surprisingly, no one seemed to respond at first, for almost no one of any position in the state read the *Nation*. Only when the article appeared in book form in 1923 and a hapless press agent for the publishers approached the governor about an endorsement did Nevadans know how their native daughter had, they thought, wronged them.

Governor James E. Scrugham was not willing to assist in the sale: he called the article a "gross libel" on Nevada and urged the publishers to send an impartial reporter to observe the "devoted and self-sacrificing efforts of the great body of our citizenry to conquer the handicap of adverse physical conditions imposed upon us by nature." Rumbling along with him, Emmet D. Boyle, former governor and by 1923 editor of the *Nevada State Journal,* opened his account with a familiar rude question "How old is Anne?" and continued a sarcastic presentation of the issue, addressing her throughout by first name. Extracting unrelated bits out of sequence, he blamed her for rambling and "clinging passionately to the possible one acre or less devoted to redlight districts." "Every well-regulated house," Boyle continued, had to have "plumbing arrangements but the lavatory . . . is hardly the point from which to view the household. Writing as plumbing inspectress, Anne has shown the mercy of leaving out the illustration of the sanitary fittings."[29]

Neither editor nor governor made any effort to respond to the arguments, but the tone of the responses outraged Anne Martin, then living in Carmel, informed of the ruckus by friends who mailed her copies of the story. She wrote in vigorous protest to the editor of the *Journal*. That publication did not reply, but the *Reno Evening Gazette* treated the letter as news, offering it page one prominent display and a hefty introduction that read in part: "If Miss Anne Martin were a man there might have been a fistfight between her . . . and Boyle."[30]

Martin admitted in her letter that she was "prohibited both by physique and personal distaste from a man's usual redress," but she requested that the *Journal* print her reply in full so that she could present the disputed passages without the editor's artful emendations. The *Gazette,* for once cooperative, complied. She closed with a challenge to Scrugham and Boyle to a written debate on the subject. At least one political commentator backed her appeal:

> . . . she must be given credit for her frankness, and, also it must be said that she never starts anything unless she is prepared to finish it . . . Miss Martin can take care of herself and she needs no sympathy because she is a woman. Let us have the debate. It will enlighten us.

But the "great show" envisioned by the columnist did not come about.[31] Neither Governor Scrugham nor Editor Boyle was finally willing to take her on. The matter faded from the public concern, although the flap remained in the minds of politicians to haunt her in years to come. Martin had reason at the time, however, to be pleased that the article was singled out by reviewers as one of the best in the series.

Perhaps resting on a successful year, perhaps taking her ease, Martin published nothing in 1923, but she took voluminous notes and read extensively for the proposed book-length publication, by then retitled "Woman the World Over." Still primarily based on the articles she had already published, the book was to include still more approaches to her single idea—the need for equal representation in legislative bodies. Like the suffragists who dreamed that the vote would make them free only to find that once won it was quickly ignored, Martin continued convinced that women lawmakers would pursue female interests and that those interests existed as common goals. How she could hold such a view in light of the continuing conflicts among women's organizations and the record is questionable. Had she been uninformed, such optimism might be less puzzling, but she was a steady and ardent reader of matters related to the cause, a woman who prided herself on knowing.

Various articles explored this theme and other related ones, most of them never appeared in print in full, some were pieced into other works. Few would have argued with her that there was not a commonly held "genuine feminist purpose" among those women becoming politically active. Sending women like Mrs. Alice Nolan of California, appointed to fill her husband's term, to Congress was a "triumph of machine politics," she complained in "A Sex War?"[32] In yet another effort she urged women to give their differences to the political world, offer their special qualities rather than imitate men. Arguing that women should set their own criteria for greatness and cease to conform to manmade standards, she pushed a variation of the same theme she had advanced so often: women had not really won equality until they learned to think for themselves, become actors and not supporters of men. Her position was not an entirely clear one: she both wanted women's clubs to develop as a force, as a women's bloc, and praised women for having less mob or crowd instinct; she both sought independence for American women and praised Englishwomen for being better at following their leaders, obeying their betters. Apparently following was fine if the ideas were women's ideas and the leader was a woman; aping men was not. "New political methods and forms of their own" would help women achieve political and economic equality, but Martin was mute on what those special forms or that special scheme might be.[33] Perhaps she saw the limitations in her own thinking and abandoned the work. More likely, she directed her attention elsewhere, to a renewed effort to return to politics and, when that failed, to a cause long cherished in a part of her mind, the cause of world peace.

When Senator Robert La Follette ran for president in 1924, Anne Martin thought she could forget what she had said in the past about the evils of men's parties and the dubious status of women in most organizations. Many of Martin's own ideas had grown from those advanced by the Wisconsin senator in a long career as a progressive. He had been a friend of suffrage and a supporter of legislation women wanted; even Martin's idol, Jane Addams, had become part of his organization. She eagerly offered her services as manager of the Nevada campaign. But when she wrote to offer her help, she was refused. To make matters worse, her 1918 Socialist opponent, Martin Scanlon, won the job. John M. Nelson, national manager for La Follette, was candid: "I regret very much my inability to get you into the Nevada organization . . . the old sores are not healed."[34]

Nelson saw no need to specify what those old sores had been. La Follette's support in Nevada came from many elements; Anne Martin at some time or another had offended most of them. Democrats remembered her opposition to Woodrow Wilson; Socialists assumed she had taken votes from them in 1918 and 1920; still other politicians considered her 1920 run a ploy engineered to split the vote. No one seemed to expect much from the woman voter.

But Anne Martin did not need any specification to explode. Although she could not market the article before the election, she wrote her fury into a piece asking "Will LaFollette Give Women Equality?" Her answer was, of course, a NO in thunder. "'Ladies entrance' will be the only open door," she insisted.[35] By the time she had found a publisher, the election was over and her anger somewhat cooled as she exposed what she saw as La Follette's folly. He had run better than expected in the state. As Martin saw it, "the Nevada election returns show that LaFollette would have carried the state by a turnover of only about 700 votes from Coolidge." She reminded readers that she had predicted as much in July and claimed that her participation could have made the crucial difference "through the money and organizers I planned to bring into Nevada, and by our vigorous, intensive methods of campaigning." She had, she boasted, outdrawn the Socialists by very large margins in both of her campaigns.[36]

La Follette's foolishness, she was sure, merely demonstrated once again that women would find no help from men's political parties. The "male dragon" in the feminist path was a monster inability to allow women to work as equals. In answer, women should follow other oppressed minorities and organize as a separate political force. They must achieve equality by the straightest route ("sex solidarity in action—just as solid as men's") expressed through the channels of women's organizations. Until that force materialized, noncooperation should be the response to male appeals for help—no auxiliaries, no ladies' aid societies, but a unity of female action to advance toward their "modest goal of half share in government . . . and life."[37]

Her continued harping on what she saw as their organizational weaknesses irritated her old friends in the NWP; actually, they did endorse some female candidates, but only shortly before elections. Showing no partiality, she scolded Carrie Chapman Catt and the LWV for advising women to work within extant parties. By 1925 she had waved her banner of sex solidarity in person and in print without result. Few women were elected to Congress, even fewer were supported, financed, or encouraged by women's organizations of any sort. She had made a stalwart effort; she had spoken her piece.

She joined others of the National Woman's Party in an effort to win acceptance of feminism's wayward child at the International Woman Suffrage Alliance (IWSA) meeting in Paris in 1926, but she played only a minor role.[38]

Martin had continued a grudging interest in the party, if only to oppose it; she kept her personal friendship with Sara Bard Field and

Mabel Vernon, responding to their concerns even though she did not return to the fold. But in 1926 she assumed a new responsibility that confirmed a new direction for her energies when she became an organizer for the Women's International League for Peace and Freedom.

In no way did she desert the cause of feminism: on any occasion she was willing to talk, to write, to give her name to causes that advanced equality for women. And her interest in what were then termed liberal or radical causes never flagged. As a member for many years of the national board of the American Civil Liberties Union she watched closely the developments in a number of major controversies. Dudley Field Malone, husband of Doris Stevens from the NWP and an old friend, was a lawyer for the Scopes "Monkey Trial," and she followed closely the trials of an old suffrage acquaintance Charlotte Anita Whitney in her many skirmishes with the law in the Red-baiting twenties.[39]

As far back as 1915 Anne Martin had been interested in the Women's Peace Party (WPP) organized that year by Jane Addams, even though Martin did not attend the meetings. Intent on her work with the Congressional Union and NWP, she found by 1918 that her candidacy precluded her joining such a group, but she was close to many of the women who formed the first group that expanded to form WILPF[40] and there had even been Nevada efforts that had failed to excite interest.[41]

By 1926, WILPF and its leader, Jane Addams, were under attack from such groups as the Daughters of the American Revolution, the National Association of Manufacturers, and the American Medical Association, the latter having seen pink in women's organizations in its continuing fight against the Sheppard-Towner Act, still controversial. Martin was not likely to be put off by public charges like that from R. M. Whitney, author of *The Reds in America,* who had described a WILPF meeting as "dominated by the spirit of Russian communism," nor by Addams' position at the top of the notorious Spider Web chart that claimed to reveal insidious connections among women's groups.[42] On her trip to Europe in 1922, Martin had met many leaders in the movement and had thanked Addams for her help: "the WILPF women were by far the most human and far-seeing we have met."[43] In the same year, Martin had offered to help after reading Addams' *The Long Road of Woman's Memory* had made her "understand so much better the basis of your wish for peace—your reasons for hoping that woman can be a big help in ending war."[44]

Shortly after the international suffrage meeting in Paris, Martin went as a delegate to the Dublin conference of WILPF, invited by Addams herself, before returning to the Continent and Geneva where the League of Nations was meeting. As she told a reporter some years later, "That meeting so thoroughly aroused my interest in its purpose that I . . . decided to spend my effort at home working for a constructive and Christian cause."[45] She offered her services, but she declined to work continuously, citing family responsibilities for her restraint. Although WILPF paid minimal travel expenses, Martin worked without salary. At the beginning she was successful, bringing in two hundred new members and $500 on her first recruiting trip in Denver and New Mexico, and she made plans for starting organizations in Nevada, Arizona, Oregon, and Washington.[46] In addition to doing the organizational work, she had placed an article on the Dublin meeting in the *Nation* that outlined the ambitious aims of the league:

> . . . to unite the women in all countries who are opposed to every kind of war, exploitation, and oppression, and who work for international disarmament and for the solution of conflicts by the recognition of human solidarity, by conciliation and arbitration, by world cooperation, and by the establishment of social, political, and economic justice of all, without distinction of sex, race, class, or creed.

The women opposed armament and conscription, seeking "complete and universal disarmament," but they extended their interests beyond peace to protection and preservation of minority groups within nations and to education of the world's youth.[47]

Martin's involvement in the peace movement was of a different sort than her previous efforts: her motives were the same as they had been in 1909 when she consciously sought a means to serve. The choice was guided as much by friendship as anything. She had admired Addams all of her life, and she could find comfort in like thinkers in the group. But her work was essentially out of the spotlight, removed from the centers of attraction. Although she attended the international congresses for many years and was once nominated for international office, she never became a leader of importance in the national movement. True, she contributed more than the women who merely paid dues and attended occasional meetings, but her efforts are in no way comparable to the full-time attention and dogged effort of her earlier endeavors for the NWP, for her own campaigns, for her writing for sex solidarity.

Martin's restrictions upon her activities as organizer were mostly self-imposed. She found time for travel, often in conjunction with her work for WILPF, but just as often on her own or in the company of Dr. Margaret Long, the familiar "Doc" who had driven her thousands of miles in her various campaigns. On trips to Europe it was Mabel Vernon who was the most frequent companion, Vernon herself being involved with first the NWP and later WILPF as speaker and organizer. Although Vernon found Martin's club in London "hoity-toity"[48] the two shared many concerns and interests. Doc Long was a member of WILPF, but she had her own practice to consider and spent time with Martin on vacation trips in the American West.

Long recalled those journeys in two different publications, *The Shadow of the Arrow*,[49] a prose account of then little-known Death Valley, and *Enchanted Desert*, a collection of quatrains in the style of the Rubáiyát of Omar Khayyám that she had privately printed.[50] Long called the latter her "Ruby at the Sign of the Rum Blossom" in correspondence with friends.[51] In the introduction, Long observed that Anne Martin and she were the "first women to enter Death Valley alone, armed with nothing more formidable than a map . . . in 1921 when that most beautiful part of our deserts was still *terra incognita* to the traveller."[52] The two returned several times during the twenties to the stark and empty area. They visited the Indian reservations of the Southwest and Martin toured Nova Scotia.

Martin had established friends and havens in New York at the New York Arts Club, in San Francisco at the Women's City Club, in Denver with Long and occasionally attempted articles and letters to editors of various publications. Apparently abandoning her earlier efforts to be a writer, she remained a responsible citizen, no doubt offended to be considered a mere clubwoman.

In 1929 in a letter to the editor of *New Republic* she asked that "woman's part in preparing the way" for peace be recognized by some attention to WILPF activity. She could not resist adding her belief that "current journalism would make a truer interpretation of our times if it put more emphasis on the contribution of women" rather than rulers, "like that Pharoah who carved his personal exploits on the monuments of Egypt, but in this case it is the President who is doing the carving," so that Martin's disinterested pleas for peace and women degenerated into a side slap at Herbert Hoover, by then President Hoover and a special sort of irritant to Anne Martin.[53]

Martin's on-again off-again friendship with Hoover dated back to Stanford days and, except for the first years in London, proved a great disappointment to her. Her family thought the split in friendship went back to English days[54] but she continued to write to him for years and tried repeatedly to persuade him to appoint her to federal office, both in the time of World War I when he was in charge of relief and later when he had become president. Her wire of congratulations on his election received only a form letter in reply. Unpublished manuscripts consistently criticize him; in the twenties she worked several times on a highly critical piece called "Understanding Herbert Hoover," and she sniped at him when she could. Still, Mabel Vernon remembered that they were friends and recalled wearing a necklace that Hoover had chosen for Anne.

If Hoover ignored her, the "sainted" Jane Addams (to use Martin's own frequent epithet) became a personal friend who visited the Martins in Carmel in 1928 and invited Martin and Long to travel with her to the 1929 WILPF congress in Prague. Martin turned down the invitation, suggesting it would be far better to name "a newcomer" if there were any vacancies in the delegation, "as you did me three years ago and perhaps enlist a new worker."[55] But the acquaintance included a good deal of contact, at Addams' residence in Chicago, for example, where both had listened to Edna St. Vincent Millay read her poetry.[56]

Other friends from her active past filled out a life of travel, organizational activity, and writing. Perhaps the most faithful and valued of the correspondents was Austin Lewis, an Oakland attorney with a long history of support for various radical causes. Martin could have met him on many occasions before their correspondence began in 1926. He had defended Wobblies in Marysville, California, and had been a member of the legal team that defended Martin's old friend Anita Whitney, charged with criminal syndicalism in 1925; he had been on the original lecture bureau of the Women's Peace party; he had translated Engels and written books about socialism; he had been Socialist candidate for governor of California in 1906; he'd known Jack London, George Sterling, and Fremont Older, liberal leaders of all sorts.[57]

Anne Martin met Lewis frequently for dinners and lunches at a particular Mexican restaurant in San Francisco, and he wrote to her most Sundays from his office in Oakland, where he carried on a similar correspondence with Mary Bulkley, a woman from Carmel Martin never could like and of whom she was intensely jealous. Lewis was married, the father of four children, but the letters were occasionally jestingly romantic, sometimes teasing Martin for her quick temper: "I'm glad you liked my last letter, for I wrote in fear and trepidation lest I might have got into trouble."[58] When Martin was in Europe, he visited the restaurant for "the sake of remembering that I had been with you and drank your health in the vino."[59] He looked forward to her return so they might develop a "companionship which is one of the most utterly charming things in a long and arduous life."[60] But although he could write to her that "you are very dear and the thought of you is very sweet," he devoted most of each letter to comments on political affairs, on mutual friends, on books they exchanged.

Lewis kept her up on Anita Whitney's continuing problems with the law.[61] Lewis could offer her mail affection: "I will light a candle for you in the cathedral in Guadalajara so you may say to yourself at dinner on New Year, 'Austin's candle is burning for me . . .' "[62] She enjoyed his uninhibited comments on Hoover ("a fat Rotarian") and on Gandhi ("that blooming saint who gets comfortably locked up when the trouble gets thick . . . to be in jail and looking at one's navel may not be so bad").[63]

By 1930 Anne Martin may not have been a public figure, but she had built a mature life that was satisfactory in many ways: she had friends to respect, work enough to offer meaning to her life, enough money to travel as she wished. If she had not won the power she had sought nor achieved the fame she would have enjoyed, she could feel she had made and still was making a contribution to society. She could cheerfully thank Addams for her help in untangling problems with California WILPF and tell her admired friend how she had raced her mother's train "the last forty miles out of the sunshine toward the fog-bank that was Carmel, and beat it into the Monterey station by five minutes."[64]

Addams' help was not enough, however, to avert a serious heart attack Martin suffered in December 1930, an attack that curtailed her activities for two years and kept her in bed, dependent on her mother, for months. She blamed the squabbles in California WILPF, particularly those with Mrs. C. E. Cumberson, for knocking her out: "No one's fault but my own," she wrote, "for not being able to stand it better."[65]

As she wrote Addams in February, "These next few weeks will show I have the will to live, and I should like to do a little more work—and after all this is sometimes a bright, pretty world." Her breakdown, as she termed it, was hard on her mother: "I should be looking after her, at her age, instead of the other way round, but she is meeting it splendidly."[66]

In August 1931, Louise Martin died after a long illness. Anne Martin was ill herself, unable to be with her mother. The *Daily Carmelite* praised Mrs. Martin for her "fine balance between homemaker and mother and social and communal neighbor, the progressive thinker and the practical worker," particularly noting the way Anne and Louise Martin had "companioned each other so loyally and understandingly." Such praise did not soothe Anne Martin, who agonized for years over her absence from her mother's side in her last hours.[67]

She remained active in WILPF, even though her participation was more limited, growing more and more impatient with the executive secretary, Dorothy Detzer, with whom she had a series of confrontations from as early as 1929. She criticized everything about Detzer—her attitude, her beliefs, her handling of the job, her organization. On finding no disarmament file in the Washington office, Martin wrote Hannah Clothier Hull, U.S. president of WILPF, of Detzer's answer: "Miss Detzer thought imperialism the enemy. I told her her place then was in the class struggle, that she should be working with the Communists or the Socialists, that she had no place in a peace agitation that put work for disarmament first." Martin argued further that of the one thousand members she had recruited in eight states, almost half had been lost because Detzer had not followed up.[68]

In late 1935 Martin became interested in a subgroup of the league, the People's Mandate to End War. The campaign was headed by Mabel Vernon, no longer with the National Woman's Party, and a woman no fonder of Detzer than Martin was. The committee goal—fifty million signatures against war—was surely as attractive as the broader efforts of WILPF, and Martin was pleased to join.[69] She was one of a small group who met with President Franklin Delano Roosevelt in the spring of 1936 to discuss disarmament in relation to the mandate, and, attractive as ever to the press for her colorful past, she was interviewed by the *Washington Post* on her dedication to peace, "the greatest of all causes I have yet worked for." People were beginning to understand, she said, that "it is braver to stand for peace than to be pushed into war." Since men who opposed war stood accused of cowardice, Martin thought it "chivalrous of women to lead the way, to make it easy for men to follow."[70]

But by the end of June, annoyed by Detzer once again, she could no longer stay in WILPF, and she resigned, accusing the league of being ineffective, tied to an ineffective executive, led by ineffective president Hull.[71] When the resignation letters—directed to all members of the national board—were not sent from the main office, Martin exploded into a second round of letters accusing Hull of suppressing freedom of speech and opinion, calling her act "one of a petty politician and unworthy of the president of the Women's International League."[72]

Responses to Martin's explosion varied. Esther J. Crooks of Maryland called the letter "childish and cheap,"[73] and Heloise Brainerd of Vermont urged Martin to examine her own attitude, for "there need be no clashes of personality among those who have the real spirit of peace and love in their hearts," and she wondered if Martin were not really "more gracious than her words sounded."[74] Rosika Schwimmer, one of the founders of WILPF and center of a noted immigration battle in the twenties, congratulated Martin on her stand. "I want to shake your hand for your letter . . . It's a pity others didn't take your straight course and told clearly how harmful Miss Detzer is to the cause of world peace, which she pretends to serve while using her job merely for her own purposes." Schwimmer asked for extra copies of Martin's letter.[75]

To cap the unpleasant summer, Martin quarreled with Doc Long and underwent yet another serious operation in August. By early 1937 she had fled to the comfort of her sister Clara's house in Portland, Oregon, where she remained for a year before she gathered her courage to return to Carmel and the house she had shared with her mother to live alone. Sara Bard Field, who lived not far away in Los Gatos, still faithful after many years, praised and respected that decision.

> I think of you constantly, knowing how severe a test of your courage it was for you to return to Carmel alone. I think I guess better than most of your friends what heroism it has taken to completely reorganize your life from one of public activity to one of private accomplishment. I am very much impressed by your turning to creative work at this time in your life.[76]

Field referred to what she called an "astonishing attack on poetry" that Martin had been making over the previous few years.

Starting not long after her illness had forced her to bed, Martin had passed her recuperation time in Denver in Margaret Long's big Colorado Boulevard house working on her autobiography and trying to write poetry. She attended poetry sessions led by local women and visiting lecturers, she wrote and rewrote, working each piece over and over again, attempting a dizzying variety of forms—ballad, cinquain, haiku, terza rima, villanelle. Field's term "attack" seems suitable for the effort. The results were disappointing to Martin and to her critics. Harriet Munro, responding for the prestigious *Poetry* magazine, summed up the truth most effectively: "They are much too long for what's in them."[77] Other notations comment on the lack of rhyme, rhythm, or cadence either mercifully or boldly. Martin had no ear and her subject matter was limited: the disappointments of her life, the nobility of her father— "Your life is like a sound and growing tree"—and of Jane Addams, the deceit of politicians, the beauty of the desert, lost love, regrets. Try as she might, even though a newspaper might print one now and then and she might place in the amateur contests in Colorado, true poetry eluded her. She had written a sturdy and serviceable prose all of her life; she appreciated literature and truly enjoyed music, but she could not grasp the music of verse.

Perhaps inspired by Sara Bard Field's respect for Emily Dickinson, Martin read much of the work of the Amherst poet, lifting lines and phrases occasionally, quoting Dickinson in her autobiography. Renunciation, loss, solitude were topics she could understand, but she seemed to know that her poetry had not succeeded. Once in a while she would send one to Austin Lewis, less frequently to Field, herself a popular poet and married to one truly successful—Charles Erskine Scott Wood could boast twenty-five printings for one of his books.[78]

Anne Martin's desire to see herself in the best possible light led to battles with Mary Austin over the latter's autobiography with its comments on Martin in London. An angry Martin insisted that Austin change parts of the book until Austin replied in exasperation:

> I wonder what you think would happen to me if I undertook to make the amount of fuss you have about everything that is said about me that is not absolutely complimentary. It is one of the prices we pay for saying what we think . . . you have been morbidly sensitive about this . . . and that is my last word.[79]

After her return to Carmel, Martin lived a lonely life for much of each year. Although the relatives in the area entertained her from time to time, she shared her home with none but her cocker spaniel, Punkin, some years later adding a rental cottage to the back of the property. Still accustomed to household help (she was close to sixty before she tried cooking, well past that age when she did her first housecleaning), she recorded in her revived diaries the coming and going of various maids and yard men, lunches in town, drives with her friends. She wrote of the terrors of old age—falls and arthritis and dependence—and the remembrance of youth, particularly after a visit to Reno to see Minnie Flanigan, who still had the campaign papers stored at her house: "It made me sad to see them all—reminds me of great youthful efforts—Mabel—disappointments" (diary, 16 September 1939). She knew that she didn't use her brain enough, and when the Doyle biography of Mary Austin, dead by then, was published with distorted comments from Martin, she was delighted to write a response for the local paper, to find "great satisfaction to create something that somebody wants."[80]

She began to organize her materials on the many campaigns to donate them to the Bancroft Library, largely through the efforts of her niece, Edna Martin Parratt, then associated with that library. Jeanne Wier, still ensconced at the University of Nevada, had already told her the Nevada Historical Society had no place for them. Martin remembered that bitterly at a Reno luncheon in Wier's honor that brought out the old venom: "Cheap show, her speech—weak, jealous woman—always been jealous of me—I fear because I gave her her job!" (28 May 1940).

While she was struggling to live on $100 a month, planning to sell her mother's diamonds, she worried less about money than about the monotony of "days so much alike" in such a life: "Must take myself in hand and do some writing . . . If only I could use consistent power in some way" (8 January 1941). A few activities drew her beyond Carmel: several trips through Death Valley with Long, testimony for the Equal Rights Amendment in Sacramento. Support of the amendment ended her long complaint that it was merely a plea to men to give women rights; she had given up expecting women to get those rights through sex solidarity, even though she still advocated it in her occasional speeches.

Even though sex solidarity was no longer her major cause her feminism had not faltered. She began a letter-writing campaign urging Stanford president Ray Lyman Wilbur to hire more women faculty, pleading with fellow alumnae to join her, distressed by a "shockingly materialistic spirit" at her alma mater. These efforts varied her life of music club meetings, Democratic women's gatherings (she had become, briefly, a fan of Roosevelt), daily walks with her dog.

When the declaration of war came in December 1941, she blamed Roosevelt for involving the country in "Britain's war," and she wrote a petulant piece, "The Pacifist's Position in War Time," complaining about a "false, hysterical blackout" in Carmel. She speculated on the silliness of such behavior in Carmel where so many of her neighbors had come "to rest and die," presenting herself as suffering the "personal and mental isolation [that was] the lot of the war-time non-conformist, the peace heretic."[81]

Most of the world paid little attention to the article in April. But when Martin sent a copy to Austin Lewis, he exploded to her and expanded on his displeasure to Mary Bulkley: "I have told her [Martin] very categorically what I think about it . . . I hinted that in the middle ages she would have been in a convent if she was good enough and that a modern concentration camp was perhaps the nearest equivalent."[82] Yet at the same time he expressed his anger over the article, he calmed down enough to continue their friendly exchanges, commenting on his pleasure in rereading Jane Austen, his sympathy with the way the area Japanese responded to their displacement with "complete self possession and sweet courtesy."[83] Clearly, Martin and Lewis had tangled over ideas many times without losing their genuine respect and affection for one another, sentiments that show through the letters up until Lewis' death.

Martin said little more publicly about the war, even though she quarreled with Long, daughter of a former secretary of the navy. She worried about her sister Margaret's three sons in the service, was delighted with their visits to her. But in her diary in 1944 she noted how she couldn't "stand to listen much to radio. War news and announcers hateful." Her brother Harry died in 1943, Austin Lewis and Lou Hoover in 1944. She could not even think of anyone to write about Lewis' death: all the old radical friends were dead.

But from her past, Mary Beard offered her a focus for her waning energies. Martin had complained to Beard, by then nationally known as part of a husband-wife historian team, of the paucity of articles on women; Beard responded with an assignment for her old NWP friend to write an entry on Josephine Butler for *Encyclopaedia Britannica*. Butler had been a pioneer in English social welfare, a feminist before the word, who had fought the English contagious diseases law on the issue of the rights of women. Martin was delighted. In the end, Martin's article—rejected more than once, returned for revision—in the 1944 edition was very short. Martin must have known her heavy research was more than was needed, but she welcomed the work, fought for careful phrasing. Her reward was a second assignment, an article on what was then called the white slave traffic (later the traffic in women and children) for the 1950 edition. Once again she over-researched, over-produced, faced revision and rejection, but she succeeded in finishing her task creditably.[84] She filled her time with activity she could respect.

During the period of the war and its aftermath, Martin began to spend more and more time in Reno. It was easier for her to work on her articles at the Washoe County Library, a short walk from her room at the Golden Hotel, than to travel to San Francisco or Berkeley. She could call on the services of the university, too, and visit old friends. Her nephews recall her living in a jumble of papers and books and magazines in the modest hotel room,[85] happy to have some purpose and direction. Gradually she became a Reno resident for much of the year, living in the hotel, eating in restaurants, entertaining herself with slot machines and bingo, attending meetings of the many women's organizations.

When a Nevada senator died mid term her friends urged her appointment to fill out the term. Martin recorded no response to such efforts; it was the very sort of empty gesture she would have scorned as a younger woman.

As if in recognition of the late return of a prodigal daughter, in 1945 she received the kind of public recognition she had wanted for so long—the university awarded her an honorary LL.D. in recognition of her work for women. It was a quarter of a century late, but Anne Martin cherished it. The citation praised her as a "native daughter, distinguished alumnus, student and scholar, inspiring teacher, disciple of world peace, pioneer in the triumphant struggle for women's rights, leader of womankind, Doctor of Laws."[86] She happily accepted, returning occasionally to walk in the graduation processions, signing her letters "Dr. Anne Martin" for the rest of her life.

With a member of the history department, she wrote an account of the suffrage movement preceded by a short memoir of her life. Most of the writing was hers and she enjoyed the review of accomplishment. She did her duty as a speaker and supporter of causes: she campaigned for the Equal Rights Amendment, using her influence with Senator Patrick McCarran in 1946 to persuade him to vote for bringing the amendment to the Judiciary Committee.[87] She backed a group demanding investigation of the state mental hospital; she supported the case of a woman social worker fired for vague allegations of misconduct; she argued for a Girls' State to parallel a model government Boys' State, and when the campaign succeeded addressed the first session, urging the girls to responsible citizenship. She made peace with the various women's organizations. She wrote letters to the editors of the local newspapers regularly and spoke on the radio at election time.

Her ideas had not changed much: she blamed men for World War II, but she told the Daughters of the American Revolution (a group she would have scorned some years before) that there was hope for a "moral revolution of women of the world to insist on the end of war and the feeding of starving peoples." Bending to the feelings of her audience, she called for "patriotic teaching of American history in the schools . . . to help record the greatest drama of freedom ever enacted by the human race."[88] To speak in such vein to a group that had once considered Jane Addams a dangerous radical required considerable mellowing. The same Anne Martin who had called the NWP "legalistic Amazons" in 1929 for their support of the Equal Rights Amendment took a public stand for it in a 1950 speech to the Reno Civic Club, taking to task modern women who were not pursuing their rights properly.[89]

Returning to the religion of her childhood, she became a regular at the Episcopal church in Reno, even though in Carmel she continued to attend meetings of the Rudolf Steiner group dedicated to study of that multitalented self-styled anthroposophist.

In April of 1951, only a few weeks after she had worked with her niece to remove personal material from the remaining papers that recorded her busy public life, she died in Carmel, victim of a series of strokes. Edna Parratt wrote to Sara Bard Field that she suffered "a series of slight thromboses April 10" and after "several strokes" died peacefully 15 April.[90] Respectful accounts in the local newspapers dutifully praised the woman they had plagued so long ago.

Field, one of the few longtime friends who had been close to Martin in the last years, wrote back to Parratt that Martin would "live in the history of the Feminist Movement as one of its most notable and persistent leaders . . . the mere record of her work will do her honor."[91]

Anne Martin had kept to the front in the progress of women during her lifetime, running to keep up, gathering strength to lead, however briefly, that forward movement to the future. Her shortcomings were many, but her efforts were sincere. If she failed to win election, she tried honorably. If she failed to persuade women to take their equality, to force their power, she nevertheless saw clearly how important that next step was. She never felt she had done enough, but she searched for reassurance constantly, as she had in notes for that oft-rewritten autobiography: ". . . a pattern is hidden in our lives from the beginning, that pattern is like the weaving of a Persian carpet or a Navajo blanket into a clearly defined and integrated design."[92] She was not sure that she ever discerned that design.

She was a maverick in an ultraconservative family, her niece believed.[93] Easily hurt, she could injure others with her rigid demands, her sarcastic responses. Her nephews remembered her as a "formidable" little woman from whom they all "scattered for cover." Yet she retained the friendship of some of her friends for decades. Martin could never quite settle between warring poles of her own self. While she longed for acceptance, she prided herself on her difference. While she could master prose, she longed for poetry. Publicly fond of being rational and arguing with facts, she was always fascinated with the supernatural, the spiritual, just as she publicly worshiped her proper Episcopalian god and was intrigued by Rudolf Steiner's surmises about the spirit. From her earliest diaries to her latest, she veered between crediting thinking and feeling as essentials to sensible life, never truly excluding either.

In many ways, she retained the nineteenth-century concepts of service with her twentieth-century urge for progress. In this she was like many other women. Her difference lay in her willingness to take action, her courage in stepping out of ranks.

Her life was a long campaign, the goals shifting and changing, the support of others varying. If it was a lost one, if there was no triumph, there was honest effort. Perhaps by 1951 she knew that she had indeed been a "forerunner and a pathfinder," so that when other women strove in any number of ways, "it would never again seem so strange."

What does such a life mean? No other woman from Nevada until 1970 was so much in the public eye on the basis of her own deeds as Anne Martin was in her time, even though she did not win many of her battles. Her life offers a single example to document the way thousands of women sought to act upon the world, to be part of the political process, to make change for themselves and their sisters. If she failed at many of her campaigns, so did most American women of her sort, of her time. She was not a mover and a shaker in either the Nevada world or the nation. But as the woman of her times, reflecting and absorbing the lights and the shadows of seventy-five crucial years for American women, she illuminates American women's lives.

She was inclined to exaggerate both her deeds and her losses, but it is no tribute to her to do the same in assessing her life. Hers was a useful public life that included considerable service to others, some basic satisfactions to the self she knew no better than most human beings do.

If Anne Martin took a long time to find direction in her life, she was in good company, only one of many women excited by new freedoms and decked with accomplishments, uncertain of how to use either. She brought the scattered suffragists in Nevada together to win the vote for her sisters and she worked hard for the federal amendment. No scholar doubts that the National Woman's Party, wrongheaded in its politics, revitalized the suffrage movement and shoved it rudely toward success, however unladylike that shoving may have seemed.

That she had the nerve, the courage, the impudence to toss a challenge at the male political world speaks well for her. She made the male politicians in Nevada sit up and take notice. When the press laughed and taunted, she endured and did not call foul. She would have been angered to admit that personal ambition urged her on (women were supposed to be altruistic), but whatever it was that made her act, she showed others how to try. There is no sure way to measure whether any Nevada woman, any woman anywhere, became more political because Anne Martin ran for office, but it is clear that her efforts were observed, received, absorbed by women who did change over the years.

Looking back over more than sixty years to her Senate campaigns, those efforts seem naive, almost foolish. The wonder is that she won five thousand votes—18 percent—of a conservative electorate with the odds, the press, the very country against her. That she did not quit public life altogether is surprising. Only those willing to go beyond the standard inaccuracies and omissions of women's lives know how the feminist struggle continued through the twenties and thirties and on until a new generation of young women revitalized, republicized, renewed that woman's work forgotten by the press and most historians. Martin and others like her remained a part of that effort, a reliable and ever ready minutewoman in the fight for equality. And if the pursuit of peace still seems vain, it is not because women like Martin and her compatriots did not earnestly hope to change human nature.

Martin's great expectations—perhaps exaggerated hopes is a better term—for the woman voter were not met, nor have they been in our time by women more free but still not truly emancipated. But women like her continue to labor after the same goal. Anne Martin's life set an example for female action—so small as a letter to the editor, a name on a petition, so bold as a knock at the Senate door—in the male-dominated world. Martin and women like her may not crowd the pages of the history books; they only, bit by bit, make change.

NOTES

Chapter 1: Native Daughter

1. Anne Martin was christened Anna Henrietta and used that name until about 1900 when she began to use Anne. Apparently friends and family used "Anna" and "Anne" almost interchangeably until that time; in the family and at school she was generally "Annie" until she was twenty.

2. Diary, 1893, Carton VIII, Personalia, Anne Martin Collection, Bancroft Library, University of California Library, Berkeley, California. This collection will hereafter be cited as AMC. Citations from the diaries, which sometimes offer specific dates and other times do not, will be made parenthetically.

3. The autobiographical documents include many rejected handwritten notes as well as two typescripts; one of thirty pages dates from about 1932, the other eight pages are from 1943. Neither of these has been specifically labeled by the library, but I have distinguished the earliest typed version as Autobiography I, the latter as Autobiography II, and any untyped notes as Autobiography N. All are in Carton I, Manuscripts, AMC.

4. Clemens, *Roughing It*, pp. 144–147.

5. Paher, *Ghost Towns and Mining Camps*, p. 17.

6. Browne, *Washoe Revisited*, p. 48.

7. Bruns, "Old Empire," p. 3.

8. See Riegel, *American Feminists*.

9. Autobiography N, no page number.

10. Autobiography I, p. 13.

11. Ibid., p. 9. Anne Martin quotes this from her own sources.

12. Ibid., p. 10.

13. See the *Reno Evening Gazette*, 16 September 1901, and *Nevada State Journal*, 17 September 1901, for example.

14. Autobiography I, pp. 3–4.

15. Ibid., pp. 6–7.

16. Autobiography N, no page number.

17. Autobiography I, pp. 11–12.

18. Totton, "Hannah Keziah Clapp," pp. 167–183.

19. The University of Nevada-Reno copy still bears Mrs. Martin's name.

20. Autobiography I, p. 17.

21. Ibid., pp. 19–20.

22. See diaries for 1888 and 1892 in Carton VIII, AMC; Autobiography I, pp. 14–15.

23. Autobiography I, p. 19.

24. In Welter, *Dimity Convictions*, pp. 6–7.

25. Ibid., p. 21.

26. In Gray, *Women of the West*, p. 2.

27. Autobiography I, p. 21.

28. Dee Brown discusses "The Great Female Shortage" in *The Gentle Tamers*.

29. Poems, Carton I, AMC.

30. Autobiography I, pp. 13–23.

31. Ibid., p. 30.

32. Ibid., pp. 30–31.

33. *Reno Evening Gazette*, 16 September 1901.

34. B. Brown, *A Tale of Three Cities*, p. 3.

35. S. Doten, *An Illustrated History of the University of Nevada*, p. 50.

36. Ibid., pp. 51–52.

37. D. Brown, *The Gentle Tamers*, p. 10.

38. Townley, "Bishop Whitaker's School for Girls," p. 171.

39. Ibid., p. 173.

40. *Reno Evening Gazette*, 12 October 1876.

41. *Annual Catalog of Whitaker Hall, A School for Girls, 1885*, Archives of the Episcopal Church, Nevada Historical Society, Reno, Nevada.

42. *Annual Catalog of Whitaker Hall, A School for Girls, 1892–93*, Archives of the Episcopal Church, Nevada Historical Society, Reno, Nevada, p. 16.

43. 1885 catalog, p. 12.

44. 1892–93 catalog, p. 13.

45. Townley, "Bishop Whitaker's School for Girls," p. 184.

46. Diaries cover 1888, 1891–1894, and 1901–1904 and will be cited parenthetically. See Carton VIII, AMC.

47. Martin, "The Johnny Rankin Album," Nevada Historical Society, Reno, Nevada.

48. Townley, "Bishop Whitaker's School for Girls," p. 177.

49. Ibid., p. 178.

50. "The Johnny Rankin Album," p. 35.

51. Kathryn Anderson, "Practical Political Equality for Women: Anne Martin's Campaigns for the U.S. Senate in Nevada, 1918 and 1920" (Ph.D. dissertation, University of Washington, 1978), pp. 27–28.

52. Townley, "Bishop Whitaker's School for Girls," pp. 179–180.

53. Ibid., p. 180.

54. M. Howard, *Facts of Life*, pp. 23–24.

Chapter 2: A Modern Education

1. S. Doten, *An Illustrated History of the University of Nevada*, p. 77.

2. *Register of the University of Nevada, 1892–93*, Archives of the University of Nevada, Getchell Library, Reno, Nevada.

3. Ruskin, "Of Queens' Gardens," Number 69 in *Sesame and Lillies*, p. 152.

4. Bruns, "Old Empire," pp. 15–16.

5. D. Brown, *The Gentle Tamers*, passim.

6. Crow, *The Victorian Woman*, p. 330.

7. Showalter, *These Modern Women*, p. 38.

8. Inez Haynes Irwin Collection, vol. I, 1891. Hereafter cited as Irwin Collection.

9. Creston, *Fountains of Youth*, p. ix.

10. In Hollis, *Women in Public*, p. 20.

11. Grand, *The Heavenly Twins*.

12. Irwin Collection, vol. III, 1894.

13. Heilbrun, "Marriage Perceived," p. 165.

14. Dobkin, *The Making of a Feminist*, p. 73.

15. Field, "Sara Bard Field: Poet and Suffragist," p. 255.

16. Showalter, *These Modern Women*, p. 81.

17. Totton, "Hannah Keziah Clapp," p. 168.

18. Ibid., pp. 171–172.

19. Ibid., p. 173.

20. Ibid., p. 175.

21. Ibid., p. 180.

22. Hannah Clapp Papers, Nevada Historical Society, Reno, Nevada. Hereafter cited as Clapp Papers.

23. Totton, "Hannah Keziah Clapp," p. 181.

24. University issue, *Reno Evening Gazette*, 6 June 1895.

25. Clipping in Clapp papers.

26. Maynard, *Walt Whitman*.

27. S. Doten, *An Illustrated History of the University of Nevada*, p. 69.

28. Ann Warren Smith, "Anne Martin and a History of Woman Suffrage in Nevada, 1869–1914" (Ph.D. dissertation, University of Nevada, Reno, 1975), pp. 25–27.

29. *Nevada State Journal*, 27 July 1894.

30. *Nevada State Journal*, 31 July 1894.

31. Autobiography I, p. 26.

32. A. Doten, *The Journals of Alfred Doten*. Doten made notes on important developments in the story over a period of months.

33. Ibid., pp. 1994–2016.

34. Lasch, "Sorority and Family in New England," pp. 29–31.

35. Smith-Rosenberg, "The Female World of Love and Ritual," pp. 316–317.

36. Ibid., pp. 330–331.

Chapter 3: The Best of Educations

1. Degler, *At Odds*, p. 145.

2. Kraditor, *The Ideas of the Woman Suffrage Movement*, p. 233.

3. Roxanne Nilan, "The Ladies at Palo Alto: Stanford University and the Coeducational Experiment" (paper, Stanford University Archives, Green Library, Palo Alto, California), p. 3.

4. Ibid., p. 10.

5. Carl Degler credits this concept of the world as extension of the home as a prime force in the betterment of women's lot. See *At Odds*, chapter 13, "The World Is Only a Large Home."

6. Nilan, "The Ladies at Palo Alto," p. 6.

7. Anne Martin File, California Historical Society Library, San Francisco, California.

8. See *The Quad* and *The Daily Palo Alto*, Stanford publications, for numerous examples.

9. Carton I, Manuscripts, AMC. This carton is divided into numbered files only in the front portion.

10. Henrietta Stadtmuller, Scrapbook, Stanford University Archives, Green Library, Palo Alto, California.

11. Ibid.

12. Nilan, "The Ladies at Palo Alto," pp. 11–12.

13. *The Daily Palo Alto*, 7 December 1894.

14. Ibid., 10 December 1895.

15. Autobiography II, p. 5.

16. *The Daily Palo Alto,* 16 March 1895.

17. Ibid., 22 October 1896.

18. Ibid., 27 October 1896.

19. *The Daily Palo Alto,* 27 April 1897.

20. Nilan, "The Ladies at Palo Alto," p. 13.

21. Ibid., p. 14.

22. Sarah Comstock, ed., *Stanford '96: An Accounting in 1926* (privately printed, 1926), p. 198.

23. D. Smith, "Family Limitation."

24. *Stanford '96,* p. 295. Quoted in Nilan, "The Ladies at Palo Alto," p. 10.

25. "Mary Sheldon Barnes," in James, *Notable American Women.*

26. Anna Henrietta Martin, "The Causes of the Baden Revolution" (M.A. thesis, Stanford University, 1897).

27. Interview with Charles Keyser, University of Nevada Archives, 1972.

28. Autobiography I.

Chapter 4: "Feminist Iron"

1. Degler, *At Odds,* p. 380.

2. *Biennial Report of the Board of Regents of the State University, 1897–1898* (Carson City, Nev.: State Printing Office, 1899), p. 22.

3. *Eleventh Register of the State University of Nevada* (Carson City, Nev.: State Printing Office, 1898), p. 20.

4. *Biennial Report,* p. 18.

5. Ibid., p. 23.

6. Class register, Anne Martin File, Nevada Historical Society, Reno, Nevada.

7. Autobiography N, no page numbers.

8. Autobiography I, p. 15.

9. Ibid., pp. 12–13.

10. Charles Keyser, Interview with James Hulse, University of Nevada-Reno Archives, NVB 23/5/7, pp. 10–11.

11. *Eleventh Register,* p. 13.

12. *Reno Evening Gazette,* 9 May 1898.

13. *Twelfth Register of the State University of Nevada* (Carson City, Nev.: State Printing Office, 1899), p. 20.

14. *Reno Evening Gazette,* 23 August 1898, p. 2.

15. Photographs, "M," Nevada Historical Society, Reno, Nevada.

16. Keyser, Interview, p. 13.

17. Photographs, "M."

18. Edna Martin Parratt to Kathryn Anderson, 24 May 1976. I am indebted to Dr. Anderson (Fairhaven College, Bellingham, Washington) for generously sharing her private correspondence with Mrs. Parratt.

19. *Stanford '96,* pp. 119–120.

20. Diary 1900 and forward, pp. 39–40, Carton VIII, AMC.

21. Ibid., p. 44.

22. Interview, Martin Mackey (nephew of Anne Martin), 19 March 1982.

23. *Reno Evening Gazette,* 21 September 1899, p. 3.

24. Ibid., 29 September 1899, p. 3.

25. *Stanford Alumnus* (Palo Alto, Calif.: 1901), p. 73.

26. Carton VIII, AMC.

27. Petersen and Wilson, *Women Artists,* pp. 85–86.

28. Gardner, *A Short History of Newnham College,* p. 22.

29. Braddock, *"That Infidel Place,"* p. 72.

30. Anne Martin to Mrs. William Kent, 11 April 1918, Box 12, AMC.

31. A note to M. Carey Thomas' diary explains the "smash" as it was understood in the women's colleges: "When a . . . girl takes a shine to another, she straightway enters upon a regular course of bouquet sendings, interspersed with tinted notes . . . locks of hair perhaps . . . the two become inseparable and the aggressor is considered . . . smashed" (Dobkin, *The Making of a Feminist,* pp. 76–77).

32. Diary, 1900ff., p. 4, Carton VIII, AMC. Subsequent references to this diary will be made parenthetically as in previous chapters.

33. Edna Martin Parratt to Kathryn Anderson, 24 May 1976.

34. Smith-Rosenberg, "The Female World of Love and Ritual," pp. 311–343.

35. *Thirteenth Annual Register of the University of Nevada* (Carson City, Nev.: State Printing Office, 1903), p. 14.

36. Autobiography N, no page number.

37. *Reno Evening Gazette,* 1 April 1901, p. 12.

38. Degler, *At Odds,* p. 320.

39. Bernard, *The Female World,* p. 507.

40. Ibid., p. 509.

41. Sklar, *Catherine Beecher,* discusses Beecher's pervasive influence.

42. Bernard, *The Female World,* p. 509.

43. Ibid., p. 512.

44. Margery Nelson, "Ladies in the Streets: A Sociological Analysis of the National Woman's Party, 1910–1930" (Ph.D. dissertation, State University of New York at Buffalo, 1976), p. 161ff.

45. There is a certain justice in that England's largest repository of books and documents devoted to the history of women, the Fawcett Library, is located now in that same Whitechapel area where so many of the leaders it treats made their first moves toward independence.

46. Carton III, AMC.

47. Nelson, "Ladies in the Streets," p. 179.

48. Ibid., p. 166.

49. Crow, *The Victorian Woman,* p. 306.

50. John Muir to Anne Martin, December 1901, Anne Martin File, California Historical Society Library, San Francisco, California, CHS 1411-1.

51. *Thirteenth Register,* p. 58.

52. *Annual Report of the Regents of the State University and Report of the President, 1901–1902* (Carson City, Nev.: State Printing Office, 1902), p. 19.

53. *Stanford Alumnus* (Palo Alto, Calif.: 1902), p. 141.

54. *Reno Evening Gazette,* 16 September 1901, p. 2.

55. Autobiography N. Martin left this out of the typed version, apparently fearing the wrong sort of response to this deathbed revelation, even though she was always interested in accounts of similar experiences.

56. Autobiography II, p. 29.

57. Autobiography I, p. 5.

58. Autobiography N.

59. *University of Nevada Bulletin,* vol. 2, no. 9 (15 June 1903), p. 1.

60. Addams, *Twenty Years at Hull House,* p. 73. This book was originally published in 1910, about the time Martin made her conscious commitment to suffrage.

61. Ibid., p. 74.

62. Small appointment book, Carton VIII, AMC.

63. Mitton, *English Woman's Yearbook and Directory,* p. 224.

64. *Votes for Women,* vol. 2, no. 69 (2 July 1909), p. 886.

65. Anne Martin File, California Historical Society Library, San Francisco, California, 1411/1.

66. Clippings, 1909, in unnumbered scrapbook, Carton VIII, AMC.

67. Interview with Martin Mackey, 19 March 1982.

68. Austin, *Earth Horizon*, p. 314.
69. Doyle, *Mary Austin*, p. 226.
70. Ibid., p. 227.

Chapter 5: Joining the Cause

1. Quoted in Mitchell, *Queen Christabel*, p. 2.
2. Ibid.
3. In Britain and America *suffragist* was the generally accepted term, while *suffragette*, a name embraced by the WSPU, had negative connotations in America. The WSPU not only accepted the term *suffragette*, it changed the name of its publication from *Votes for Women* to *The Suffragette*. When the National Woman's party began its peaceful demonstrations, American newspapers used the term derogatorily, as did Nevada newspapers later on in Anne Martin's career.
4. O'Neill, *The Woman Movement*, p. 83.
5. An appointment book in Carton VIII, AMC, places Martin in London on the date O'Neill notes (p. 83).
6. *Fabian News,* vol. 19, no. 1 (December 1907), p. 95.
7. *First Annual Report of the Women's Social and Political Union, Including Balance Sheet and Subscription List for the Year Ending February 28, 1907.*
8. NWSPU, *Fifth Annual Report, Including Cash Statement and Subscription List for the Year Ended February 28, 1911, and Accounts of the Women's Press, January 1–December 31, 1910* (London: The Woman's Press, 1910), p. 43. Yet another contributor in that list is Alice Paul, who would turn her British experience to action in the United States and be Martin's ally and enemy over the years.
9. Kamm, *Rapiers and Battleaxes*, pp. 146–147.
10. Ibid., p. 154.
11. Crow, *The Victorian Woman*, p. 340.
12. Anne Martin to *The Women's Journal*, 14 May 1914, Box VIII, AMC.
13. *Votes for Women*, vol. 3 (11 February 1909), p. 101. Martin read most of James' works and must have been gratified by the change in attitude of an author who had personified and ridiculed the feminist in *The Bostonians* some years earlier.
14. *Votes for Women*, vol. 2 (25 June 1908), p. 269.
15. Haig, *This Was My World*, p. 161.
16. Ibid., p. 165.
17. Ibid., p. 155.
18. Quoted in Fulford, *Votes for Women*, p. 137.
19. Anne Martin File, California Historical Society Library, San Francisco, California, 1411/1, includes a black-bordered announcement canceling that presentation because of the death of King Edward in May 1910.
20. Fawcett, *Woman's Suffrage*, p. 86.
21. *Votes for Women*, vol. 5 (16 June 1911), p. 612.
22. Strachey, *The Cause*, p. 311.
23. Miscellaneous Suffrage Materials, Carton VII, AMC.
24. Strachey, *The Cause*, p. 305.
25. "Anne Martin," Photograph Files, Bancroft Library, University of California-Berkeley, Berkeley, California.
26. Autobiography II, p. 5.
27. Quoted in Raeburn, *The Militant Suffragettes*, p. 173.
28. The militant movement is well documented. In addition to works already cited, thorough accounts appear in Rover, *Woman's Suffrage and Party Politics in Britain*, and Rosen, *Rise Up, Women!*, among many others. *The Vote*, the publication of the Women's Freedom League, which broke off from the WSPU over Mrs. Pankhurst's authoritarian methods and the campaign of

vandalism that followed Black Friday, and *Votes for Women*, later *The Suffragette*, offer close documentation. Papers of the WSPU (except for those seized in police raids in 1910) are preserved at the Museum of London. The account here draws from all of these as well as from Martin's own unclassified collection of flyers and papers from the campaign in Carton VII, AMC.

29. Fawcett, *Woman's Suffrage*, p. 63.
30. Quoted in O'Neill, *The Woman Movement*, pp. 83–84.
31. Ibid., p. 85.
32. Anne Martin, "The Suffragette Problem in England: Personal Experiences," Carton I, Manuscripts and Notes, AMC. Published in a slightly altered version in the *Reno Evening Gazette*, 7 January 1911.
33. Ibid., p. 13.
34. Ibid., pp. 15–16.
35. Morgan, *Suffragists and Liberals*, p. 71.
36. Mitchell, *Queen Christabel*, p. 160.
37. Brailsford, *The Treatment of Women's Deputations by the Metropolitan Police*, p. 9.
38. Martin, "The Suffragette Problem," pp. 22–24.
39. Ibid., pp. 17–19.
40. Mitchell, *Queen Christabel*, p. 161.
41. Martin, "The Suffragette Problem," p. 21.
42. Scrapbook VII, AMC.
43. J. C. Hopper to Anne Martin, 19 November 1910, Box 3, AMC.
44. Clipping, undated, Scrapbooks, vol. II, AMC.
45. *Votes for Women* (25 November 1910), p. 122.
46. Clipping, undated, Scrapbooks, vol. II, AMC.
47. Anne Martin to *Manchester City News*, 27 July 1911, Carton I, AMC.
48. C. Pankhurst, *Unshackled*, p. 166.
49. Scrapbook II, AMC.
50. L. E. Morgan-Browne, "The Purple, White and Green," in Scott, *Bread and Roses*, p. 109.
51. Cicely Hamilton, "The March of Women," in Scott, *Bread and Roses*, p. 114.
52. Dangerfield, *The Strange Death of Liberal England*, pp. 127–130.
53. From *Pittsburg Dispatch*, n.d., Scrapbook II, AMC.

Chapter 6: Leading at Last

1. Jeanne Wier, "A History of the Suffrage Movement in Nevada, 1900–1913," unpublished manuscript, Jeanne Wier Collection, Nevada Historical Society, Reno, Nevada. Hereafter cited as JWC.
2. Ann Warren Smith, "Anne Martin and a History of Woman Suffrage in Nevada, 1869–1914" (Ph.D. dissertation, University of Nevada, Reno, 1975), gives a detailed description of the organization from the first resolution in the legislature in 1869 to the winning of the vote in 1914.
3. A. A. Hubbard to Jeanne Wier, 25 January 1911, "Suffrage Materials," JWC.
4. Weinstein, *The Decline of Socialism in America*, p. 60.
5. Smith, "Anne Martin," pp. 62–69.
6. Anna Howard Shaw to Jeanne Wier, 21 March 1911, JWC.
7. J. E. Stubbs to Anna Howard Shaw, 24 February 1911, Anne Martin Collection, Nevada Historical Society, Reno, Nevada.
8. Flexner, *Century of Struggle*, pp. 263–265.
9. Anne Martin, "Reno, Nevada," unpublished manuscript, Carton I, AMC, pp. 1–2.
10. Ibid., pp. 4–5.
11. Ibid., pp. 7–8.
12. Ibid., pp. 10–11.
13. A. Smith, "Anne Martin," p. 97.

14. *Reno Evening Gazette,* 12 February 1912, p. 3.

15. Anne Martin, "The Winning of Nevada," *Suffragist,* 7 November 1914, p. 3.

16. A. Smith, "Anne Martin," p. 100.

17. "Suffrage, 1912," Carton VII, AMC.

18. Most of the out-of-town clippings are preserved in volume IV of the Scrapbooks of the AMC; the "Woman on Horseback" article appeared first in the *Gazette,* 16 November 1912, p. 8, illustrated by a striking and dramatic picture of Martin.

19. Scrapbook IV, AMC.

20. Ibid.

21. Anne Martin, "An American View of English Militancy," *Reno Evening Gazette,* 22 June 1912.

22. Maud Gassaway to Anne Martin, 3 October 1912, AMC, Box 3.

23. The long correspondence between Anne Martin and Bird Wilson shows Wilson as the most trusted of suffrage workers after Mabel Vernon. The chilling of that friendship in the 1916 campaign was a major blow to Martin.

24. Gilman was a rare feminist thinker in her cooler assessment of the value of the ballot, but she willingly participated in campaigns all over the country for minimal fees to support the more ardent suffragists.

25. Bird Wilson to Anne Martin, 22 October 1912, Box 7, AMC.

26. Boyer, "My Home for Many Years," pp. 133–136.

27. Earl, "Nevada Suffragets," p. 17.

28. Bird Wilson to Anne Martin, 11 October 1912, Box 7, AMC.

29. *The Woman's Journal,* vol. 43, no. 47 (30 November 1912), p. 380.

30. A. Smith, "Anne Martin," pp. 120–123.

31. Ibid., pp. 123–124.

32. Carton VII, AMC.

33. Riegelhuth, "Memoirs of a Pioneer," p. 41.

34. Minnie Blair to Anne Martin, 16 January 1913, Box 1, AMC.

35. Clippings, mostly unidentified, in Felice Cohn Papers, Nevada Historical Society, Reno, Nevada.

36. A. Smith, "Anne Martin," pp. 139–141.

37. "Tonopah Suffragists Declare War upon Society President," *Tonopah Bonanza,* 13 March 1913, p. 1.

38. Anne Martin to Mrs. P. E. Keeler and the *Tonopah Bonanza,* 15 March 1913, Box 8, AMC.

39. Editorial, *Tonopah Bonanza,* 20 March 1913.

40. Marjorie Brown to Anne Martin, n.d., from Palace Hotel, Box 1, AMC.

41. Esther Givens to Anne Martin, n.d., Box 3, AMC.

42. Bird Wilson to Anne Martin, 27 March 1913, Box 7, AMC.

43. Clipping in Scrapbook IV, AMC.

44. Miscellaneous Suffrage Materials, Carton VI, AMC.

45. Bird Wilson to Anne Martin, 29 April 1913, Box 7, AMC.

46. Minnie Bray to Anne Martin, 11 November 1913, Box 1, AMC.

47. Gertrude Webster to Anne Martin, 16 November 1913, Box 7, AMC.

48. Edith West to Anne Martin, 28 March 1913, Box 7, AMC.

49. A. Smith, "Anne Martin," pp. 160–162; see also *Nevada State Journal,* 6 October 1913, p. 6; 10 October 1913, p. 8; 14 October 1913, p. 8.

50. Degler, *At Odds,* p. 350.

51. Anna Howard Shaw to Anne Martin, 18 October 1913, Box 6, AMC.

52. *Nevada State Journal,* 27 October 1913, p. 4.

53. Anne Martin to Suffrage Presidents, 5 November 1913, Box 9, AMC.

54. "From Other Editors," *Reno Evening Gazette,* 24 November 1913, p. 4.

55. It seems quite possible that at least some of Martin's accusations were right. See Flexner, *Century of Struggle,* pp. 304–318, and Degler's chapter, "Who Opposed Suffrage?" in *At Odds.*

56. Deckard, *The Women's Movement*, p. 293.

57. Buhle and Buhle, *The Concise History of Woman Suffrage*, pp. 417–421.

58. *Minutes of the Suffrage Convention* (NAWSA, 1913), pp. 87–91.

59. A. Smith, "Anne Martin," p. 170.

60. Anne Martin to Agnes Ryan, 30 July 1914, Box 9, AMC.

61. Earl, "Nevada Suffragets," p. 18.

62. *Nevada State Journal*, 14 February 1914, p. 8.

63. Untitled typescript, apparently an account of the convention, in "Miscellaneous Suffrage Materials," Carton VII, AMC.

64. *Nevada State Journal*, 4 December 1913.

65. Flexner, *Century of Struggle*, p. 269.

66. A. Smith, "Anne Martin," p. 190.

67. Ostrander, *Nevada, The Great Rotten Borough*, pp. 140–142.

68. Anne Martin to Margaret Foley, 19 September 1914, Box 9, AMC.

69. Suffrage Materials, Carton VII, AMC, and *Manhattan Post*, 21 March 1914, among others.

70. Anne Martin to Suffrage Presidents, 25 March 1914, "Form Letters," Carton VII, AMC.

71. Vernon, "Mabel Vernon," p. 42.

72. Nelson, "Ladies in the Streets," p. 177.

73. Vernon, "Mabel Vernon," p. 44.

74. Maude McCreery to President and Executive Committee of the Nevada Equal Franchise Society, 12 May 1914, Box 4, AMC.

75. There is a possibility that this letter was not sent: it appears in the carton of manuscripts rather than in the suffrage files; still, that omission from public files would make sense with so consciously vindictive an attack. "Manuscripts and Notes," Carton I, AMC.

76. Vernon, "Mabel Vernon," pp. 44–45.

77. Ibid., pp. 129–131.

78. Field, "Sara Bard Field," pp. 248–253, passim.

79. Anne Martin to Key Pittman, April 1914, Box 8, AMC.

80. Key Pittman to Anne Martin, 10 April 1914, Box 6, AMC.

81. Anne Martin to Key Pittman, 21 April 1914, Box 8, 1914.

82. Key Pittman to Anne Martin, 12 May 1914, Box 6, AMC.

83. Anna Howard Shaw to Anne Martin, 16 June 1914, Box 6, AMC.

84. Anna Howard Shaw to Anne Martin, 26 June 1914, Box 6, AMC.

85. Anne Martin to *San Francisco Examiner*, 1 May 1914, Box 8, AMC.

86. Harper, ed., *The History of Woman Suffrage*, vol. 5, p. 421.

87. Anne Martin to Agnes Ryan, 30 July 1914, Box 8, AMC.

88. "The Winning of Nevada," *Suffragist*, 7 November 1914, p. 13.

89. Vernon, "Mabel Vernon," p. 146.

90. Undated letter to Margaret Foley, "Margaret Foley," unprocessed (as of May 1981) collection, Schlesinger Library, Radcliffe College, Cambridge, Massachusetts. Hereafter cited as MFC.

91. Notebook, MFC.

92. Folder 47, MFC.

93. Bird Wilson to Anne Martin, 5 October 1914, Box 7, AMC.

94. A. Smith, "Anne Martin," p. 222.

95. Mrs. F. A. Weeks to Anne Martin, 10 October 1914, Box 7, AMC.

96. Undated clippings, MFC.

97. Scrapbook V, AMC.

98. Field, "Sara Bard Field," pp. 250–253.

99. Mrs. George Bailey to Anne Martin, 5 October 1914, Box 1, AMC.

100. Sara Bard Field Ehrgott, "The Clash in Nevada," *Outwest Magazine* (August 1914), pp. 52–53.

101. Ibid., p. 51.

102. Letter dated 3 July 1914, Suffrage Miscellany, Carton VII, AMC.

103. Anne Martin to Suffrage Presidents, 14 October 1914, Box 8, AMC.

104. Anne Martin to V. L. Ricketts, Editor of the *Reno Evening Gazette,* 10–14 April 1914, Box 7, AMC.

105. Bird Wilson to Anne Martin, 19 October 1914, Box 7, AMC.

106. Maude Younger to Anne Martin, 29 September 1914, Box 7, AMC.

107. Maude Younger to Anne Martin, 5 October 1914, Box 7, AMC.

108. Laura Gregg Cannon to Anne Martin, 9 July 1914, Box 2, AMC. Cannon wrote more letters than most of the organizers; her fifty-nine letters in the collection are particularly rich in detail.

109. *Official Returns of the Election of November 7, 1914*, compiled by George Brodigan, pp. 18–25.

110. Maude Younger to Anne Martin, 19 October 1914, Box 7, AMC.

111. Ehrgott, "The Clash in Nevada," p. 48.

112. Earl, "Nevada Suffragets," p. 19.

Chapter 7: Clamor in the Streets

1. Autobiography II, p. 6.

2. Anna Howard Shaw to Anne Martin, 26 June 1914, Box 5, AMC.

3. Autobiography I, chapter 2.

4. Irwin, *Angels and Amazons,* pp. 355–356.

5. Flexner, *Century of Struggle,* p. 277.

6. Bird Wilson to Anne Martin, 20 October 1914, Box 7, AMC.

7. Clipping from *New York Tribune,* 25 December 1914, Equal Franchise Society File, Nevada Historical Society, Reno, Nevada.

8. Anne Martin to Minnie Flanigan, 16 January 1914, Box 8, AMC.

9. Anne Martin to Suffrage Presidents, 4 February 1915, Box 8, AMC.

10. Mrs. H. L. Norton to Anne Martin, n.d., but by context 1915, Box 5, AMC.

11. Bird Wilson to Anne Martin, 4 February 1915, Box 7, AMC.

12. Bird Wilson to Anne Martin, 22 February 1915, Box 7, AMC.

13. Martin, out correspondence, Box 8, is filled with these exchanges.

14. Anne Martin to Mary Ogden White, 11 February 1916, NC 167, Nevada Historical Society, Reno, Nevada.

15. Anne Martin to Anna Howard Shaw, 17 May 1915, NC 67, Nevada Historical Society, Reno, Nevada.

16. Myra Beane to Margaret Foley, unprocessed collection, folder 47, Schlesinger Library, Radcliffe College.

17. Martin, "Nevada Women," pp. 4–5.

18. Ibid.

19. Program for the Woman Voters' Convention, Carton III, AMC.

20. Scrapbook V, and Sara Bard Field typescript, pp. 340ff., discuss the colorful trip; a Bancroft Library publication offers more detail. See "When Sara Comes, It's Always a Holiday," *Bancroftiana* no. 76 (October 1980) (Berkeley: University of California, 1980), pp. 1–3.

21. Irwin, *The Story of Alice Paul,* p. 326.

22. Sochen, *The New Woman.*

23. Quoted in Sidney Roderick Bland, "Techniques of Persuasion: The National Woman's Party and Woman Suffrage, 1913–1919" (Ph.D. dissertation, George Washington University, 1972), p. 186.

24. Kraditor, *The Ideas of the Woman Suffrage Movement,* p. 227. It is also true that as the years passed, some left the CU, as Kelley did when she fought the central officers over protective legislation.

25. Sochen, *The New Woman,* p. 98.

26. Nelson, "Ladies in the Streets," pp. 161–163.

27. Irwin, *The Story of Alice Paul,* p. 121.

28. Inez Haynes Irwin, "The Adventure of Feminism" (unpublished manuscript in Inez Haynes Irwin papers, Schlesinger Library, Radcliffe College), p. 456.

29. Florence Wise to Alice Paul, 5 November 1915, Box 7, AMC.

30. Irwin, *The Story of Alice Paul,* p. 131.

31. Ibid., p. 327.

32. Ibid., p. 131.

33. Ibid., pp. 116–117.

34. Flexner, *Century of Struggle,* pp. 279–282.

35. Ibid., p. 283.

36. Irwin, *The Story of Alice Paul,* pp. 132–137.

37. Flexner, *Century of Struggle,* p. 279.

38. Irwin, *The Story of Alice Paul,* p. 152.

39. Flyer to "Women Voters of Nevada," n.d., but by context summer 1916, Carton III, AMC.

40. Ibid.

41. Bland, "Techniques of Persuasion," p. 189.

42. *Nevada State Journal,* 15 June 1916, Scrapbook II, p. 177, AMC.

43. On one occasion, she remembered, "He congratulated me on my crowd and I sympathized with him for having so few." In Field, "Sara Bard Field," p. 356.

44. Vernon, "Mabel Vernon," Vol. 1, p. 55.

45. Clipping in Carton IV, AMC.

46. Anne Martin's letters to Minnie Flanigan over the period of February to April cover the plans, Box 7 and the *Bulletin* of the Civic League, 3 May 1916, printed details.

47. Undated clipping in Carton IV.

48. Anne Martin to Minnie Flanigan, 27 July 1916, Box 7, AMC.

49. Anne Martin to Key Pittman, 5 August 1916, Box 7, AMC.

50. Helen Belford et al. to Nevada Women's Civic League, but also read into the *Congressional Record* by Senator Pittman, printed and sent out in many copies by the government printing house. Carton IV, AMC.

51. From April 1916 until March 1917, CU and the Woman's Party were treated as separate organizations, the first for all women, the second for voting women.

52. Carrie Chapman Catt, "Crisis in the Suffrage Movement," *New York Times,* 3 September 1916, reprinted in Janeway, *Women,* p. 93.

53. Buhle and Buhle, *The Concise History of Woman Suffrage,* p. 434.

54. Anne Martin to Sara Bard Field, 22 September 1916, Box 8, AMC.

55. Mae Packer to Mabel Davis, 17 September 1916, Box 4, AMC.

56. Bird Wilson to Anne Martin, 30 September 1916, Box 7, AMC.

57. Anne Martin to Bird Wilson, 2 October 1916, Box 8, AMC.

58. Anne Martin to National Woman's Party, 25 September 1916, Box 8, AMC.

59. Anne Martin to NWP, night letter, 28 October 1916, Box 8, AMC.

60. Scrapbook V has the records.

61. Vernon, "Mabel Vernon," p. 65.

62. Ibid.

63. *Suffragist,* 4 November 1916, Carton IV, AMC.

64. Unsigned letter to Mabel Vernon, 28 October 1916, Box 4, Mabel Vernon Collection, Bancroft Library University of California, Berkeley, California; hereafter cited as MVC.

65. Box 8 is full of frantic questions and careful delaying letters.

66. Evans, *The Feminists,* p. 195.

67. Gruber, *Women in American Politics,* p. 6.

68. Kraditor, *The Ideas of the Woman Suffrage Movement,* p. 195.

69. Flexner, *Century of Struggle,* p. 277.

70. Anne Martin to Alice Paul, 20 November 1916, Box 8, AMC.

71. *Suffragist,* 9 December 1916.

72. Quoted in Sinclair, *The Better Half,* p. 304.

73. *Carson Daily Appeal,* 13 November 1916, p. 2.

74. Nevada Branch, *Woman's Party Bulletin,* 14 November 1916.

75. Anne Martin to C. F. Horton, 22 November 1916, Box 8, AMC.

76. Paul, "Conversations with Alice Paul," vol. 1, pp. 211–212.

77. Flexner, *Century of Struggle,* p. 386 n.

78. Ibid., p. 293.

79. Stevens, *Jailed for Freedom,* pp. 76–77.

80. Ibid.

81. Field, "Sara Bard Field," p. 361.

82. Bland, "Techniques of Persuasion," p. 185.

83. Nelson, "Ladies in the Streets," p. 178.

84. Kettler, "The Suffragists," p. 16.

85. Bland, "Techniques of Persuasion," p. 186–188.

86. Flexner, *Century of Struggle,* p. 283.

87. Bland, "Techniques of Persuasion," pp. 111–112.

88. Flexner, *Century of Struggle,* pp. 294–295.

89. Ibid., p. 285.

90. Statement of Miss Anne Martin, Carton I, AMC.

91. Irwin, *The Story of Alice Paul,* p. 259. This quotation appears in a number of phrasings, depending perhaps more on the literary leaning of the writer than the actual words. See Stevens, *Jailed for Freedom,* p. 102, and newspaper accounts in Scrapbooks III and IV for variations.

92. Stevens, *Jailed for Freedom,* pp. 104–106.

93. Ibid., p. 106.

94. Mabel Vernon to Minnie Flanigan, 17 July 1917, Box 5, MVC.

95. Stevens, *Jailed for Freedom,* pp. 107–109.

96. Kettler, "The Suffragists," pp. 20–21.

97. *Suffragist,* 28 July 1917.

98. Some months later, the sentences were declared null by District of Columbia courts, a fact often forgotten by a press delighted with such sensational material.

99. *Suffragist,* 10 December 1917, p. 17.

100. Lou Henry Hoover to Anne Martin, 7 August 1917, Martin File, 1411/1, California Historical Society, San Francisco.

101. Bird Wilson to Anne Martin, 23 November 1917, Box 7, AMC.

102. Vernon, "Mabel Vernon," p. 133.

103. See Carton V, AMC.

104. Autobiography II.

105. Flexner, *Century of Struggle,* pp. 286–287.

Chapter 8: The Senate Campaigns

1. Anderson, "Practical Political Equality for Women," p. 85. My sense of the campaigns is deeply indebted to Anderson's work.

2. Ibid., pp. 86–88.

3. Anne Martin to Mrs. William Kent, 28 May 1918, Box 13, AMC.

4. Paul, "Conversations with Alice Paul," pp. 453–455.

5. Anne Martin, "Speech of Miss Anne Martin," delivered at the Brown Palace Hotel, Wednesday, 17 April 1918, Carton VI, AMC.

6. Vernon, "Mabel Vernon," p. 45.

7. *Reno Evening Gazette,* 11 March 1918.

8. "Topics in Brief," *Carson Daily Appeal,* 20 March 1918.

9. Ibid., 6 April 1918.

10. "He Bids Her Goodnight," reprinted in the *Reno Evening Gazette*, 14 March 1918. The *Gazette* wrote little, but happily seized negative reports from the state papers all out of proportion to the coverage it gave other events.

11. *Tonopah Times*, 14 March 1918.

12. *Carson Daily Appeal*, 7 March 1918.

13. *Carson Daily Appeal*, 2 March 1918.

14. Ibid.

15. *San Francisco Examiner*, n.d., Scrapbook VI, AMC.

16. *Mason Valley News*, 12 October 1918.

17. Anne Martin to Ella Riegel, 25 May 1918, Box 13, AMC.

18. Letters between Martin and Kent, Martin and Riegel, and other women are almost entirely devoted to fund raising from March to May. See Box 13, AMC.

19. Mary Austin to Anne Martin, 3 April 1918, Box 10, AMC.

20. Carton VI contains records of contributions and statements required by the Nevada Corrupt Practices Act.

21. Anderson, "Practical Political Equality for Women," pp. 48–49.

22. Vernon, "Mabel Vernon," p. 86.

23. Anderson, pp. 57–58.

24. Margaret Whittemore to Mabel Vernon, September 1918, Box 3, MVC.

25. The many letters and wires exchanged are in Box 12 (Wilson's) and Box 13, AMC.

26. Anne Martin to Mrs. Carrie Orr and others, 21 March 1918, marked "Form letter not sent." Box 13, AMC.

27. "Woman Suffrage: Remarks of Honorable Charles Henderson of Nevada in the Senate of the United States, Saturday, September 28, 1918" (Washington: U.S. Government Printing House, 1918), pp. 2–4, Carton VI, AMC.

28. Ibid.

29. Chafe, *The American Woman*, p. 26.

30. Freda Kirchwey in *Everywoman*, 21 April 1918, p. 4.

31. Ella Riegel to Mabel Vernon, 27 August 1918, Box 3, MVC.

32. Margaret Long to Mary Goodman, n.d., but probably 1940, Margaret Long Papers, Sophia Smith Collection, Smith College, Northampton, Massachusetts. Hereafter cited as MLP.

33. "Gats Wage Desert War to Elect Anne Martin First Woman Senator," *Newport News* (Virginia) *Times Herald*, n.d., Carton IV, AMC.

34. Margaret Long to Mabel Vernon, 17, 26, and 27 October 1918, Box 3, MVC.

35. Jessica Granville-Smith, 18 October 1918, Box IV, MVC.

36. Margaret Long, Travel Diary 1918–1919, "Abe's Journal," Fallon, 1 July 1918, Margaret Long Papers, Box 20, folder 1, University of Colorado, Boulder, Colorado. Quoted in Anderson, "Practical Political Equality for Women," p. 194.

37. The clipping in Scrapbook VII shows no date, but seems to have been from mid October.

38. Reprinted in *New York Sun*, 4 August 1918, Scrapbook VII, AMC.

39. *Tonopah Times*, undated clipping, Scrapbook VII, AMC.

40. Mollie Condon to Mabel Vernon, 31 July 1918, Box 2, MVC.

41. Ibid.

42. *Carson Daily Appeal*, 1 November 1918.

43. See Elliott, *History of Nevada*, pp. 222–223.

44. Scrapbook VII, n.d., AMC.

45. Scrapbooks VI and VII, AMC, cover the campaign.

46. Anne Martin to Sara Bard Field, 2 September 1918, Box 13, AMC.

47. *Tonopah Bonanza*, 28 September 1918.

48. Scrapbook VII, AMC.

49. Winnifred Harper Cooley to Anne Martin, n.d., but probably early October, Box 10, AMC.

50. Jessica Granville-Smith to Mabel Vernon, October 1918, Box 3, MVC.

51. Out Correspondence in Box 13 and Box 10 is stuffed with requests and regrets.

52. Flyer in Carton V, AMC.

53. Carton V, AMC.

54. Ibid.

55. Mabel Vernon to Mrs. Koeding, 30 October 1918, Box 6, MVC.

56. Ann Penn Aston to Anne Martin, 9 October 1918, Box 10, AMC.

57. Rita Breeze to Anne Martin, 7 October 1918, Box 10, AMC.

58. Elbert Howard to Anne Martin, n.d., but apparently early 1919, Box 11, AMC.

59. Robert Manion to Anne Martin, 23 October 1918, Box 11, AMC.

60. *Oakland Tribune*, 20 November 1918, Scrapbook VII, AMC.

61. *Political History of Nevada*, prepared by Malcolm McEachin, Secretary of State (Carson City, Nev.: State Printing Office, 1940), pp. 43–44, Carton II, AMC.

62. Anderson treats strategy in, "Practical Political Equality for Women," pp. 197–204.

63. Anne Martin to Campaign Helpers, 15 November 1918, Box 13, AMC.

64. Glass, "Nevada's Lady Lawmakers," p. 3 offers a discussion of women who ran for state offices and served in the legislature.

65. Hulse, *The Nevada Adventure*, p. 242.

66. Kathryn Lincoln to Mabel Vernon, 25 October 1918, Box 3, MVC.

67. Alice Valentine to Mabel Vernon, 14 October 1918, Box 3, AMC.

68. Pearl Karaus to Mabel Vernon, 30 December 1918, Box 3, MVC.

69. Kirchwey, Scrapbook VII, AMC.

70. *Carson Daily Appeal*, 19 August 1918.

71. Flexner, *Century of Struggle*, p. 209, and Sinclair, *The Better Half*, p. 304.

72. Lemons, *The Woman Citizen*, p. 10.

73. Ibid., pp. 10–12; Deckard, *The Women's Movement*, p. 200; Flexner, *Century of Struggle*, pp. 298–299, for example.

74. Lemons, *The Woman Citizen*, pp. 7–10.

75. Ibid., p. 15.

76. Lemons' chapter on World War I, "the first hour in history for the women of the world," offers a helpful account of these years (pp. 3–41).

77. *Reno Evening Gazette*, 25 February 1919.

78. *Carson Daily Appeal*, 12 March 1919.

79. Autobiography N, Carton I, AMC.

80. Unlabeled clipping, 17 January 1919, Scrapbook VII, AMC.

81. William P. Dillingham to Anne Martin, 10 April 1919, Box 14, AMC.

82. William Ralston to George Bartlett, n.d., but clearly 1919, George Bartlett Papers, NC 432, University of Nevada Special Collections Library, Reno, Nevada.

83. Anne Martin to J. A. H. Hopkins, 2 July 1919, Box 14, AMC.

84. Anne Martin, "Land Monopoly and Its Evils Discussed by a Woman Candidate for U.S. Senator," *Reconstruction* (October 1919), pp. 306–309.

85. Martin, "What Women Should Vote For," pp. 155ff.

86. Ibid., p. 165.

87. Lemons, *The Woman Citizen*, p. 148.

88. Ibid., p. 154.

89. Ibid., pp. 154–157.

90. Lemons offers a detailed history of the bill from conception to repeal in 1929 (pp. 153–177).

91. Martin, "Everywoman's Chance to Serve Humanity: An Everlasting Benefit You Can Win in a Week," *Good Housekeeping* (February 1920), pp. 20–21ff., and Martin, "We Couldn't Afford a Doctor," pp. 19–20ff.

92. Martin, "Land Monopoly," pp. 306–310.

93. Martin, "If I Were a Senator," pp. 162–163.

94. Ibid., p. 162.

95. Press Release, Anne Martin's Headquarters, 5 April 1920, Carton V, AMC.

96. Clipping from *Independent Woman*, n.d., but clearly 1919, Scrapbook VIII, AMC.

97. Anne Martin to Will Hays, 17 April 1920, Box 16, AMC.

98. Anne Martin to Mrs. Nelson Woods, 21 June 1920, Box 16, AMC.

99. Edith Howard to Anne Martin, Box XIV, AMC.

100. Anne Martin to Harriot Stanton Blatch, 24 June 1920, Box 16, AMC.

101. *Carson Daily Appeal,* 14 October 1920.

102. Katherine Mullen to Anne Martin, 9 June 1920, Box 15, AMC.

103. Elizabeth Kent to Anne Martin, 2 May 1920, Box 15, AMC.

104. Harriot Stanton Blatch to Anne Martin, 18 June 1920, Box 14, AMC.

105. Mrs. H. O. Havemeyer to Anne Martin, 20 October 1920, Box 14, AMC.

106. Doris Stevens to Anne Martin, 21 October 1920, Box 15, AMC.

107. Helen Clegg Winters to Anne Martin, n.d., but apparently October 20, Box 15, AMC.

108. Mrs. Victor DuPont to Anne Martin, Box 14, AMC.

109. Helen Hoy Greeley to Anne Martin, 27 July 1920, Box 14, AMC.

110. Mabel Vernon to *Tonopah Times,* 20 August 1920, Box 3, MVC.

111. *Carson Daily Appeal,* 24 April 1920.

112. Scrapbooks 8 and 9 are full of the accusations.

113. Anne Martin to *Reno Evening Gazette,* 17 May 1920, Box 16, AMC.

114. Margaret Long to Anne Martin, 20 June 1920, Box 15, AMC.

115. Anne Martin to *Reno Evening Gazette,* 21 June 1920, Box 15, AMC.

116. Anne Martin to *Reno Evening Gazette,* 26 June 1920, Box 15, AMC.

117. Margaret Long to Anne Martin, 27 June 1920, Box 15, AMC.

118. Anne Martin to Nevada Editors, form letter, 26 June 1920, Box 16, AMC.

119. Karl Martin to Anne Martin, 14 July 1920, Box 15, AMC.

120. Roger Baldwin to Anne Martin, 29 August 1920, Box 4, AMC.

121. *Reno Evening Gazette,* 3 August 1920, Box 15, AMC.

122. George Johnson to Mabel Vernon, 9 October 1920, Box 4, MVC.

123. Walter C. Clark to Anne Martin, 1 August 1920, Box 14, AMC.

124. D. S. McFarlane to Anne Martin, 23 October 1920, Box 15, AMC.

125. Margaret Long to Anne Martin, 20 June 1920, Box 15, AMC.

126. J. D. Lorraine to Mabel Vernon, 14 October 1920, Box 4, MVC.

127. Margaret Long to Anne Martin, 8 June 1920, Box 15, AMC.

128. Katherine Mullen to Mabel Vernon, n.d., apparently late August or early September, Box 4, MVC.

129. Carbon of a letter from George Hampton to Warren E. Stone, 16 April 1920, Box 16, AMC.

130. Flyers, Carton V, AMC.

131. Katherine Mullen to Mabel Vernon, 15 August 1920, Box 4, MVC.

132. Katherine Mullen to Mabel Vernon, 11 September 1920, Box 4, MVC.

133. Lola Maverick Lloyd to Mabel Vernon, Box 4, MVC.

134. Carton VI, AMC.

135. Margaret Long to Mrs. Verner Z. Reed, 16 November 1920, MLP.

136. Anne Martin to Mabel Vernon, 3 September 1920, Box 14, AMC.

137. Letters are in Box 14, AMC.

138. Italo-Gasso and Olio Company to Mabel Vernon, 28 October 1920, Box 2, MVC. The typed letter is on company stationery but bears no signature.

139. Chan, *Sagebrush Statesman.*

140. Form letters to supporters, 1920, Carton VI, AMC.

141. Anne Martin to Helen Hoy Greeley, 18 November 1920, Box 16, AMC.

142. Ibid.

143. Anne Martin to Alonsita Walker, n.d., but apparently late 1919 or early 1920, Box 9, AMC.

144. *San Francisco Call,* 20 December 1920, Carton IV, AMC.

145. *Fernley Enterprise,* 28 August 1920, Vol. X, AMC.

146. Anne Martin to Helen Hoy Greeley, 30 August 1920, Box 14, AMC.

147. Anne Martin to L. Selma, 20 October 1920, Box 16, AMC.

148. Form letters, 1920, Carton VI, AMC.

149. "Women Are Half the People," 10 October 1920, Box 7, MVC.

150. Flexner, in her chapter "Who Opposed Suffrage?" in *Century of Struggle,* and Degler in chapters 13 and 14 in *At Odds,* delineate some of these ideas. See also Kraditor, *The Ideas of the Woman Suffrage Movement.*

151. Martin, "What Women Should Vote For," p. 15.

152. "What Use Will Women Make of Political Power?" Carton I, AMC, is the original of the *Good Housekeeping* article. Martin's personal reaction did not appear in the printed version.

153. *Official Returns of the Election of November 2, 1920,* compiled by George Brodigan, pp. 42–43.

154. Theresa Carlson to Anne Martin, 26 November 1920, Box 14, AMC.

155. Marie Michel to Anne Martin, 26 November 1920, Box 15, AMC. Michel's story of her life was among the books Anne Martin left to the University of Nevada Special Collections department.

156. Mrs. Simmons to Anne Martin, n.d., but apparently 1920, Box 14, AMC.

157. Anne Martin, "Parties, Principles and the Woman Voters," Carton I, folder 4, AMC.

158. Harriot Stanton Blatch to Anne Martin, 18 June 1920, Box 14, AMC.

159. Ostrander, *Nevada, The Great Rotten Borough,* has chronicled the political life of the Silver State in detail.

160. Sochen, *Movers and Shakers.*

161. Kirchwey, in *Everywoman,* 21 April 1918, p. 4.

Chapter 9: Dr. Anne Martin

1. *Reno Evening Gazette,* 23 May 1942.

2. Poems, Carton I, AMC.

3. Martin, "Labor Is Watching Its Leaders."

4. Martin, "Women's Inferiority Complex."

5. Ibid.

6. Lemons, *The Woman Citizen,* p. 49.

7. Crystal Eastman, "Alice Paul's Convention," reprinted in Cook, *On Women and Revolution,* pp. 57–60.

8. Lemons, *The Woman Citizen,* p. 49.

9. Chafe, *The American Woman,* pp. 25–26.

10. Lemons, *The Woman Citizen,* pp. 157–159.

11. Ibid., p. 171.

12. Chafe, Lemons, and O'Neill distinguish in a variety of ways between the two major divisions of the movement of the twenties. The terms used here follow their distinctions: "hard-core" or "pure" feminists, here termed "feminists," were those who sought legal equality above all other causes; social reformers—sometimes called "social feminists"—were opposed to legal equality measures, fearing the loss of hard-won protective legislation.

13. Lemons, *The Woman Citizen,* p. 184.

14. Ibid., p. 48.

15. Vernon, "Mabel Vernon," pp. 81–83.

16. Anne Martin to Jane Addams, 29 May 1922, Addams Correspondence, Schlesinger Library.

17. Anne Martin, "Jane Addams' Work for Peace," *Time and Tide,* 24 October 1922.

18. Martin, "Equality Laws vs. Women in Government," pp. 165–166.

19. Martin, "The Next Step for Women," p. 159.

20. Ibid., pp. 159–165.

21. Martin, "Equality Laws vs. Women in Government," p. 166.

22. Anne Martin, "British and American Women in Politics," *New York Times Magazine,* 5 November 1922, p. 14.

23. "Aspects of British and American Feminism," Carton I, AMC, an earlier version of the previous article.

24. Summary of "Woman Today and Woman Tomorrow," Carton I, AMC.

25. Martin, "Women and Their Magazines," pp. 91–93.

26. *San Francisco Call,* 28 October 1922, in Carton IV, AMC.

27. Martin, "Nevada: Beautiful Desert of Buried Hopes," pp. 89–92.

28. Ibid.

29. *Nevada State Journal,* 16 July 1923.

30. *Reno Evening Gazette,* 31 July 1923.

31. Unlabeled clipping, Carton IV, AMC.

32. Anne Martin, "A Sex War?," pp. 2–4, Carton I, AMC.

33. Anne Martin, "Women, Give Your Differences," Carton I, AMC.

34. John M. Nelson to Anne Martin, 28 August 1924, Box 4, AMC.

35. Anne Martin, "Will LaFollette Give Women Equality?," Carton I, AMC.

36. Martin, "Feminists and Future Political Action."

37. Ibid.

38. Eastman, *On Women and Revolution,* p. 173.

39. Carton IV is filled with clippings of the trials.

40. Records of the Women's Peace party and the Women's International League for Peace and Freedom are deposited at the Swarthmore Peace Archive at Swarthmore College, Swarthmore, Pennsylvania. Henceforth cited as WILPF. Charter member list, Box I, Series A; Council list, Box 3, folder i, WILPF.

41. Women's Peace party correspondence, Nevada Peace party, Roll 12.8, WILPF.

42. Lemons's chapter 8 in *The Woman Citizen* gives a thorough account of the running battle between rightists and "Reds" in the twenties (pp. 209–225).

43. Anne Martin to Jane Addams, 29 May 1922, Jane Addams Correspondence, Roll 7, Schlesinger Library.

44. Anne Martin to Jane Addams, 26 December 1922, Jane Addams Correspondence, Schlesinger Library.

45. *Rocky Mountain News,* 1 May 1928.

46. Anne Martin to Executive Board, 16 July 1926, WILPF.

47. Martin, "The Woman's Peace Congress at Dublin."

48. Vernon, "Mabel Vernon," p. 79.

49. Long, *The Shadow of the Arrow.* Long dedicated the book to Anne Martin.

50. Long, *Enchanted Desert.* A copy is in the Anne Martin Collection left to Special Collections, Library, at the University of Nevada-Reno.

51. Margaret Long to Mary Goodman, 9 February 1943, MLP.

52. Long, *Enchanted Desert,* pp. 7–12.

53. Anne Martin, *New Republic,* 30 October 1929.

54. Personal interview with Martin Mackey, 18 January 1982.

55. Anne Martin to Jane Addams, 21 May 1929, Addams Correspondence, Schlesinger Library.

56. Anne Martin to Jane Addams, n.d., inscribed "Birthday Wish 1930," Addams Correspondence, Schlesinger Library.

57. Sources for Lewis's life include the Austin Lewis Papers, Bancroft Library, and "Austin Lewis" in the *History of San Francisco,* Lewis Frank Byington (ed.), Oscar Lewis (assoc. ed.), 3 vols. (San Francisco: S. J. Clarke Publishing Company, 1931), vol. 2, and his obituary in the *San Francisco Chronicle,* 27 June 1944, p. 9.

58. Austin Lewis to Anne Martin, 17 March 1926, Anne Martin File, California Historical Society, San Francisco. Hereafter cited as AMF.

59. Austin Lewis to Anne Martin, 25 August 1929, AMF.

60. Ibid., 29 September 1929, AMF.

61. Ibid., 2 August 29, AMF. Whitney's stellar career as a radical is recorded in Richmond, *Native Daughter*.

62. Austin Lewis to Anne Martin, 19 December 1930, AMF.

63. 11 May 1930, AMF.

64. Anne Martin to Jane Addams, 1931, Box 9, AMC.

65. Anne Martin to Emily Balch, WILPF, 15 January 1930, Box 9, AMC. One date is probably an error; she consistently gave 1930 as the date for her heart attack.

66. Anne Martin to Jane Addams, 10 February 1930, Addams Correspondence, Schlesinger Library. Another doubtful date.

67. *Daily Carmelite,* 17 August 1931.

68. Anne Martin to Hannah Clothier Hull, 2 November 1933, Box 9, AMC.

69. Mabel Vernon to Anne Martin, 19 November 1935, Box 7, AMC.

70. *Washington Post,* 6 April 1936.

71. Anne Martin to Hannah Clothier Hull, 30 June 1936, Box 9, AMC.

72. Anne Martin to WILPF board members, 16 July 1936, Box 9, AMC.

73. Esther J. Crooks to Anne Martin, 23 July 1936, Box 7, AMC.

74. Heloise Brainerd to Anne Martin, 4 August 1936, Box 7, AMC.

75. Rosika Schwimmer to Anne Martin, 27 July 1936, Box 7, AMC.

76. Sara Bard Field to Anne Martin, 1938, AMF.

77. Harriet Munro to Anne Martin, 1932, Carton I, AMC.

78. Sara Bard Field to Anne Martin, n.d., AMF.

79. Mary Austin to Anne Martin, 3 January 1933, AMF.

80. Anne Martin to Ray Lyman Wilbur, 22 June 1941, Box 7, AMC.

81. *Carmel Cymbal,* 12 April 1942.

82. Austin Lewis to Mary Bulkley, 13 May 1942, Austin Lewis Papers, Bancroft Library.

83. Austin Lewis to Anne Martin, 6 May 1942, AMF.

84. Papers and notes on the two articles are spread through Carton I and the Nevada Historical Society File.

85. Interview, Martin, Peter, and Douglas Mackey, 19 March 1982.

86. Austin E. Hutcheson (ed.), *The Story of the Nevada Suffrage Campaign,* University of Nevada Bulletin 42, no. 7 (August 1948), p. 19.

87. Patrick McCarran to Anne Martin, 19 January 1946, Box IV, AMC.

88. Clipping, May 16, 1947, in Carton VI, AMC.

89. *Reno Evening Gazette,* 23 March 1950.

90. Edna Martin Parratt to Sara Bard Field, 21 April 1951, AMF.

91. Sara Bard Field to Edna Martin Parratt, 28 April 1951, AMF.

92. Autobiography N.

93. Edna Parratt to Kathryn Anderson, 22 May 1978, AMF.

BIBLIOGRAPHY

Books

Addams, Jane. *Twenty Years at Hull House*. With autobiographical notes. New York: Signet, 1960.

Allen, Peter C. *Stanford, from the Foothills to the Bay*. Stanford, Calif.: Stanford Historical Society, n.d.

Atherton, Gertrude. *My San Francisco, a Wayward Biography*. New York: Bobbs-Merrill, 1946.

Austin, Mary. *Earth Horizon: Autobiography*. New York: Houghton Mifflin, 1932.

Banner, Lois. *Women in Modern America*. New York: Harcourt Brace Jovanovich, 1974.

Bashkirtseff, Marie. *The Journal of a Young Artist, 1860–1884*. Translated by Mary J. Serrow. New York: Cassell and Company Limited, 1889.

Becker, Susan D. *The Origin of the Equal Rights Amendment: American Feminism between the Wars*. Westbrook, Conn.: Greenwood Press, 1981.

Bernard, Jessie. *The Female World*. New York: The Free Press, 1981.

Boulding, Elise. *Women in the Twentieth Century World*. New York: John Wiley and Sons, Sage Publications, 1977.

Boyd, Nancy. *Three Victorian Women Who Changed Their World: Josephine Butler, Octavia Hill, Florence Nightingale*. New York: Oxford University Press, 1982.

Braddock, M. C. *"That Infidel Place"—A Short History of Girton College, 1869–1969*. London: Chatto and Windus, 1969.

Brailsford, E. L. et al. *The Treatment of Women's Deputations by the Metropolitan Police*. London, 1911.

Brown, Bertha Bender. *A Tale of Three Cities: Reno, Carson, San Francisco, The Saga and Humor of an Old Pioneer Family*. Healdsburg, Calif., n.d.

Brown, Dee. *The Gentle Tamers: Women of the Old Wild West*. New York: Putnam, 1958.

Browne, J. Ross. *Washoe Revisited: Notes on the Silver Regions of Nevada*. Oakland, Calif.: Biobooks, 1957.

Buhle, Mary Jo. *Women and American Socialism, 1870–1920*. Urbana: University of Illinois Press, 1982.

———, and Paul Buhle. *The Concise History of Woman Suffrage*. Urbana: University of Illinois Press, 1978.

Butler, Rupert. *Emmeline Pankhurst: Portrait of a Wife, Mother and Suffragette*. London: George Harrop and Company Limited, 1970.

Caffrey, Kate. *The 1900s Lady*. London: Gordon and Cremonesi, 1976.

Carroll, Berenice A., ed. *Liberating Women's History: Theoretical and Critical Essays*. Urbana: University of Illinois Press, 1976.

Chafe, William H. *The American Woman: Her Changing Social, Economic and Political Roles, 1920–1970*. New York: Oxford University Press, 1972.

Chamberlin, Hope. *A Minority of Members: Women in the United States Congress*. New York: Praeger, 1973.

Chan, Loren. *Sagebrush Statesman: Tasker L. Oddie of Nevada*. Reno: University of Nevada Press, 1973.

Clemens, Samuel L. *Roughing It*. New York: Harper and Brothers, 1913.

Comstock, Sarah. *Stanford '96, an Accounting in 1926*. Privately printed for the class, 1926.

Cook, Blanche Wiesen, ed. *On Women and Revolution*. New York: Oxford University Press, 1978.

Cooley, Winnifred Harper. *The New Womanhood*. 3rd edition. New York: Broadway Publishing Company, 1904.

Coolidge, Olivia. *Women's Rights: The Suffrage Movement in America, 1848–1920*. New York: Dutton, 1972.

Cott, Nancy F. *The Bonds of Womanhood: Woman's Sphere in New England, 1780–1835*. New Haven: Yale University Press, 1977.

————, and Elizabeth H. Pleck. *A Heritage of Her Own: Toward a New Social History of American Women*. New York: Simon and Schuster, 1979.

Creston, Dormer (Dorothy Julia Baynes). *Fountains of Youth: The Life of Marie Bashkirtseff*. New York: E. P. Dutton, 1937.

Cross, Barbara, ed. *The Educated Woman in America: Selected Writings of Catherine Beecher, Margaret Fuller, and M. Carey Thomas*. New York: Teachers College Press, 1965.

Crow, Duncan. *The Edwardian Woman*. New York: St. Martin's Press, 1978.

————. *The Victorian Woman*. New York: Stein and Day, 1972.

Currell, Melville E. *Political Woman*. London: Croom Helm, 1974.

Dangerfield, George. *The Strange Death of Liberal England*. London: McGibbon and McKee, 1933.

Deckard, Barbara Sinclair. *The Women's Movement: Political, Socioeconomic, and Psychological Issues*. 2nd edition. New York: Harper and Row, 1979.

DeFord, Miriam Allen. *They Were San Franciscans*. Caldwell, Idaho: Caxton Printers, 1941.

Degen, Mary Louise. *The History of the Woman's Peace Party*. Johns Hopkins University Studies in Historical and Political Science, series 57 no. 3. Baltimore: Johns Hopkins, 1939.

Degler, Carl. *At Odds: Women and the Family from the Revolution to the Present*. New York: Oxford University Press, 1980.

————. *"Is There a History of Women?" An Inaugural Lecture Delivered before the University of Oxford on 14 March 1974*. Oxford: Clarendon Press, 1975.

Delamont, Sara, and Lorna Duffin, eds. *The Nineteenth Century Woman*. London: Croom Helm, 1978.

Despard, Charlotte. *Women in the New Era*. London: Suffrage Shop, 1910.

Detzer, Dorothy. *Appointment on the Hill*. New York: Holt, 1948.

Dobkin, Marjorie Housepian, ed. *The Making of a Feminist: Early Journals and Letters of M. Carey Thomas*. Kent, Ohio: Kent State University Press, 1979.

Doten, Alfred R. *The Journals of Alfred Doten, 1849–1903*. Edited by Walter Van Tilburg Clark. Reno: University of Nevada Press, 1973.

Doten, Samuel Bradford. *An Illustrated History of the University of Nevada*. Reno: University of Nevada, 1924.

Doyle, Helen McKnight. *Mary Austin, a Woman of Genius*. New York: Gotham House, 1939.

Eastman, Crystal. *On Women and Revolution*. Edited by Blanche Wiesen Cook. New York: Oxford University Press, 1978.

Eliot, George (Marian Evans). *Middlemarch*. New York: Belford Clarke, 1884.

Elliott, Russell. *History of Nevada*. Lincoln, Nebr.: University of Nebraska Press, 1973.

Evans, Richard J. *The Feminists: Women's Emancipation Movements in Europe, America and Australasia, 1840–1920*. London: Croom Helm, 1977.

Faber, Doris. *Petticoat Politics: How American Women Won the Right to Vote*. New York: Lathrop, 1967.

Faderman, Lillian. *Surpassing the Love of Men: Romantic Friendship and Love between Women from the Renaissance to the Present*. New York: William Morrow Company, 1981.

Faragher, John M. *Women and Men on the Overland Trail*. New Haven: Yale University Press, 1979.

Fawcett, Millicent Garrett. *Woman's Suffrage: A Short History of a Great Movement*. London: The People's Books, n.d.

Flexner, Eleanor. *Century of Struggle: The Woman's Rights Movement in the United States*. Revised edition. Cambridge: Belknap Press of Harvard University Press, 1975.

Fulford, Roger. *Votes for Women: The Story of a Struggle*. London: White Lion, 1976.

Gardner, Alice. *A Short History of Newnham College*. Cambridge: Bowes and Bowes, 1921.

Githens, Marianne, and Jewel L. Prestage. *A Portrait of Marginality: The Political Behavior of American Women*. New York: McKay, 1977.

Gorham, Deborah. *The Victorian Girl and the Feminine Ideal*. Bloomington: Indiana University Press, 1982.

Grand, Sarah (Frances Elizabeth MacFall). *The Heavenly Twins*. New York: Cassell Publishing Company, 1893.

Gray, Dorothy. *Women of the West*. Mill Valley, Calif.: Les Femmes, 1976.

Grimes, Alan. *The Puritan Ethic and Woman Suffrage*. New York: Oxford University Press, 1967.

Gruber, Martin. *Women in American Politics*. Oshkosh, Wis.: Academia Press, 1968.

Haig, Margaret (Viscountess Rhondda). *This Was My World*. London: Macmillan, 1933.

Hamilton, Richard. *Restraining Myths: Critical Studies of United States Social Structure and Politics*. New York: Wiley, 1975.

Harper, Ida Husted, ed. *The History of Woman Suffrage in Six Volumes*. Vol. 5 (1900–1920). New York: National Association for Woman Suffrage in America, 1922.

Harris, Barbara. *Beyond Her Sphere: Women and the Professions in American History*. Westport, Conn.: Greenwood Press, 1978.

Harrison, Brian. *Separate Spheres: The Opposition to Woman's Suffrage in Britain*. London: Croom Helm, 1976.

Hartman, Mary S., and Lois Banner, eds. *Clio's Consciousness Raised*. Harper Torchbooks. New York: Harper and Row, 1974.

Hellerstein, Erna Olafson, Leslie Parker Hume, and Karen M. Offen, eds. *Victorian Women: A Documentary Account of Women's Lives in Nineteenth Century England, France, and the United States*. Stanford, Calif.: Stanford University Press, 1981.

Hogeland, Ronald W., ed. *Women and Womanhood in America*. Lexington, Mass.: D. C. Heath, 1973.

Holliday, Laurel. *Heart Songs: The Intimate Diaries of Young Girls*. Guerneville, Calif.: Bluestocking Books.

Hollis, Patricia. *Women in Public: 1850–1900, Documents of the Victorian Woman's Movement*. London: Allen and Unwin, 1979.

Howard, Maureen. *Facts of Life*. New York: Penguin Books, 1978.

Hulse, James. *The Nevada Adventure*. 3rd edition. Reno: University of Nevada Press, 1973.

———. *The University of Nevada, a Centennial History*. Reno: University of Nevada Press, 1974.

Irwin, Inez Haynes. *Angels and Amazons: A Hundred Years of American Women*. New York: Doubleday, Doran and Company, 1933.

———. *The Story of Alice Paul and the National Woman's Party*. Fairfax, Va.: Dellinger's Publishers Limited, 1977.

James, Edward T., ed. *Notable American Women, a Biographical Dictionary*. Cambridge: Belknap Press of Harvard University Press, 1971.

Janeway, Elizabeth. *Women: Their Changing Roles*. The Great Contemporary Issues. New York: Arno Press, 1973.

Jeffrey, Julie Roy. *Frontier Women: The Trans-Mississippi West, 1840–1880*. New York: Hill and Wang, 1979.

Jordan, David Starr. *The Voice of the Scholar*. San Francisco: Paul Elder and Company, 1903.

Josephson, Hannah. *Jeannette Rankin: First Lady in Congress, a Biography*. New York: Bobbs-Merrill, 1974.

Kamm, Josephine. *Rapiers and Battleaxes: The Women's Movement and Its Aftermath*. Foreword by Mary Stocks. London: George Allen and Unwin Ltd., 1966.

Kenney, Annie. *Memoirs of a Militant*. London: Edward Arnold and Company, 1924.

Key, V. O. *Politics, Parties and Pressure Groups*. 5th edition. New York: Crowell, 1964.

Klein, Viola. *The Feminine Character: History of an Ideology*. Urbana: University of Illinois Press, 1971.

Kraditor, Aileen S. *The Ideas of the Woman Suffrage Movement, 1890–1920*. Garden City, New York: Anchor Books, 1971. (Originally Columbia University Press, 1965.)

———. *Up from the Pedestal: Selected Writings in the History of American Feminism*. New York: Quadrangle Books, 1968.

Lagemann, Ellen Condliffe. *A Generation of Women: Education in the Lives of Progressive Reformers*. Cambridge: Harvard University Press, 1979.

Lasch, Christopher. *The New Radicalism in America, 1889–1964*. New York: Knopf, 1965.

Lawrence, F. W. P. *Women's Fight for the Vote*. London: Women's Press, 1910.

Lemons, J. Stanley. *The Woman Citizen, Social Feminism in the 1920's*. Urbana: University of Illinois Press, 1973.

Levine, Daniel. *Jane Addams and the Liberal Tradition*. Madison: State Historical Society of Wisconsin, 1971.

Long, Margaret. *Enchanted Desert*. Privately printed, 1941.

———. *The Shadow of the Arrow*. Caldwell, Idaho: Caxton Printers, 1950.

Maynard, Mila Tupper. *Walt Whitman, the Poet of Selfhood*. Chicago: Charles H. Kerr and Company, 1903.

Melder, Keith. *Beginnings of Sisterhood: The American Woman Rights Movement, 1800–1860*. New York: Schocken, 1977.

Mitchell, David. *Queen Christabel: A Biography of Christabel Pankhurst*. London: McDonald and Jane's, 1977.

Mitton, G. E., ed. *English Woman's Yearbook and Directory*. London: Adam and Charles Black, 1910.

Morgan, David. *Suffragists and Liberals: The Politics of Woman Suffrage in England*. Oxford: Basil Blackwell, 1975.

Newcomer, Mabel. *A Century of Higher Education for American Women*. New York: Harper and Brothers, 1959.

O'Neill, William. *Everyone Was Brave: The Rise and Fall of Feminism in America*. Chicago: Quadrangle Books, 1969.

———. *The Woman Movement: Feminism in the United States and England*. New York: Barnes and Noble, 1969.

Ostrander, Gilman. *Nevada, The Great Rotten Borough, 1859–1964*. New York: Alfred A. Knopf, 1966.

Paher, Stanley. *Ghost Towns and Mining Camps*. Berkeley: Howell-North, 1970.

Pankhurst, Dame Christabel. *Unshackled: The Story of How We Won the Vote*. Edited by Lord Pethick-Lawrence. London: Hutchinson, 1959.

Pankhurst, E. S. *The Suffragette: The History of the Women's Militant Suffrage Movement, 1905–1910*. New York, 1911.

Pankhurst, Sylvia. *The Suffrage Movement*. Introduction by Dr. Richard Pankhurst. London: Virago, 1977.

Paul, Rodman. *Mining Frontiers of the West, 1848–1880*. New York: Holt, Rinehart and Winston, 1963.

Petersen, Karen, and J. J. Wilson. *Women Artists: Recognition and Re-Appraisal, From the Early Middle Ages to the Twentieth Century*. New York: Harper and Row, 1976.

Powell, John J. *Nevada: The Land of Silver*. San Francisco: Bacon and Company, 1876.

Pugh, Martin. *The Women's Suffrage Movement in Britain, 1867–1928*. London: The Historical Association, 1980.

Raeburn, Antonia. *The Militant Suffragettes*. Introduction by J. B. Priestley. London: Michael Joseph, 1973.

Ramelson, Marian. *The Petticoat Rebellion: A Century of Struggle for Women's Rights*. London: Lawrence and Wishart, 1967.

Richmond, Al. *Native Daughter: The Story of Anita Whitney*. San Francisco: Anita Whitney Seventy-fifth Anniversary Committee, 1942.

Rickey, Elinor. *Eminent Women of the West*. Berkeley: Howell-North Press, 1975.

Riegel, Robert E. *American Feminists*. Lawrence: University of Kansas Press, 1963.

———. *American Women: A Story of Social Change*. Rutherford, N.J.: Farleigh Dickinson Press, 1970.

Rosen, Andrew. *Rise Up, Women! The Militant Campaign of the Women's Social and Political Union*. London: Routledge and Kegan Paul, 1974.

Rover, Constance. *Love, Morals and the Feminists*. London: Routledge and Kegan Paul, 1970.

———. *Women's Suffrage and Party Politics in Britain, 1866–1914*. London: Routledge and Kegan Paul, 1967.

Ruskin, John. *Sesame and Lillies*. New York: H. M. Caldwell Company, n.d.

Russell, Dora. *The Tamarisk Tree: My Quest for Liberty and Love*. London: Elbe-Pemberton, 1975.

Ryan, Mary P. *Womanhood in America from Colonial Times to the Present*. New York: New Viewpoints, 1975.

Scott, Anne Firor. *The American Woman: Who Was She?* Englewood Cliffs, N.J.: Prentice Hall, 1971.

Scott, Diana, ed. *Bread and Roses: An Anthology of Nineteenth and Twentieth Century Poetry by Women Writers*. London: Virago Press, 1982.

Shaw, Anna Howard, with the collaboration of Elizabeth Jordan. *The Story of a Pioneer*. New York: Harper, 1915.

Showalter, Elaine, ed. *These Modern Women: Autobiographical Essays from the Twenties*. Old Westbury, N.Y.: Feminist Press, 1978.

Sinclair, Andrew. *The Better Half: The Emancipation of American Women*. New York: Harper and Row, 1965.

Sklar, Kathryn Kish. *Catherine Beecher: A Study in Domesticity*. New York: Norton, 1973.

Smith, Henry Nash. *Mark Twain of the Enterprise: Newspaper Articles and Other Documents, 1862–1864*. Berkeley: University of California Press, 1957.

Smith, Page. *Daughters of the Promised Land: Women in American History*. Boston: Little, Brown and Company, 1970.

Sochen, June. *Movers and Shakers: American Woman Thinkers and Activists, 1900–1970*. New York: Quadrangle Books, 1973.

———. *The New Feminism in Twentieth Century America*. New York: Heath, 1971.

———. *The New Woman: Feminism in Greenwich Village, 1910–1920*. New York: Quadrangle Books, 1972.

Spacks, Patricia Meyer. *The Female Imagination*. New York: Alfred A. Knopf, 1975.

Spender, Dale. *Women of Ideas and What Men Have Done to Them from Aphra Behn to Adrienne Rich*. London: Routledge and Kegan Paul, 1982.

Springer, Marlene, ed. *What Manner of Woman? Essays in English and American Life and Literature*. New York: New York University Press, 1977.

Stevens, Doris. *Jailed for Freedom*. New York: Liveright Publishing Corporation, 1920.

Strachey, Ray (née Costelloe). *The Cause: A Short History of the Women's Movement in Great Britain*. London: G. Bellan Sons, Ltd., 1928.

Thomas, M. Carey. *The Making of a Feminist: Early Journals of M. Carey Thomas*. Edited by Marjorie Housepian Dobkin with a foreword by Millicent Carey McIntosh. Kent, Ohio: Kent State University Press, 1978.

Thompson, Margaret E., and Mary D. Thompson. *They Couldn't Stop Us!* Ipswich: Ancient House Press, W. E. Harrison and Sons Ltd., 1957.

Vicinus, Martha, ed. *A Widening Sphere: Changing Roles of Victorian Women*. Bloomington: Indiana University Press, 1977.

Walkowitz, Judith R. *Prostitution and Victorian Society: Women, Class, and the State*. Cambridge: Cambridge University Press, 1980.

Weinstein, James. *The Decline of Socialism in America, 1912–1925*. New York: Monthly Review Press, 1967.

Welter, Barbara. *Dimity Convictions: The American Woman in the Nineteenth Century*. Athens: Ohio University Press, 1976.

West, Rebecca. *The Post Victorians*. London: Ivor Nicholson and Watson, 1933.

Women's Social and Political Union. *The Trial of the Suffragette Leaders, London 1908*. London: The Woman's Press, 1908.

Woolf, Virginia. *A Room of One's Own*. New York: Harper, 1972.

———. *Three Guineas*. New York: Harper, 1966.

Wren, Thomas. *A History of the State of Nevada, Its Resources and Its People*. New York: Lewis, 1904.

Yonge, Charlotte Mary. *Womankind*. New York: Macmillan, 1877.

Articles

Cook, Blanche Wiesen. "Female Support Networks and Political Activism: Lillian Wald, Crystal Eastman, Emma Goldman." *Chrysalis* 3 (Fall, 1977): 43.

Degler, Carl. "What Ought to Be and What Was: Women's Sexuality in the Nineteenth Century." *American Historical Review* 79, no. 5 (December 1974): 1467–1490.

Earl, Philip. "Nevada Suffragets Battle for the Vote." *Nevada* (Fall, 1974).

Fry, Amelia. "Along the Suffrage Trail: From West to East for Freedom Now." *American West* 6, no. 1 (1969): 16–25.

Gallagher, Robert S., ed. " 'I was Arrested, of Course.' " *American Heritage* 25 (February 1974): 16–24.

Glass, Mary Ellen. "Nevada's Lady Lawmakers." *Nevada Public Affairs Report* (October 1975).

Heilbrun, Carolyn. "Marriage Perceived, 1873–1941." *What Manner of Woman? Essays on English and American Life and Literature*. Edited by Marlene Springer. New York: New York University Press, 1977.

Howard, Anne. "Anne Martin: Western and National Politics." In *Beyond ERA, Nevada Public Affairs Report* (Fall, 1983).

Kirchwey, Freda. Article in *Everywoman*, 21 April 1918, p. 4.

Larson, T. A. "Dolls, Vassals and Drudges—Pioneer Women in the West." *Western History Quarterly* 3, no. 1 (1972): 4–16.

———. "Emancipating the West's Dolls, Vassals, and Hopeless Drudges: The Origins of Woman Suffrage in the West." University of Wyoming Publication 37 (1971): 1–16.

———. "Women's Role in the American West." *Montana: Magazine of Western History* 24, no. 3 (1974): 2–11.

Lasch, Christopher. "Sorority and Family in New England, 1839–1846." In *The World of Nations*. New York: Knopf, 1973.

Lemons, J. Stanley. "The Sheppard Towner Act: Progressivism in the 1920's." *Journal of American History* 55, no. 4 (1969): 776–786.

Lerner, Gerda. "New Approaches for the Study of Women in American History." *Journal of Social History* 3, no. 1 (Fall, 1969): 53–62.

Martin, Anne. "English and American Women in Politics." *New York Times Magazine*, 5 November 1922, pp. 12–13.

———. "Equality Laws vs. Women in Government." *Nation*, 16 August 1922, pp. 165–166.

———. "An Everlasting Benefit You Can Win in a Week." *Good Housekeeping* 70 (February 1920): 20ff.

———. "Family Income and Infant Mortality." *Good Housekeeping* (April 1920).

———. "Feminists and Future Political Action." *Nation*, 18 February 1925, pp. 185–186.

———. "If I Were a Senator." *Independent Weekly Review*, 1 May 1920, pp. 16–30.

———. "Josephine Butler." *Encyclopaedia Britannica* (1951).

———. "Labor Is Watching Its Leaders." *Nation*, 2 March 1921, pp. 335–337.

———. "Nevada: Beautiful Desert of Buried Hopes." *Nation*, 26 July 1922, pp. 89–92.

———. "Nevada Women and the National Freedom: A Vital Resume of the Suffrage Question." *Everywoman* (August 1915): 4–5.

———. "The Next Step for Women." *Sunset* (April 1922).

———. "Political Methods of American and British Feminists." *American History Magazine, New York Times* 20 (June 1924): 396–401.

———. "We Couldn't Afford a Doctor." *Good Housekeeping* 70 (April 1920): 19–20.

———. "What Women Should Vote For." *Good Housekeeping* 69 (November 1919): 15ff.

———. "White Slave Traffic (Traffic in Women and Children)." *Encyclopaedia Britannica* (1951).

———. "Women and Peace." *New Republic*, 30 October 1929, pp. 299–300.

———. "Women and Their Magazines." *New Republic*, 20 September 1922, pp. 91–93.

———. "Women's Inferiority Complex." *New Republic*, 20 July 1921, pp. 210–212.

———. "Women's Peace Congress at Dublin." *Nation*, 18 August 1926, pp. 156–157.

———. "Women's Votes and Women's Chains." *Sunset* 48 (April 1922): 12–14.

Millholland, Inez. "The Changing Home." *McClure's* 40 (March 1913): 214.

O'Neill, William. "Feminism as Radical Ideology." In *Dissent: Explorations in the History of American Radicalism*. Urbana, Ill., 1968.

Riley, Glenda Gates. "Origins of the Argument for Improved Female Education." *History of Education Quarterly* 4 (1969): 455–470.

———. "The Subtle Subversion: Changes in the Traditionalist Image of the American Woman." *Historian* 32 (February 1970): 210–227.

Rosenberg, Rosalind. "In Search of Woman's Nature, 1850–1920." *Feminist Studies* 3 (Fall, 1975): 141–154.

Smith, Daniel Scott. "Family Limitation, Sexual Control, and Domestic Feminism in Victorian America." *Feminist Studies* 14 (Winter–Spring, 1973): 40–57.

Smith-Rosenberg, Carroll. "Beauty, the Beast and the Militant Woman." *American Quarterly* 23 (October 1971): 562–584.

———. "The Female World of Love and Ritual: Relations between Women in Nineteenth Century America." In Nancy F. Cott and Elizabeth H. Pleck, *A Heritage of Her Own: Toward a New Social History of American Women*. New York: Simon and Schuster, 1979.

Stevens, Doris. "The Home as Joint Stock Company." *Nation*, 27 June 1926.

Stewart, Robert. "A Lady of New York." *Christian Century*, 24 December 1894.

Taylor, William, and Christopher Lasch. "Two 'Kindred Spirits': Sorority and Family in New England." *New England Quarterly* 36 (1963): 25–41.

Totton, Kathryn. "Hannah Keziah Clapp: The Life and Career of a Pioneer Nevada Educator, 1824–1908." *Nevada Historical Society Quarterly* (Fall, 1977): 167–183.

Townley, Carrie. "Bishop Whitaker's School for Girls." *Nevada Historical Society Quarterly* 3 (1976): 191ff.

Tucker, Janice Law. "The Suffrage Prisoners." *American Scholar* 41, no. 3 (1972): 409–423.

Unpublished Materials

Manuscript Collections

Jane Addams Correspondence, Schlesinger Library, Radcliffe College, Cambridge, Massachusetts.

George Bartlett Papers, Special Collections, Getchell Library, University of Nevada, Reno, Nevada.

Hannah Clapp Papers, Nevada Historical Society, Reno, Nevada.

Felice Cohn Papers, Nevada Historical Society, Reno, Nevada.

Equal Franchise Society Papers, Nevada Historical Society, Reno, Nevada.

Margaret Foley Papers, Unprocessed collection (as of May 1981), Schlesinger Library, Radcliffe College, Cambridge, Massachusetts.

Inez Haynes Irwin Collection, Schlesinger Library, Radcliffe College, Cambridge, Massachusetts.

Austin Lewis Papers, Bancroft Library, University of California, Berkeley, California.

Margaret Long Papers, Sophia Smith Collection, Smith College, Northampton, Massachusetts.

Anne Martin Collection, Bancroft Library, University of California, Berkeley.

Anne Martin File, California Historical Society Library, San Francisco, California.

Anne Martin File, Nevada Historical Society, Reno, Nevada.

Mabel Vernon Collection, Bancroft Library, University of California, Berkeley, California.

Jeanne Elizabeth Wier Collection, Nevada Historical Society, Reno, Nevada.

Women's International League for Peace and Freedom Papers, Swarthmore Peace Archive, Swarthmore College, Swarthmore, Pennsylvania.

Oral Histories

Boyer, Florence. "Las Vegas Nevada: My Home for Many Years." Oral History Project, University of Nevada-Reno, 1966.

Bruns, Eugenia May. "Old Empire on the Carson River: My Native Town." Center for Western North American Studies, Oral History Project, University of Nevada-Reno, 1966.

Field, Sara Bard. "Sara Bard Field: Poet and Suffragist." Regional Oral History Office, Bancroft Library, University of California, Berkeley, 1976.

Kettler, Ernestine Hara. "The Suffragists: From Tea Parties to Prison." Feminist Research Project, Sherna Gluck, Interviewer. Regional Oral History Office, Bancroft Library, University of California, Berkeley.

Paul, Alice. "Conversations with Alice Paul: Woman Suffrage and the Equal Rights Amendment." Regional Oral History Office, Bancroft Library, University of California, Berkeley, 2 vols., 1975.

Riegelhuth, Katharine. "Memoirs of a Pioneer of Eureka and Reno, Nevada." Oral History Project, University of Nevada-Reno, 1977.

Vernon, Mabel. "Mabel Vernon: Speaker for Suffrage and Petitioner for Peace." Suffragist Oral History Project, Regional Oral History Office, Bancroft Library, University of California, Berkeley, 1976.

Other Unpublished Materials

Anderson, Kathryn. "Practical Political Equality for Women: Anne Martin's Campaigns for the U.S. Senate in Nevada, 1918 and 1920." Ph.D. dissertation, University of Washington, 1978.

Becker, Susan. "An Intellectual History of the National Woman's Party, 1920–41." Ph.D. dissertation, Case Western Reserve University, 1975.

Bland, Sidney Roderick. "Techniques of Persuasion: The National Woman's Party and Woman Suffrage, 1913–1919." Ph.D. dissertation, George Washington University, 1972.

Martin, Anna Henrietta. "The Causes of the Baden Revolution." M.A. thesis, Stanford University, 1897.

Nelson, Marjory. "Ladies in the Streets: A Sociological Analysis of the National Woman's Party, 1910–1930." Ph.D. dissertation, State University of New York-Buffalo, 1976.

Nilan, Roxanne. "The Ladies at Palo Alto: Stanford University and the Coeducational Experiment." Paper, Stanford University Archives, Green Library, Palo Alto, California.

Smith, Ann Warren. "Anne Martin and a History of Woman Suffrage in Nevada, 1869–1914." Ph.D. dissertation, University of Nevada-Reno, 1975.

Stadtmuller, Henrietta. Scrapbook, Stanford University Archives, Green Library, Palo Alto, California.

INDEX